HOME

A Portrait of
an American Community

TOWN

by Peter Davis

A TOUCHSTONE BOOK
Published by Simon and Schuster
NEW YORK

Copyright © 1982 by Peter Davis

First Touchstone Edition, 1983
Published by Simon and Schuster
A Division of Gulf & Western Corporation
Simon & Schuster Building
Rockefeller Center
1230 Avenue of the Americas
New York, New York 10020
TOUCHSTONE and colophon are trademarks of Simon & Schuster
Designed by Eve Kirch
Manufactured in the United States of America
10 9 8 7 6 5 4 3 2 1
10 9 8 7 6 5 4 3 2 1 Pbk.
Library of Congress Cataloging in Publication Data
Davis, Peter W.
  Hometown.
  1. Hamilton (Ohio)—Social life and customs.
I. Title.
F499.H2D38   977.1'75   81-21363
                                  AACR2
ISBN 0-671-24556-2
ISBN 0-671-47059-0 Pbk.

For my children and their grandparents

CONTENTS

Was the discovery of America a blessing or a curse to mankind? If it was a blessing, by what means are we to conserve and enhance its benefits? If it was a curse, by what means are we to repair the damage?
    —Essay topic proposed to the
    Academy of Lyons in 1780 by
    Abbé Raynal, first prize 1200 francs

I
GETTING THERE

Though no traveler's manual would contain any of what is found here, this is a kind of guidebook. Motels and restaurants are not listed, natural delights and scenic treasures are only incidental. Yet it is a guide in the sense that I try to map the passions of one American town, to find coordinates for the conflicts and harmonies that unite and divide the townspeople. Such passions involve a stream of confrontations—between men and women, teams, races, schools, workers and bosses, rich and poor. Occasionally an individual confronts his own destiny; finally the community confronts itself.

Wondering where to go, knowing only that the right place should be neither too large for a small compass nor too small to contain a full range of experience, I hit highways and airports. The country rings out in its names: Lowell, Massachusetts; Utica, New York; Selma, Alabama; Santa Rosa, California; Muncie, Indiana; Kalamazoo, Michigan; York and Lancaster, Pennsylvania; Denton, Texas; Dubuque and Cedar Rapids, Iowa. I also went to the Census Bureau.

Deep in the Census catacombs, the chief of the Demographic Statistics Branch of the Population Division, one Richard L. Forstall, demanded my purpose.

To understand America by going into one community and penetrating its society as deeply and widely as possible.

"Is that all? Where are you from yourself?"

Never mind, he couldn't have heard of it.

"Try me."

"A small town in San Bernardino County in California."

"Does it have a name?"

"I told you, you've never heard of it, even the natives describe it by the distances from larger towns nearby. All right, it's called Upland."

"Oh sure, more than thirty thousand people now, just above Ontario, fifteen miles or so from Fontana where the Kaiser steel mill shifted the whole job pattern when it was built back in the forties."

Wise guy. So he, too, was a western aborigine. Southern Californians are so smug. "You win. What made you leave the West for Washington?"

"I've never been to California in my life. Twenty years with Rand McNally, then the Census. Now, what can I do for you?"

Tell me where I can go to combine categories of social research with techniques of storytelling. Where I can observe activities the way an anthropologist might, as Robert and Helen Lynd did in *Middletown,* and then tell about them as Sherwood Anderson did in *Winesburg, Ohio.* Stories of marriage and morals, work and leisure, politics, crime, punishment, religion, caste and class. Stories of real people using not only fact but fantasy, not only information but impression, attitude, legend—diverse tidings that disclose particular truths in a community.

With a permanently quizzical expression and a high forehead behind which might have been stored all the significant binary digits of the United States population, Richard Forstall attacked several dozen reference books as though they were keys to unlocking the century's best-kept secret.

Pausing during his hunt, Forstall said the town should have a population between fifty and one hundred thousand since below fifty the complete array of situations and institutions is lacking, and above one hundred the community becomes too complex. "You have to find a place," he said, "big enough to have everything its people need and small enough so you can figure out what the hell is going on." The town should be northern enough to be industrial, southern enough to have a gently rural aspect, western enough to have once been on the frontier, eastern enough to have a past. No single integer can ever contain the whole, but it can contain processes that reflect those of other integers. In the meditations of Martin Buber, "a nation is a community to the degree that it is a community of communities."

Forstall of the Census pored over his maps, scrutinized his demographic charts, probed his commercial and population surveys. He searched his city directories as if they were an encyclopedia of the zodiac and he an astrologer. He conjured his *County and City Data Book* the way a necromancer entreats tarot cards to deliver their mysteries. There seemed no limit to the sources at his disposal nor to his determination to canvass them all. At length, when we would have realized it had grown dark had his nook in the labyrinthine Census contained a window, he looked up. The quizzical expression never left him. "You could do worse," Richard Forstall concluded, "than to go to Hamilton, Ohio."

The first recorded event in Hamilton was a public hanging. The last, and in some ways main, event in this book is what many Hamiltonians called an attempted lynching. In 1793, a young soldier deserted the Fort Hamilton compound, which was not yet a town but only a defensive perimeter against the Indians, to return to his sweetheart in New York. Caught a few miles downriver, he was brought back to the garrison where he was, an early chronicler noted, "swung off without a murmur." In 1978, a respected citizen of Hamilton was accused of a crime few people had previously thought of as a crime and which no one wanted to talk about until the alleged incident became a public scandal—the occasion for the town to examine itself as it never had. The resemblance between the calamities is less than identical, more than coincidental. In each case the collective impulse was to get rid of someone whose presumed deed threatened what was perceived as the integrity and structure of the community.

The birth of Fort Hamilton came about when a federal judge, John Cleves Symmes, held peace talks in the Northwest Territory with an Indian chief, Little Turtle of the Miamis, in 1789. They met on a bright October morning, maples crimson in the vanishing dew, at the confluence of the Ohio and Miami rivers, three months after the storming of the Bastille, eight years after Cornwallis surrendered at Yorktown. It was a defining moment, casting all that followed in a new light for the whites, a new shadow for the Indians. Judge Symmes, a genial dreamer from New Jersey with a summer home on eastern Long Island, hoped "that it would be given to me to found a settlement that will become the great metropolis of the entire West." He promised his side would start no more skirmishes if an agreement could be reached on the division of land. Chief Little Turtle, hopeful but skeptical, said his own side had given no trouble in the first place, and asked for proof of the judge's friendly mission. Judge Symmes produced as verification that "the thirteen fires had sent me hither," the Great Seal of the United States, which, then as now, showed a spread eagle holding a leafy stalk in one talon, a spray of arrows in the other. Little Turtle responded with an interpretation of the seal that was a prophecy of the intentions of the infant country.

Judge Symmes had told the Chief, as he wrote a friend in Congress, that while the weapons in one claw did signify power, the tree branch in the other was "an emblem of peace." Little Turtle looked hard at the Seal and then replied "that he could not perceive any intimations of peace from the attitude the Eagle was in, having her wings spread as in flight; when folding of the wings denoted rest and peace. That he could not understand how the branch of a tree could be considered as a pacific emblem, for rods designed for correction were always taken from the boughs of trees. That to him the Eagle appeared from her bearing to hold a large whip in one claw, and such a number of arrows in the other, and in full career of flight, to be wholly bent on war and mischief. I need not repeat to you my arguments to convince him of his mistake. . . ."

Despite Little Turtle's misgivings, a bargain was struck. Whites from the East got the river basins, the Miami tribe took the headwaters and uplands. It seemed politic to name the first fort along the Miami River after the secretary of the treasury; perhaps Alexander Hamilton could convince Congress to appropriate funds for more troops to protect the western settlements. New migrants from the East paid little attention to Judge Symmes's agreement with Little Turtle, and fighting was soon general on the frontier. Little Turtle won several famous victories, including the humiliating defeat of an army contingent from Fort Hamilton, but General Anthony ("Mad Anthony") Wayne, a dashing hero of the Revolution, arrived with reinforcements to destroy Indian power in the Northwest Territory forever. The early citizens of Hamilton were eulogized affectionately many years later by a town orator who recalled them as "practical eradicationists" where Indians were concerned. "Our pioneer forefathers were not idealists and perhaps they were not, properly speaking, reformers; they were practical eradicationists. They acted upon their well-founded belief that the most certain road to successful competition with savage man and beast was to exterminate them, and as a consequence the community was soon rid of both, and the joy of prosperity and happiness took root and grew apace."

The first businesses were taverns. By 1810, there were two hundred and ninety-four Hamiltonians with seventy wood houses and a stone jail. By 1830 the town had one thousand residents and was no longer merely a marketplace for farmers to sell their produce. During the 1850s Hamilton became a station for fugitive slaves on the Underground Railroad; a black built Hamilton's first flour mill, though he was not allowed to own it. The population had grown to over seven thousand by the Civil War, and the town was a thriving textile and paper mill center. After the war, cotton factories, sawmills, banks, law firms, foundries and machine shops all flourished. Hamilton was connected to the nearest larger cities, Cincinnati and Dayton, by a canal, a turnpike, and several railroads.

"Education, Free as Air" was the motto of the public schools that were built in the mid-nineteenth century, when the town was eager to unite the feuding settlements on either side of the Miami River under one civic government. The East Side was the downtown section, where most of the factories and trade were situated; across the river were newer homes, smarter shops, and they called it "West Side Best Side." The town was the seat of Butler County, whose sheriff was indicted for bribery; Hamilton's own officials often trafficked in bootleg liquor. A local historian rued the "shocking murders committed during drunken brawls." Yet growth and prosperity remained the rule.

By the town's centennial in 1891, the eighteen thousand Hamiltonians made stoves, paper, safes, wool, ink, patent medicines and wood products. The Chamber of Commerce bragged that "we hold the reins to the world trade lanes." There were three banks, eleven hotels, six undertakers, fifteen blacksmiths, eighteen dry-goods stores, forty-nine lawyers, two daily and three weekly newspapers, two brass bands, twenty-seven doctors, eighteen churches, and—inevitably—ninety-eight saloons.

The town kept growing, though not as fast as before. Much of it was destroyed by a flood in 1913; corrupted by Prohibition in the 1920s and 1930s when it was a hideout for John Dillinger; devastated by the Depression; diminished by the flight of industry to the Sunbelt in the 1960s and 1970s. It survives, however, and perseveres.

I went to Hamilton not so much looking for as assuming change. The prevalence of change is a given in America. Yet what I found was an astonishing, striking, virtually genetic resemblance between Hamilton's past and its present. The desire to sell, build, expand, advertise, migrate, win, get more for the children—all of this has been in Hamilton for over one hundred fifty years. Dazzled by the vividness and clutter of technology, Hamiltonians themselves remark on how much has changed in the town. Buildings are replaced, everything runs by computer, people are ciphers. Sidewalks are no longer safe, everyone gets mad at his neighbor too easily, public officials are dishonest, kids leave town if they get an education. Yet each of these complaints echoes one in the nineteenth century. The bootlegging city marshal of the 1870s is mirrored in the sheriff who in the 1970s was convicted of embezzlement, conflict of interest, and income tax evasion. The rapid pace of change disturbed those Hamiltonians of the 1890s who longed for "the gentler days gone by" when families stayed together, indeed for their own youth: "The maypole surrounded by a bevy of girls dressed in every color of the rainbow, a beautiful sight that reminded many a heart, whose youthful throb had become chilled, of the merry times of long ago." New buildings were condemned for shoddy workmanship; fighting in the streeets made evening walks perilous.

As for technology, Hamiltonians proudly and somewhat fearfully recorded the "radical changes" that had made the 1890s different from the early nineteenth century—the railroad, telegraph, telephone, electric light, microphone. These made them feel they lived in a time the world had never known, and of course they were right. But so had their own grandparents been right when they declared that canals, steamboats, and daguerreotypes had changed the world forever.

When the town celebrated its 1891 centennial, Hamilton High School had a history of twenty-nine years. Only thirty-six percent of its graduates still lived in Hamilton, compared with forty-four percent of the class of 1950 who were in town three decades later. Comparisons can be misleading when life expectancy, methods of record-keeping, and population size are as different as they are between nineteenth- and twentieth-century Hamilton. Yet it seems clear that despite hometown nostalgia for a stabler past, Hamilton's young were at least as unlikely to remain nestlings one hundred years ago as they are today. Hamiltonians who look back longingly are those, obviously, who still live there. *Their* parents did stay. But not all their aunts and uncles did. The point is not that Hamiltonians are wrong to think their children footloose; the point is only that they always were. America was not where you started but where you started over. In Europe the frontier was a border where you had to stop; in America the frontier was a horizon stretching as far as the imagination. We move a lot, one fifth of us changing homes every year, and always have.

Blinded by speed, inventions, new means of transportation, we focus on change to the exclusion of permanence. What generation since the founding of the Republic has not thought itself living in transition, has not longed for the time when children obeyed, a dollar was worth a dollar, the boss knew all his workers by their first names? It is hard to escape the conclusion that permanence, continuity, relative fixity are paid insufficient attention in a society that, even when fearful of it, reveres and generally profits from change. In thrall to the gospel of change, we overlook what is continuous; one of the most enduring features of the American landscape is change itself.

What changes far less than is suspected by most social researchers and commentators, it seems to me after six years of observing Hamilton, is the nature of family relationships. When the novelist William Dean Howells was growing up in Hamilton in the 1840s, he noticed that "Between the young and the old there is a vast gulf, seldom if ever bridged. The old can look backward over it, but they cannot cross it, any more than the young, who can see no thither side." More than a century later, "generation gap" was coined and pushed as an insight into a current phenomenon. Howells himself did not present his recollection as anything new; he was simply paying attention to his own childhood, making observations as applicable to the 1980s as they were to the 1840s. Howells also found Hamilton's class structure oppressive, even as a boy, criticizing "social cruelties which are the modern expression of the savage spirit otherwise repressed by civilization." The continuities are not necessarily reassuring, but they are still continuities. The novelist Fannie Hurst, a child in Hamilton sixty years after Howells, was equally aware of the generation gap and of social distinctions that would have circumscribed her, as a Jew, had she stayed in her hometown all her life. Yet neither was alienated, both enjoyed their Hamilton childhoods. "I am treating myself to a debauch of nostalgia," Fannie Hurst said when she returned to Hamilton after several decades. Howells, too, loved Hamilton. "The home of my happiest years," he wrote, "what an incomparable town for a boy to be a boy in." Though a New Englander for half a century, the writer never tried out a new pen without inscribing on the nearest piece of paper:

William Dean Howells

Hamilton, Ohio

As for Hamilton's being split into factions, the West and East Sides never liked each other, blacks and whites have been uneasy for over a century, rich and poor have been estranged since the town's first industrialist, John Woods, refused to give his employees a five-cent-a-day raise in 1836. Hamilton's mayor, Frank Witt, worried about the city's divisions in the late 1970s. Just forty, he was a three-term mayor already and had an eye that fixed itself well beyond Hamilton. Both his friends and enemies expected higher office for him; God only knew where he would go from here. "Remember this and you'll know Hamilton," Mayor Witt said as a January afternoon darkened outside his flag-decked, municipally correct office in the City Building. "We are a deeply fragmented community. We're *nice* to each other so much of the time we get the idea that's all there is. But since the problems and misunderstandings remain pretty consistent year after year, I have to assume we don't actually like each other as much as we claim to. Maybe nice is what you have to be or you'd be swinging at each other all the time. Still, if you don't recognize your divisions, it's going to be pretty hard to heal them." The bright, ambitious young mayor—shrewd, handsome, supple—was perfectly in tune with his predecessors who, in the 1890s, were already mourning the loss of a sense of community in Hamilton.

The town's past and present seem to contain each other the way an orange contains a seed that is itself the beginning of a new orange. Change is, as always, everywhere. To deny it is to baffle the sounds of our time. Yet there is a correspondence between nineteenth- and twentieth-century Hamilton, an essence in what happened there over one hundred years ago leading very certainly, on direct course, to what the town is today. In the world around Hamilton, there is a sense in which the nineteenth century—from Darwin to Verne to Marx to Edison to Einstein to Freud—can even be said to have *dreamed* the twentieth. It is not a simple *plus ça change*. Much does change; even more remains. Hamilton's identity is composed of elements that evolve and accrue gradually, incrementally, yielding to the latest patents and annual trends only the way the Grand Canyon does to wind.

As one approach to Hamilton is through its past, another is overland.

If Hamilton were Canterbury, pilgrims would arrive by various routes—from Dayton to the northeast, Cincinnati to the southeast—of which none is at once more ordinary, yet more beguiling, than the back way from the Cincinnati airport. The airport lies across the Ohio River fifteen miles deep into Kentucky. Heading north, the road commences with determination but quickly loses momentum to wind through alfalfa fields and spruce woods until it reaches a moribund river settlement on the Kentucky side. From a piece of land that bulges into the water, a ferry service plies the river to Ohio as it has since 1817. The crossing—from South to North, farm to factory, from a state that prides itself on horse breeding to one represented in the Senate by the first American to orbit the earth—takes only a few minutes, as though all passages were so deceptively facile and painless. The transition seems conclusive, obscuring for the moment the fact that there is a manufacturing South as well as a rural North.

But true to type, on the Ohio side the riverscape is abruptly industrial. The highway sweeps left past asphalt, chemical, and salt plants, the inevitable automobile graveyard, more of Cincinnati's metropolitan detritus. On the right is North Bend, the ancient river village where Judge Symmes persuaded Little Turtle to abandon a sizable portion of his territory.

Leaving the Ohio, a two-lane blacktop juts north along the Miami River. A refinery and a sand and gravel works feed off the river, which stays to the right of the road. The rural North asserts itself as industry ends and farms begin. On the left are fields of rye, corn, alfalfa, winter wheat, tomato, and melon. Barns are lettered with huge pleas to "Chew Mail Pouch Tobacco." The way is lined with small firm stone houses, mobile home parks, wooden shacks, vegetable stands, a mossy cemetery, boys fishing in the river in June or sledding down to its edge in January. Two small towns with antique stores punctuate the route, then more fields with statuesque, well-groomed scarecrows, fields where in one season everything is planting and in another everything is gathering.

In anticipation, the road widens to three lanes. Finally, around a late hill on the left and a crook in the river on the right, the towers of Hamilton—churches, department stores, county offices, banks, the senior citizens highrise, the courthouse, and the Civil War monument—suddenly become the horizon. A bridge crosses the Miami to the east bank where first the fort against the Indians, then the frontier settlement, and later the town itself were all built. Hamilton grows and decays, reconstructs and declines in cycles that never quite reveal themselves until they are over. A newcomer sees the spires, the confident and accommodating houses, the downtown window displays, hears rain on the river and a high school band warming up, watches the open market spring to life around the courthouse on a Saturday morning—and figures he has come home. But no. The big thing, as anywhere, is still to get ahead. The next thing is still not to fall too far behind. Places like Hamilton are variously called the nation's heartbeat and the middle of nowhere, incubators and stagnant pools. Depending on how it is observed, Hamilton is a city, a self-contained town, a suburb, a satellite in the orbits of both Cincinnati and Dayton, a minor metropolitan cluster, a county seat, a bump on the plain, a galactic microdot where 63,189 people wait to see what will happen next.

II
THE WEDDING

Bobby Jackson had a hangover on the morning of his marriage to Nancy Sloneker, who had a bad cold. As he drove to the Cincinnati airport to pick up several friends coming in for his wedding, he did not think it was so bad he had not recovered from the bachelor party the night before. The hangover kept him from worrying.

Exposure to brazen adolescent germs was an occupational hazard; they should pay teachers extra for showing up in class during a flu epidemic. Nancy Sloneker picked the beginning of Christmas vacation as the right time for her wedding because she would not have to be back at school for two more weeks. Her sore throat had struck in the cafeteria halfway through the noon recess on Thursday, and by Saturday morning it had branched out into her head and chest, leaving her with a nose —every bride's dream—that Santa's own Rudolph would have been proud to brandish.

Still, it was not only her sentimental Aunt Em who found her beautiful by the time Nancy was fidgeting with her bouquet in the basement of the small old United Presbyterian Church in a country parish a few miles north of Hamilton. Aunt Em and

other relatives who tiptoed downstairs for a peek all said they
had never seen such a perfect bride. The Slonekers were Hamiltonians but had rural roots that drew them back on important
occasions to the church in the village of Seven Mile (just that far
from the original site of Fort Hamilton) where the first Sloneker
had settled after coming west from Pennsylvania before the
Civil War. Bobby was already at the church when the Slonekers
arrived. Handsome, sturdy Bobby, good old Bobby, Nancy
thought, right on time. But what her mother said was, "For once
in his life."

Nancy's mother, hurrying back and forth in the church basement between her family and the groom's, was very pretty herself, Nancy plus a couple of decades, her brown hair just
starting to fleck with gray. Since the families were observing the
traditional ban on the bride and groom seeing each other before
the ceremony, the parents were emissaries. Nancy, in white,
stayed with her bridesmaids in a little room at the bottom of the
stairs. In honor of the season, the bridesmaids wore red and
green dresses. One of them powdered most of the red off
Nancy's nose while the bride bit her lip and smiled, bravely
clutching her veil the way she had once held an ice cream cone
she hadn't wanted to dribble all over a new Easter dress.

Upstairs the guests filed into the little church as the organist
played "Moon River" and "The Way We Were." In their gray
sharkskin suits with white and black striped ties, the ushers
seated people on either side of the aisle according to which
family they were connected to. Then they unrolled white paper,
very soft and only a little crinkly, for Nancy to walk down the
aisle on.

Coming out of the bathroom in a corner of the basement,
Nancy's mother encountered Bobby on his way in. "What's the
matter, do you have a nervous kidney, Bob?" she asked. "That's
not what's nervous," Bobby said to his mother-in-law-to-be as he
shut the door.

Nancy adjusted the veil, her nose having been dulled to a
pink blush. Her father was at the door. Compact, handsome,

Malcolm Sloneker with the open features and smiling, disappointed eyes of a born salesman. Better looking than Bobby? a bridesmaid had asked Nancy. No, different. Her father's hair was light brown, almost sandy, Bobby's was dark. Bobby's look was more piercing, her father's more accepting. Mac Sloneker held out his arm for his daughter. "Sounds like our song upstairs," he said as the first bar of Mendelssohn rolled down into the basement.

Bobby stood with his best man as Nancy and Mac Sloneker negotiated the aisle. Nancy seemed to quiver—with anxiety, anticipation, an incipient sneeze, regret? Nervously feeling for the knot on his tie, Bobby glanced out for comfort at Nancy's Aunt Em, who was putting a reassuring handkerchief to her eyes.

"Good friends and family," said the young minister, Ed Brown, as he began his fortieth wedding, "we are gathered today to witness the marriage of this fine young couple. True friendship and physical love are involved here." At this moment, the Sloneker-Jackson wedding was the essence of what weddings were supposed to be in America, the ritual start of a bright, faithful, lasting life together for a radiant couple in their middle twenties.

The small church contained only eleven rows of benches, and thirty-four stocky candles provided almost the only illumination, one posted at the aisle end of each bench, the remainder at the altar. Set off by the red and green bridesmaids and the sharkskin ushers were the bride, groom, and minister. Nancy's dress was made of a fabric called "candlelight ivory satin," its train long enough that the tiny page, her nephew, had almost tripped over it as he lurched down the aisle behind her. Standing solemnly between bride and groom, Ed Brown kept his hair short and his sideburns long, a square-cut, earnest minister who, to make ends meet, also served another parish besides the one at Seven Mile. He had a retreating chin which, together with the long sideburns, made the lower part of his cheery face look like a vanishing question mark. Since he wanted to stay abreast of the times, Reverend Brown had written his own mar-

riage service. "Young people were coming up to me asking what
it meant to 'plight a troth,'" he had said, "and since I wasn't so
sure myself I thought I'd compose my own. Some of the older
members think the mention of physical love has no place in a
marriage service, but I think it belongs."

The making of physical love has a place in Hamiltonian lore
as solid as the cutting of a baby's first teeth or a retirement
ceremony. It is not only a rite of passage but a destination. The
story is told of a young drifter, a James Dean type, who came to
Hamilton in the 1950s—though others say it happened in the
'30s, that he rode into town on the top of a boxcar at the bottom
of the Depression—and took up with a kind but fading prostitute. His name was Sam and he was about eighteen; she was
called Rose and she could have been his mother. Before he met
Rose, Sam went around cadging drinks and meals, rolling
drunks for their last dimes. He was arrested twice but was never
kept in jail longer than overnight because even there he caused
trouble. Then Rose took him in. She had been the favorite of
the upper class in general and of a certain prominent businessman in particular. Some heads of households had even, as they
might in Europe, sent their sons and nephews to her. It was said
Rose taught Sam all she knew about life and love.

He ripened, got along better with everyone, and found steady
work at a small newsstand-soda parlor which, with Rose's help,
he soon owned. On the side Sam took a few bets. Polite society
ignored Sam and Rose, especially since Rose was no longer
doing business, but the liaison found its way into local gossip.
Rose took up gardening and sent a sunflower to the spring
floral show. It was rejected, so she sent it to the orphanage. As
soon as Sam began to pay attention to a younger girl his own
age, before he even knew the direction his feelings were taking,
Rose threw him out. He argued there was nothing to be jealous
of, and she said it was not jealousy. On his own, Sam had to see
the younger girl secretly since she came from a good family who
knew about Sam and Rose and could not abide a drifter around
their hope and pride.

Virtuous tongues clucked, "Wouldn't you know it?" and

"Serves her right" when Rose found she was in an advanced stage of tuberculosis. Sam came back to Rose and nursed her in her final weeks, which cost him the girl from the good family. When Rose died, the police raided Sam's newsstand for taking horse bets, and it turned out he had only been allowed to operate because, unknown to him, Rose had been paying protection. In jail, Sam's leg was gashed during a fight in which he defended the honor of both Rose and the well-born girl who had left him. When the judge asked where Sam was from, he said he had grown up in Hamilton, though he had been there less than a year altogether. The judge told him to get out of town. The last anyone saw of Sam he was limping along highway 129 to the west, looking for a ride. It was heard, years later, that Sam had settled two states away, in southern Illinois, where he prospered as the owner of several cafés and the father of three daughters, one of whom he named Roseanne.

Only two people in the Seven Mile Presbyterian Church cried during the wedding, sniffled really. They were Bob's mother, who came originally from a large Italian-American family, and Aunt Em. Aunt Em was actually Nancy's great-aunt, an artist whose watercolors sold under her married name, Emily Larsh Dicks. Her great-uncle, an exemplary Hamiltonian, had been the nineteenth century orator who eulogized the town's "practical eradicationist" Indian-killers. He was remembered as a kindly old man who collected butterflies. Aside from Aunt Em and Bob's mother, very little emotion was visible among the guests in the church.

As she prepared to drop the name Sloneker for Jackson, however, Nancy's joy beatified her face, dancing in her eyes and giving her smile the intensity of light. The Reverend Ed Brown looked up at the vaulted stained-glass windows presiding on either side of his church and told the bride and groom to put aside their illusions. "You must sustain your unity and deepen your love. Love is patient and kind, never haughty or selfish." Perhaps the young minister was projecting his own innocence onto the wedding couple. Isn't one of the problems with love precisely that it is often, especially when charity is most needed, both haughty and selfish? Surely it is much more than that, but might not a nascent pair of mates be well forewarned to expect from love small generosity along with great insistence upon getting its own? Marion and Dottie Parish, who ran the Mental Health Center in Hamilton, found the most frequent complaints among married couples, as always, were sex and money. Jealousy, scorn, resentment showed up in infidelity, incompatibility, economic rage. "It starts with not getting along in the living room, then pretty soon they don't get along in the bedroom either," Marion Parish often said. But that described a different world, not this community of grace. That was the Hamilton of wrath, not of Nancy Sloneker's radiance. That was for later or never; this evening was candles and veils. Ed Brown asked Mac Sloneker if he gave away his daughter. With just the right tone of assent, the father of the bride answered, "Her mother and I do."

Surveying his dominion of happiness, Ed Brown asked Bob Jackson if he was ready to take the young lady standing next to him as his wife. "I do. I will," Bob said, and proceeded to tell Nancy he would comfort and cherish and love her, as the minister directed.

Nancy's own vow sounded less responsive to Ed Brown, or even to Bob Jackson, than to her own feelings. "I, Nancy, ask you, Bob, to be my wedded husband. Sharing joys, bearing your sorrows, in poverty or in riches. I promise to love and care for you always."

With a nod to reality—"It's not easy to build a deep personal relationship, even in marriage"—Ed Brown asked for the ring. When Nancy's finger had been encircled, the reverend prayed, "Loving Father, strengthen Bob and Nancy. Let them be faithful to each other and to Thee." He barely had time to say they were now married before they embraced.

As Bob and Nancy posed for the traditional wedding picture after the service, the photographer said he was sure the seventy percent deposit had not been necessary in their case. They stood at the altar, then, for a photograph with both sets of parents,

achieving a kind of Norman Rockwell perfection. A teacher who
worked with Nancy was able to say, perhaps wishing she were at
the altar herself, "Thank God she made it at last." For the six
principals—a bride and a groom, two mothers and two fathers
—fulfillment seemed a demonstrable fact. This unblemished
union, made not only in heaven but in Hamilton, was the delight of their families, the envy of their friends. Statistics showing divorces surpassing marriages in many parts of the country
were as remote from this scene as novas in distant galaxies. This
was a beginning that scorned all endings, whether by death or
divorce. It scorned drudgery as well, and trouble, scorned the
gossip that would surface the first time the Jacksons quarreled
in public. In a sense, the moment denied both the past and the
future, ratifying the ritual of wedding while denying the reality
of courtship and marriage. Nothing that Bob and Nancy would
do or endure had any existence other than the pop-flash of
their wedding photograph, glossy testimonial to faith, family,
and love.

In his anthropological study of a French community, the
American scholar Laurence Wylie finds that freedom ends with
marriage. No one is considered grown-up in Wylie's Vaucluse
until "he has tasted excess to the point of preferring moderation." After marriage, individuals settle like stones in a pond,
declining in possibility to the point where they will never be
more than themselves again. Life becomes so centered around
the family that everyone outside the circle of kinship is on some
level an enemy. A characterization of family life in rural France
told more about Bob and Nancy Jackson by contrast than comparison. For Bob and Nancy, their intimacy seemed to enrich
rather than exclude their friendships, their possibilities as individuals were enhanced rather than limited by family responsi-
bilities, and nothing in their guileless countenances betrayed
any excess it would be necessary to trade in for moderation.

In the Vagabond Lounge just west of town, two Hamiltonians
met for a beer after dinner and a long day at the Champion
Paper Company, one of the town's industrial mainstays. "I'm

not saying my wife's the best woman I ever met," the first man said. "I'm saying she's the best *person,* the best person I ever met in my life."

"Whether she's the best wife, Kelly, or person or whatever, I have to agree with you she's one awful good woman," the second man said.

"The best," Kelly said. "She's the routine best and I appreciate her. I never did anything to harm her or to go against her. I can be in a bar someplace and maybe talk to some woman, but I'll never touch her. Maybe she'll come over and sit down beside me and talk to me sort of intimate-like, but by God when I leave that bar I'm walking out of there by myself."

"That's right. Same with me. Once and again, though, you might want to party a little bit."

"Well, once and again, ha ha. Nobody's perfect."

"That's it, Kelly. That's the whole thing. Nobody's perfect."

Sex, which has been an obsession in America since New England ministers issued their proclamations in the 1600s limiting how, when, and where it could take place, is now far more open than it was even a generation ago. You can discuss it, read about it, watch it on the screen, have group encounters centered around it, and best of all you can *do* it. Without being condemned. The sheriff of Butler County banned the magazine, *Hustler,* from Hamilton's newsstands, but the ban was so ineffective that the magazine did not even bother to go to court and have it overturned. The change from Puritan days is complete as long as one remembers that sex was and remains an American obsession. Real change in behavior is much less clear. The change seems in the direction of honesty, allowing attitudes and behavior to be more in line with each other. In *Middletown,* the Lynds noted chastely that "the marriage ceremony relaxes the prohibition upon the mutual approaches of the two persons to each other's persons and as regards the sexual approach makes 'the wrongest thing in the world the rightest thing in the world.' " While "the prohibition" remained in the 1920s and

1930s, it was nowhere near universally honored. The Lynds also observed "an increasing aggressiveness on the part of the girls in the activity preliminary to mating." In their sequel, *Middletown in Transition,* the Lynds did an actual survey and found that seventy percent of unmarried people in their twenties were having sexual relations. That was in the 1930s and hardly accorded with the public standards of the time. In the late 1970s, however, after the widely acclaimed "sexual revolution," slightly over fifty percent of those surveyed in the senior class at both Hamilton high schools still listed themselves as virgins. This figure will decline, of course, by the time the seniors reach the age of the *Middletown* sample, but the indication is strong that behavior has not changed nearly as dramatically as both radicals and hand-wringers claim.

Where attitudes have brought about changes in behavior, it has often been among those who are trying hardest to live by the ideals they profess, especially college students. Tom Rentschler, a Hamilton banker, was married as a senior in college in the mid-1950s. "It's hard to believe this story now," he said as his twenty-fifth anniversary approached. "It's even hard for me to talk about it now, but Dody and I used to go away on weekends when we were in college and we were going together, though we weren't about to get married yet. One time we went on a double date overnight after a football game. We checked into a motel, feeling terribly grown-up, the boys in one room, the girls in another, and the four of us sat up all night talking in that motel. Now the funny thing is that what we were talking about all night was mostly sex, but all we did was talk about it and not do it. I can't imagine kids today spending a night like that, but I think we were protected in some ways. Protected from getting into situations we couldn't handle either physically or emotionally. I think that kids now, by having all the bars down, sometimes get themselves into very frightening predicaments it's not really good for them to be in. This is not a matter of morality but growth." It might please Tom Rentschler—as it would disappoint others—to know that where sex is concerned, there is still a great deal more talk than action in Hamilton. The double standard itself rides on, boys "gaining" sexual experience while girls "lose" their virginity.

If, in nuclear terminology, the wedding of Bob and Nancy would have been called fusion, the reception would certainly have been fission. Families, in-laws, generations, and individuals all seemed to divide, even to come apart. Virtually nothing was as it had seemed at the wedding.

There was the question, first, of money. The wedding, while hardly lavish, had been marked by dignity and quiet class, suggesting prosperity. The Sloneker name is illustrious in Hamilton, one wing of the family having founded the Ohio Casualty Insurance Company, the town's biggest employer and a corporation with vast holdings. "But that's not us; I always say they're the quality Slonekers, we're the quantity Slonekers," said Mac Sloneker, a salesman of foam-core steel doors for home and office, as he bounced around the reception he was giving for his daughter.

Gonzaga Hall, an annex of Hamilton's Mercy Hospital, was the scene of the reception. Upstairs from Gonzaga Hall was the Catholic hospital's detoxification unit for alcoholics. In keeping with the setting, though not because of it, no hard liquor was served to the guests downstairs. The Slonekers could not afford an expensive affair and contented themselves with a champagne punch. "Not that we're complaining," one of the Jackson relatives said. "The rehearsal dinner at Eaton Manor cost $378. Nancy's gown was $250 with the veil. The whole shebang must have set Mac Sloneker back at least $1,200, and that would hurt any of us." The champagne punch tasted a little weak, more like lemonade, but was obviously deceptive. From the way people began to talk, it may have been spiked with sodium pentothal.

As soon as Mrs. Edna Jackson, Bob's grandmother, remarked that she surely was glad to see him married since she had worked so hard to put him through school, the occasion began to unravel. The safety and contentment of hometown roots, so much on display in the little church where the wedding was held, turned out to be an illusion. What was planned merely as a celebration became a public event revealing private truths. At first there were only obvious questions: Why did *you* put him through school? Aren't those his parents posing for pictures with the newlyweds? What are their names? First Edna Jackson, then other relatives in both the Jackson and Sloneker families, gave sketches of feuding clans, of bitterness going back several generations, of skeletons dancing out of the closet onto the manicured front lawn. The reception became a renunciation of the vision that in a heartland town relationships are kind and well-fastened, family patterns are easily repeated, marriages endure.

Edna Jackson was a bitter old lady, acutely conscious of the hardships she had borne, running hard against the popular image of saintly grandmothers gamely weathering every storm to emerge triumphant in their golden years. She was retired after three and a half decades as a paper sorter in the Champion mills. "First of all," she began, "that's not Bobby's father over there. It's his stepfather. Bobby's father, my son, was divorced from his mother when their marriage went sour. Bobby's father remarried, but the woman was hateful. She wouldn't take care of Bobby nor his brother. Bobby's pa worked at the Beckett Paper Company, which his own pa had too, so we were all in the paper business. When he was only thirty-four, Bobby's father died of ulcers, which left Bobby with me since his stepmother was no good to him and his mother wasn't around at that time. Bobby was only thirteen, and I took care of his schooling and room and board. My job at Champion was tough, and it got tougher on the swing shift when I worked from eleven P.M. to seven in the morning. The bosses at Champion were nice and gave me time off to look after Bobby, but the work itself was awful hard. I had the worst grade of paper to sort because the good paper goes out on rolls. Actually, it's even tougher now at Champion because you can't see the defects as easily with the artificial light they've put in there. When they brought in the air conditioning, the artificial lights became necessary because you couldn't open the windows during the day shift any more. My own husband, Bobby's grandfather, died at forty-six of hardening of the arteries while he still worked for Beckett Paper, so I've been on my own since then. I learned to drive when I was fifty-six because the bus service was going off in Hamilton. Finally, Bobby's mother remarried—that nice man with the beard. They took Bobby up to live with them in Kalamazoo, but he had met Nancy while he was in grammar school before they took him away. My twin sister is my best friend now. I'd never marry again, even for love. We have this one younger sister who convinced our father to sell his farm and then talked him out of all the money. He had worked all his life as a machinist and then moved out to his farm. But when our younger sister got him to sell the farm he had to come back to Hamilton, where he died unhappy, with her keeping the money. I guess I have no real good memories except when my grandkids were young."

By vivid contrast, Bob Jackson's mother, now Mrs. Gorman Howard, was cheerful and delighted for her son. She and her husband have one child of their own, and she was happy living in Kalamazoo, where Mr. Howard worked for General Motors. In mood and tone, in all the colorations and impulses that define personality, Mrs. Howard was no more like her former mother-in-law, Mrs. Jackson, than a piece of quartz is like a tangerine. It was not clear how they had ever coexisted in the same town, much less family. A Jackson cousin surveyed them both, Bob's grandmother sitting alone with her resentments in a corner while his mother with her wavy black hair hugged friends and relations in the center of the room, borrowing their handkerchiefs to dry her eyes. "Old Mrs. Jackson had a strike on against Mrs. Howard because Mrs. Howard is a Catholic," the cousin said. "Mrs. Jackson didn't really want her son to marry anyone, certainly not a girl from a big Italian family that seemed to be making noise all over Hamilton."

"I was a Caesar," Mrs. Howard said. She was happy and proud, seeming to dominate about an acre of Gonzaga Hall with her exuberance. "Before I was a Jackson I was a Caesar. There were nine of us kids in my family and we were very close, very emotional. I had no way of dealing with someone like Bob's grandmother. She had no idea what to do with me, either. Actually, she treats me much better now than when I was married to Bob's dad. Isn't this a great occasion?" But Mrs. Howard was as full of relief as she was of joy. "You know, this hasn't been so easy. They've gone with each other, on and off, ever since they were kids. Twice before, they were about to be married. The first time Nancy called it off. The second time Bobby did. Bobby cancelled, got scared really, after the gowns had already been ordered two years ago. That was pretty late, and all of Nancy's family were awful mad at him, except for her father. He seemed to understand. After that, Nancy got a lot smarter."

So the course of true love could run anything but smoothly and still find a way? Was that the late-century message of Bobby and Nancy? "This is their third shot at it," old Mrs. Jackson said from her perch in a darkened corner of the hall. "Let's hope they hit the bull's-eye this time," she added, with what could not quite be called a rush of optimism.

After one of the break-ups, Nancy went to France. She went out with other men and learned the language so well that she was now a French teacher. After their second near-miss, Nancy simply moved to Florida. "That brought Bobby to his senses," a Sloneker relative said. "She did so well without him that he decided he could not do without her. He followed her to Florida, and she took him back." The consensus among the Slonekers was that Nancy was a little more sophisticated, a little sharper than Bobby, and would tend to become the head of her new family. The Jacksons, for their part, felt Nancy had been a spoiled girl who learned a lesson when Bobby broke up with her.

Nancy's grandfather, a house painter named Stanley Sloneker, sailed around the hall in a Colonel Sanders goatee with his own version—no doubt the original one—of his son's remarks about the quantity and quality Slonekers. "I always say there's two Slonekers in Butler County. Them that has. Them that doesn't. And I don't." He was proud, though, that his family got to the United States before the Civil War, which meant he shared a common great-great-grandfather with the chairman of Ohio Casualty, Howard Sloneker.

The divorce of Bob Jackson's parents was mirrored in Nancy's family. "Nancy was terribly upset when her father and mother broke up," an aunt said. "She never thought such a thing could happen, had no idea there was anything wrong. Always saw her father as a complete homebody, which he was. But her mother likes to go out. Nothing wrong with that, she just does."

Nancy's pretty mother, according to family gossip that wafted through Gonzaga Hall, had run off from Hamilton to work for a Republican congressman, leaving Mac Sloneker with two sons and a daughter. When the congressman lost his seat, he lost Barbara Sloneker too. She stayed in Washington, where she worked for several other Republican congressmen before marrying the lobbyist for a manufacturers' association. Her determination, ambition, intelligence, and good looks had gotten Barbara Sloneker, now Barbara Mack, to Washington, but at the wedding she looked back fondly, perhaps twisting her memory slightly to suit her buoyant mood. "People are content here in Hamilton, and that's one thing I miss in Washington," Barbara Mack said, momentarily forgetting that it had been her own *dis*content that had propelled her out of Hamilton in the first place.

Mac Sloneker had never remarried. He accepted his wounds and finished raising his daughter and sons alone. Like Bob Jackson's mother, Mac Sloneker had been one of nine children himself. Divorce was not something he had ever imagined, and relatives said it left him deflated. A business colleague at the reception, who had known him since before his divorce, said, "It just kind of took the rah-rah out of Mac." As the reception began to wind down, Mac Sloneker leaned against a wall, looking exhausted but also satisfied. He and Nancy's mother had scarcely seen each other since she left him, but they had brought the wedding off with warmth that was not forced. They had been polite to each other at first, then something more than polite that could not yet be called at ease. After all, he had come through, maybe turned a little corner.

Nancy's great-aunt, Emily Larsh Dicks, who had cried at the wedding, wished she had been able to do a watercolor of the scene inside the church. Not that Aunt Em, as Nancy still called her, was utterly romantic about weddings. She had had two herself, both ending in divorce. Her second husband, with whom she had been very much in love, died after they were divorced. "World War II," she said, "ruined that man, destroyed his values." Aunt Em was especially fond of Nancy, and she had thought a good deal about the marriage to Bob. She looked at the young couple sympathetically but perceptively. "Well, they're on their own now, to make it or break it. Nancy and Bobby are a bit scrappy," Aunt Em said, partly to herself, but with an almost musical note of prophecy. "That could help them actually, or it could hurt them. I hope they won't scrap too much."

The party swirled around Bob and Nancy, at times lavishing toasts and flashbulbs on them, at times almost forgetting them in the alternating current of gaiety and reminiscence. The groom's morning hangover was only a memory, but his bride's cold seemed to be picking up tempo for her wedding night. Bob Jackson looked to the future. "We plan to stay here even though Hamilton used to be more thriving before several of the big companies left for the South," he said. "A few years ago I'd have felt I had to become a teacher, or at least some kind of white-collar worker, but the truth is I love to work with my hands. I'm doing carpentry now, and maybe some day I'll be a contractor. I can do that here as well as anywhere, and Nancy loves her family an awful lot, so we'll stay in Hamilton."

Sensing that her reception was in danger of losing track of its main attraction, Nancy blew her nose, cleared her throat and yelled to an old college boyfriend across Gonzaga Hall. "HENRY!" A blond, bearded young man turned around and was issued a summons by the bride. "Henry, you fink, come over here immediately!" When Henry had trudged obediently through the crowd to Nancy's side, she beamed at Bob and said, "Well, this is Henry. Remember?" Turning to Henry, Nancy said triumphantly, "Henry, I don't know if you've met my husband."

With that, Bob and Nancy Jackson sped away to their honeymoon hotel in Cincinnati, their wedding over, their marriage begun.

Six months later, Bob Jackson played softball one warm evening while Nancy watched him from the stands. School was out for the summer, and Nancy was expecting to get bored, though boredom for her was not a time of restless discontent but of hot-weather dormancy, part of an organic cycle she would accept tolerantly, hospitably. Bob, at third base, handled every ball hit to him the way a lapidary handles diamonds, and at bat he made two singles and a double, but his team still lost. Over four thousand men and women participate in Hamilton's softball leagues and on most summer nights a dozen games are played.

The Jacksons had just bought a new Volkswagen Dasher and were thinking about a house of their own. "It's too expensive to build, but we hope to buy someday," Nancy said. Their rented home had a garden of about seventy feet by forty feet, and in that space the Jacksons were practicing a vegetable version of Noah's ark. With their four green thumbs, they grew corn, tomatoes, lettuce, radishes, onions, carrots, several kinds of squash, spinach, and canteloupe. Nancy canned some of this; the rest they ate or gave away to friends.

Bob had returned to Miami University at Oxford, Ohio, to get a degree in secondary education as a science teacher, but he did not really plan to teach unless he had to. "He gets so much more enjoyment out of working with his hands, that's what he should do," Nancy said. "I'd like to have a boy and a girl, but we're not looking that far into the future. It'll get here soon enough. Right now we have a golden retriever who just had three puppies."

Nancy accommodated herself to the monotony of summertime as she someday would to pregnancy. "Bob gets tired of my having to work so hard during the winter, correcting papers half the night. We get on each other's nerves at times, but he's really such a sweetie. He cooks and does the dishes when he comes home early and I get home late."

How did they get on each other's nerves?

"Oh, I don't know, just dumb stuff."

As part of the Jacksons' initiation into adulthood, their home was burglarized one day while they were at work. Like others, they felt violated, invaded, almost raped; they might as well have been living in Chicago or New York. "Getting broken into put us in a bad mood for a while," Nancy said, "but we came out of it."

The Jacksons entertained about once a week and had three separate groups of friends. There were her high school classmates (not Bob's, he had lived in Kalamazoo after junior high); Bob's buddies, most of whom were computer operators, softball players, or both; and the teachers Nancy worked with. "We went steady for two months in the seventh grade. Then Bobby left town. After that, I hung around with 'the dirty dozen,' " Nancy said.

"The dirty dozen" were Nancy's eleven closest girl friends and herself, and when she recalled their nickname she pronounced it in such a way as to indicate she meant the clean dozen, at least as far as their own (not necessarily their parents') group standards were concerned. Ten of the twelve went on to college, the same number as were married by the time they were twenty-five. Eight still lived in Hamilton. Only one went to a big city, Los Angeles. One went to a medium-sized city, Nashville, where she married a country and western singer. One went to Naples, Florida, one to Youngstown, Ohio, and another left for a distant Ohio town, but later returned to Hamilton. These informal statistics—no trend, obviously, but an indication of the group Nancy Jackson belonged to—are comparable to the percentage of nineteenth-century Hamiltonians who chose to stay in their hometown.

Two of Nancy's dirty dozen had been divorced, and one had

remarried. Three, including Nancy, had lived with their husbands before getting married. This was hardly what middle-class women would have done in the 1870s, though among the working class it was not uncommon to "set up housekeeping" before a match was ritualized. "A lot of the parents," Nancy said, "still don't like it, but what can they do? Some kids leave town in order to live together, then come back after they marry. The parents don't like marijuana either, but they can't stop it. They all know we smoke now and then." When reminded that many students, if not actually a majority, at the high schools claimed they would leave Hamilton as soon as they graduated, Nancy laughed. "That's what they say. Now let's see what they do."

After his softball game, Bob brought a six-pack from his car, gave most of it away, then put his fielder's glove on his head while he opened a can for himself. "Too bad we lost, but the other team went to the semi-finals last year."

"You were terrific," Nancy said.

"Married life is great," Bob said expansively. "It's fun getting to know each other's habits. But there's hard things about being married, too. It's going to take me five, six years to adjust to the other person, I can already tell."

"That's me," Nancy said, "the other person." She threw a look into the air that asked, "Can you believe he called me 'the other person'?"

"I still like to do things by myself sometimes," Bob said.

"He goes out with the guys and doesn't always say where he is," Nancy said, "like when you went fishing. For two days I had no idea where you were."

"You're the one who stayed out all night."

"I called at least."

"It was two-thirty in the morning by the time you did call," Bob said.

"And you wouldn't answer the phone," Nancy said. "What if I was lying dead in a ditch?"

"It was too late to call. You shouldn't have been out all night."

"I told you—a couple of the girls were drunk and it was their car so I had to drive them home. But I did call you to say I was sleeping over."

"Yeah, at two-thirty."

"And you didn't even answer the phone."

"I was still tired from being waked up the night before by your father wanting to know where your brother is. How am I supposed to know where your brother is?"

"See what I mean?" Nancy said. "Dumb stuff."

Nancy Jackson has what some would criticize as limited horizons and others would admire as the ability to be content. In the cocoon of Hamilton, she does not become wild with Bovary-like fantasies nor stir-crazy like a refugee from *Peyton Place*. In the slow summer, she grows her perfect garden. Possibly when she has had her children and they are half-grown she may feel the cocoon somewhat constricting. Nancy respects the fierce self-reliance she finds in Ayn Rand, the primacy of the individual over the group. But she likes the group she is in too much to want very often to declare her independence of it. In twenty years someone may ask Nancy if she is happy, and she will be likely to say, "Most of the time, yes. Once I thought it would be nice if we went somewhere else, maybe France for a year or two. But he got better jobs here and the babies came and we didn't go anywhere and come to think of it we're probably much better off this way after all."

Bob and Nancy Jackson worked hard enough to buy their own home a few miles north of town just after Nancy got pregnant. Their first child, a boy, was born the same week Nancy's father, Mac Sloneker, was promoted from master salesman to manager of quality assurance for his company. Patrick Jackson was baptized Easter Sunday, 1979, in the Seven Mile Presbyterian Church where his parents were married.

III

THE GAME

In repose, before their team has made its appearance, the Taft cheerleaders could almost be mannequins. Care has made no crease on any of the eight upturned faces whose wholesome purity is marred only by the scent of honey-licorice coughdrops hanging over the two of them that have colds. They are not, however, innocent of apprehension. One chews on her lip, another toys with an ear-level pimple she can only wish she had disposed of earlier. Does it matter to them in their accordion pleats whether they look better than the Garfield cheerleaders, or which team will win, or what moods their boyfriends will be in after the game? Perhaps they are not naive about the world but simply immune to it. At sixteen and seventeen, they have known pressures equivalent to those faced by board chairmen at angry stockholders' meetings. Selected by a scrutiny far more rigorous than the basketball team itself had undergone, the cheerleaders have seen their every flaw magnified in videotaped tryouts that were then shown to a panel of judges with Olympian authority. Yet now they are placid. The cheerleaders sit still, skirted and sweatered in their school's red and black, pompoms at rest in all eight of their sought-after laps, and wait.

Though no player has yet burst from the locker room, the gymnasium is ruled by sweat and wintergreen and the routine Friday night din of fifteen hundred voices, not yet in full yell, but warming up like a symphony orchestra. The game is being played at Garfield on Hamilton's older, shabbier East Side, but the Taft parents and fans have one side of the gym to themselves. The two halves of the gym emphasize the differences between the schools, the divisions in Hamilton. The Taft side is tweed and cashmere, Garfield tends toward chinos and leather jackets, dungarees and workshirts.

Looking fitter than most of the athletes who will presently appear, Mayor Frank Witt sits just behind the Taft bench; his daughter Amy had sung with the Taft Treble-Aires in the pregame concert under the direction of the town's favorite music teacher, the effervescent Sam Shie. Mayor Witt had jogged four miles in the YMCA at lunchtime, putting far behind him a heart condition he developed during his last election campaign, drawing closer to the day when he will seek a broader constituency than Hamilton. He spends mornings at his supermarket, a secure if not lavish economic base, afternoons running the town from city hall. His energy and drive are infectious, symbols of the town's hopes for an economic revival. Frank Witt's own hopes, many Hamiltonians know, cannot forever be contained in a small-city mayoralty. "I don't know where I'm going," he has said, "but I'm having an awful good time getting there."

The Garfield side is divided between Appalachian whites, come north to man factories after their farms gave out, and blacks, who hope their children will break out of Hamilton to find money and equality in Chicago, Los Angeles, or Atlanta. A local character, known as Flatiron, describes the Garfield atmosphere. "On the big hill right above the school is the old home where the county has stashed its down-and-outers ever since the 1840s, and that's pretty much the Garfield story," says Flatiron, a former steelworker who got his nickname after his nose was mashed in a foundry accident. With little to do but collect his pension and disability payments, Flatiron spends his time looking into Hamilton folklore. "What you get these days at Garfield," he says, "is peacetime teenagers whose parents both work, yet never see more than eleven thousand dollars between them in a single year. They send their young to a school at the foot of Poorhouse Hill in a neighborhood appropriate to that designation. The southern whites and the blacks have weak affection for each other. Sometimes right in the hallway they fight like bearcats, but for this game they hate Taft more. In ten years, if they don't leave town, they'll be competing for the same jobs, working for the folks on the other side of the gym. Garfield teachers with kids send them to Taft, never the other way 'round. Now and then Garfield gets its mad up and gives Taft a run for its big bucks. Not this year."

For the children of Taft and Garfield high schools, this game is a way of telling time, of establishing a relationship with Hamilton's past. Banners from old championship seasons drape the gym. The game between Taft and Garfield redeems a dreary record, settles ancient grudges. To the players and their classmates, the game is the season, and the season is the cusp of their future.

If adolescence is anything, it is winning and losing. Grades, dates, sex, a driver's license, complexion, approval, graduation, scholarships, college admission—success and failure looming on all fronts. School becomes victory for brains, beauty, and jocks, defeat for practically everyone else. It is especially a defeat for those from homes that have not prepared them for books and literacy, a defeat passed through the generations like watch fobs and lace doilies. In Hamilton, the traditional channel for adolescent energies, as well as the most consistent metaphor for the wins and losses of adolescence, is athletics. Games, of course, have to be both more and less than metaphor, for they themselves *are* the wins and losses, not merely an index to success and failure elsewhere. Games occupy a region in the community mind where dreams and reality mingle. Yet they are also metaphorical, for they involve the aggression, hostility, exultation and despair that are expressions—postponed, displaced—of triumph and disaster in other arenas.

Not that the Taft-Garfield game represents a crisis confined to adolescence. The community at large is always aroused by the game, which inspires bets, office pools, and barroom arguments. Since Hamilton does not have professional or college sports, it is making no great claim to say that a seat at the Taft-Garfield basketball game is the hottest ticket in town, but extremes are reached that would scarcely be imaginable to those unfamiliar with American sports mythology. Fistfights over seats have broken out among Garfield fans, and Taft parents have used basketball season tickets as courtroom pawns in their divorce settlements.

With amnesia about their own adolescence, some parents ascribe to teenagers an omnipotence in the form of unlimited sexuality and vigor. Among the schoolchildren, therefore, are athletes and beauty queens who become temporary stars in the firmament of local life. The players are infinitely skilled, the cheerleaders infinitely sexy, available for safe fantasies because of the under-age taboo and because, like movie stars, they are unattainable anyway. Work controls the practical side of Hamilton, but this game unleashes its psychic life, its dreams of heroism, beauty, potency, triumph.

During the season, Taft had won twice as many games as it had lost; Garfield had done the opposite. Taking no chances, Taft's practice sessions the week before the game achieved the fervor of war councils. While the team ran plays, its mascot, a boy with muscular dystrophy, hobbled around under a sideline basket taking contorted shots that he was repeatedly successful in sinking. Coach Marvin McCollum paced the court squinting intently at his varsity. It was a squint with a twinkle. McCollum's apparent war council was also a play, and the play was not a melodrama, but a kind of ethical romance with moments of self-mockery. The romance was in the love of victory, the ethics in the means by which victory was pursued.

McCollum was as calm as he was concentrated. When mistakes were made he gestured a player to the sidelines for quiet advice. He never shouted. He watched his charges making power lay-ups, throwing elaborate twenty-foot hook shots, trying turn-around fadeaways, scrimmaging against the second team. McCollum was a moralist fond of trite sayings and mangled parables from sources as disparate as Lao Tze and Tennyson. In the practice for Garfield, these flowed with a happy mixture of earnestness and whimsy. McCollum believed all of them, but he knew they were, after all, slogans and not the Sermon on the Mount. He seemed to use them both as inspiration and tension-breakers.

Having beckoned Mike Grubbs, a senior guard, to his side after Grubbs missed a bounce pass that should have led to an easy basket, McCollum gave a brief lecture on concentration. Then he interrupted himself with:

> *If you can't be a highway be a trail,*
> *If you can't be a sun be a star,*
> *If you can't be the best, be the best man you are.*

When Grubbs returned to the scrimmage, McCollum explained that he loved basketball, but he loved teaching even more. "If you do it right, coaching is teaching. If you don't, it's a crime against youth," he said. A moment later, McCollum darted his dark, glowing eyes at a forward who had fired a long, missed jump shot instead of passing to the center open under the basket. McCollum motioned the forward, Sam Marcum, to join him, and delivered a haymaker. "There is no 'I' in T-E-A-M." When one of his two top players, Andy Kolesar, a tall, muscular guard, lunged in the wrong direction for a pass that ended up behind him, McCollum intoned:

> *You can pitch a no-hit ballgame,*
> *Pass and run with easy grace,*
> *But it's just another loss if a teammate's out of place.*

"Right, Coach. Sorry," Kolesar said, as he hurried gratefully back to his teammates. Kolesar, a senior, had enjoyed and endured McCollum's maxims for three years; they took the sting out of a rebuke, and they were fun to try to remember.

McCollum himself had played baseball and basketball as a student. He came out of World War II with a knee wound that gave him a permanent limp. Though he also had diabetes, he did well enough as a semi-pro pitcher so that the Dodgers offered him a contract with a Class B farm team. "Which was not that hard to turn down," he said, watching his basketball players in their final practice for Garfield, "because all I had was control, and I knew it even if they didn't." McCollum was Taft High's first basketball coach when the school opened in 1959, and there had never been another. He was as different from the screaming drill sergeant coaches as Casey Stengel was from Vince Lombardi. But when his top player, a rangy junior forward named Scott Grevey, loafed after a loose ball, McCollum enfolded him in an anthology of bromides.

> *Good, better, best.*
> *Never let it rest.*
> *Until your good is better, and your better best.*

"I wondered which one I'd get. Sorry, Coach," said Grevey, both of whose older brothers had been coached by McCollum. The eldest, Kevin Grevey, became a star with the Washington Bullets of the National Basketball Association. Scott Grevey had been around McCollum's parables most of his life. "We'll get them for you on Friday night, Coach. I promise."

"It's not winning, it's being our best," McCollum said, immediately launching another proverb:

> *In times of our distress,*
> *And in our triumphs too,*
> *The game is more than the player of the game,*
> *The ship is more than the crew.*

Grevey begged for mercy and rushed back into the scrimmage.

On the West Side, in the newer residential area, Taft had a student body compounded of Hamilton first families, the upper middle class, and some poorer children just up from Appalachia. One student who found herself between the extremes was Sue Barber, an attractive, intelligent junior who was also number one on the girls' tennis team. She had fine, pleasing features and laughing eyes, with the unspoiled sense of possibility that characterizes teenaged Americans at their freshest. Still, she saw the social fences already up, not only between Taft and Garfield, but among Taft students themselves. It was already better to live on a hill than in the flats. "The cliquey kids from Sanders Hill are what our parents call 'the element,'" Sue Barber said. "Then there are the rednecks. If you want to get in with the element, you have to try to connect your name with theirs, and theirs are the names that go way back in Hamilton to the early nineteenth century. On the first day of school, one of the redneck boys walked in with shiny shoes and short pants, probably the first member of his family ever to make it to high school. A girl from Sanders Hill was sitting in the front row in history, and when this boy walked in she just cracked up, which meant her best friend and her boyfriend had to laugh too, and right away half the class was laughing at this poor boy. I just thought it was so cruel. I don't like the element, but then I don't identify with the rednecks either. Between us and Garfield, the tennis scores tell a lot. Our tennis team was ten and four last year. Garfield, with a shorter schedule against weaker teams, was zero and eight. That tells you who gets to play tennis and who doesn't."

Taft's athletic symbol was the tiger; counting pictures, statues and figurines, the school principal had twelve representations of tigers carefully mounted in his office. "I'm a very sports guy, the whole nine yards," said Hank Miller, a stocky dark-haired former coach who greeted Taft's problems with a patient, fixed smile. "I fight fires as they start, it's better not to worry too much beforehand, and I think the school is an expression of the principal's personality. For the last several years we haven't dared to have assemblies, which I hope we can soon. We have simply been unable to get the whole student body together for fear of what would happen. I don't want to tell tales out of school, but we have had our problems. Of course, this *is* a school, isn't it? You know, people have given us the stigma that we prepare for college. This is not entirely so." Taft was sending thirty-three percent of its graduates to four-year colleges, as opposed to Garfield's seventeen percent. With a principal who considered it a "stigma" to have a reputation for being a college preparatory school, it seemed entirely possible that Taft's thirty-three percent could be whittled away without too much difficulty.

Across town at Garfield's last practice before the Taft game, Coach Don Gillespie's problem was completely different from Marvin McCollum's at Taft. Where McCollum had to make sure his players were sufficiently inspired against the crosstown rivals they were supposed to beat easily, Gillespie had to find out if he could field a team at all. His top player, a graceful guard named Robbie Hodge, had been in a Volkswagen accident the week before that left him with a whiplash. Two of his starters had been lost because of suspensions; one had been truant, the other told a teacher to kiss his ass. Garfield had two administrators who described themselves as spending "one hundred percent of our time on disciplinary problems." Gillespie, in his mid-thirties, was Hamilton's first black coach and had played for McCollum in high school. He was very fond of his old coach, but he did not think McCollum's genial methods of handling players would work at Garfield. "The homes my fellows come from," Gillespie said, "they simply don't *hear* anything softer than a holler."

On the court, Robbie Hodge moved with ease and confidence among his taller teammates, showing no effects of the Volkswagen accident. At five-nine, he was the shortest member of the squad, but he could outjump everyone else, including a six-three forward. Most of the players were black, but Hodge, a white senior, managed to be the playmaker and everyone's friend at the same time. Hodge's passes were bullets, often fumbled by less skillful players. Gillespie would shake his head. "Taft averages four inches taller among the starters. All we've got are quick hands and fast legs. If we can't hang onto the ball we're dead." When Hodge or his most talented teammate, a lanky black forward named Calvin Chapman, grew tired of the rest of the squad's mistakes and began to play tricks with the ball, Gillespie shouted, "Hodge and Chapman, I warned you, no more razzle-dazzle! Drop for ten!"

He would yell to keep order, but behind his loud voice, Gillespie was not stern. He was a diligent, patient coach who expected his athletes to give as much as he did. Where McCollum was fatherly, Gillespie was brotherly. With soft, brown eyes, a gently sloping mustache, and a determined chin set in dark flesh that was beginning to run just a little toward pudge, Gillespie might be on his way in a prosperous business career instead of a trainer of adolescents. In fact, he also worked as a probation officer and owned a commercial office cleaning business. Besides coaching boys' basketball and girls' track, Gillespie taught vocational training and was chairman of the Occupational Work Experience Department at Garfield. With all his duties and outside jobs, Don Gillespie had still found time to move his family out of Hamilton to an integrated Cincinnati suburb. He made the move, even with strong ties to Hamilton that included bringing his family back for church each Sunday, because he wanted his children to go to an integrated school. Garfield itself was integrated, with thirty-seven percent black students, but Hamilton's feeder schools—both elementary and junior high—were predominantly either white or black. Gillespie's choice, if he stayed in Hamilton, was for his children to attend all-black ghetto schools for the first nine years of their education, or else to be the token blacks in the upper-middle-class schools on the West Side.

Moving to a better Hamilton neighborhood would not have been easy for Gillespie anyway. On the West Side is a tree-lined street of frame houses in a middle- to lower-middle-class neighborhood. The street is called Progress Avenue, and it intersects with Liberty Street, a fortuitous junction, many would agree, just the way things ought to be in America. *Life* magazine did an article in the 1940s on Progress Avenue as America's most typical street. Yet, at the end of the 1970s, a Hamilton city official declared that an unspoken covenant still existed to prevent blacks from living on Progress Avenue itself.

Don Gillespie's brother, a decorated combat pilot from Vietnam, returned to Hamilton to look for a place to live. Home from the war, Captain Lawrence Gillespie offered to pay one landlord a year's rent in advance if he could take the apartment he liked. The landlord, a prominent Hamilton attorney, refused. When several of the town's most powerful white businessmen intervened on Captain Gillespie's behalf, the landlord told them to go into the real estate business, sign notes guaranteeing mortgages on multimillion dollar apartment complexes, and then *they* could rent to black war heroes. Lawrence Gillespie thanked his white supporters, went into exile, and became the personal pilot to the Prime Minister of Guyana.

"The situation in Hamilton is socially stagnant," Don Gillespie said, as his basketball players took their final practice shots. "This is a status quo town and not just for black people. But the young blacks say, 'Hurry up and let me get old enough to move out of here.' I myself had roots here and wanted to stay; in fact I still hope to move back someday. When I was a kid I served parties at the homes of rich white families, which gave me advantages later. I felt I knew the whole community. I didn't resent being a servant, it was just an apprenticeship. My own father is a businessman himself, though he's not a Beckett. The Becketts have the roast prime ribs in this town—we had a little bit of salami. We lived in the Second Ward ghetto when I was a kid, but it seems poorer now, more hopeless. Some of my students who come from there have a very dim view of themselves. The black junior high allows them to practice stupidity as long as they don't become discipline problems. They get good at dumbness. We have to try to correct the junior high's mistakes when they come to Garfield, but teachers do the same things kids do—they make up their minds on certain students who have a bad rep or poor grades, and they stick to their initial impression. It's doubly hard for a kid to get out of his rut when his teacher is helping him stay in it. The cliché is accurate. These kids aren't failing school; school is failing them."

There was a sense that Don Gillespie did not quite belong away from his hometown because he still cared too much about it. He had the objectivity of an outsider, having grown up black in Hamilton, yet this was combined with the insight and affection of an insider. Knowing the town's problems intimately, he was wary of plunging back into Hamilton as a contestant for community stewardship. He was a little afraid he might become corroded with bitterness, as had one local black leader, or be bought off with an impotent municipal title, as had another. So Don Gillespie had chosen to leave, thereby depriving both the town and himself of a unique potential for leadership.

A white teacher stopped by the practice on his way home, putting on a deep southern accent as he greeted Don Gillespie. "How's the team, boy?"

Affecting an obsequious manner and a black lower-class accent of his own, Gillespie trotted out his ritual answer. "We might could surprise some folks, boss."

"Ah'm so sorry y'all moved outa town," the white teacher continued. "Ah told you boys to wait a little longer and y'all could move inta any neighborhood you lahk."

"All I wanted, boss, was to move next door to you, and you went and blocked me ev'y time."

"Be patient is what Ah said. Rome was not built in a day. Jes' give us a little moah time, hear?"

Gillespie shooed the other teacher away, unamused by the minstrel routine but unwilling to break it, and summoned his players. They were slow to assemble, Robbie Hodge horsing around with his best friend, a black guard named Tony McCoy, the rest of the squad trying long, idle hook shots from well past the key. Hodge and McCoy were partners on and off the court, known to everyone as salt and pepper. "Fellas, I said get your asses over here!" Gillespie bellowed. Now they crowded around him, chicks to a familiar roost. "I don't know what I can tell you," Gillespie began. "Taft figures they're going to kill us. They're thinking state tournament and we're just a little pebble in the road, they can roll right over us. The paper says, I quote, 'The Taft Tigers should encounter no difficulty with the Garfield Griffins.' End of quote, end of city rivalry, end of our self-esteem. Men, and that's what you are, I appeal to your potential, because you all have it. I appeal to your competitive instincts. Most of all, I appeal to your pride."

Waiting for the game to begin in the steamy Garfield gym, Flatiron, the old steelworker, muses on the relationship of the sport to its environment. "Basketball has always been a perfect game for the Midwest," he says. "This is a vast area of small towns tied together at first by interurban tracks and later by Model T's that enabled fans to follow their teams from town to town. There wasn't a damn thing to do in most middlewestern towns once the hunting season ended, so the local gym became the town hall for a few months. This crosstown matchup only goes back twenty years because before that Hamilton had just one high school, the Big Blue they called them, and they took state championships like brass rings at a county fair. When they built the two high schools they split the town, but they started a pretty hot rivalry. It should just about end tonight. Taft could take this by thirty or forty points."

The gym explodes as the Taft team breaks onto the court, each player leaping dramatically through a paper banner held up by the cheerleaders. The banner is torn down the middle by the first player, his teammates in close pursuit, each emerging from the head and haunches of a brightly striped tiger. Next, the Garfield players do a loop around their own gym, and the crowd volume turns to thunder. A few boos for the Tigers since they are, after all, in enemy territory, and for the Griffins since they have, after all, a dismal record.

The jump ball is controlled by Taft as the gymnasium's contained energy is released on the court. After furious scrambling,
a Garfield forward dashes for the basket and misses. Taft's six-
two senior guard, Andy Kolesar, controls the rebound and slows
down the play, setting his team's own preferred pace. Taft
scores first on an easy shot by its star junior forward, Scott
Grevey, from inside the key. The Tigers lope to their end of the
court while the Tigerettes—Taft's cheerleaders—give the yell
that means their boys have drawn first blood. Garfield's Griffins,
named after the mythical hybrid between a lion and an eagle,
retaliate with a long jumper by their star, Robbie Hodge, admi-
rable not only for its accuracy but its trajectory. High school
ballplayers, when they jump, often fire the ball straight at the
basket, making a score impossible unless their aim is perfect;
Hodge's shot, taken when he is high off the court, describes an
arc like the dotted lines on a globe showing the voyage of Ma-
gellan.

With the score at two apiece, Taft's full-throated cheer is simply "Go!" repeated ten times, though the Tigerettes pronounce
it "Geaow." A free-lance cheer wafts down from the Garfield
stands. "Tiger thinks he's cool, but Griffin ain't no fool. We
gonna get 'em, you just bet 'em, we got the jive-ass school!" The
city's racial partition is reflected on the court and the sidelines.
Garfield has three black starters, Taft none. Three out of five
Garfield cheerleaders are black, only one out of eight on the
Taft side.

Taft controls the game easily at first, not yet hot, passing the
ball too much, waiting to shoot until the best opportunity has
passed—but still in command. Garfield, by contrast, is disorga-
nized, scrambling hard for each loose ball, inconsistent in its
shots, hustling in every direction. By fighting for every loose
ball, the players keep the game even until it is tied at ten, Taft
scoring each basket first and Garfield responding. A pattern is
established in a personal duel. Andy Kolesar, Taft's leading
scorer all season, cannot shake the player assigned to guard
him, the five-nine Tony McCoy. It is a one-on-one that looks

like a confrontation between Mutt and Jeff. The same height as his best friend, Robbie Hodge, McCoy haunts Kolesar all night, crowding him, blocking his drives, stealing passes intended for him. Though giving away five inches in height, McCoy becomes Kolesar's shadow, his ghost, his tight-fitting glove.

Taft's Scott Grevey is ready to fill the void left by McCoy's neutralization of Kolesar. Grevey, Coach McCollum said, was improving every week; as a six-two junior, he appeared ready to join the family tradition of high school stardom, a college scholarship, followed by the NBA like his brother Kevin. The previous summer, Coach Gillespie of Garfield had taken twelve Hamiltonians to play basketball in Poland. Both Andy Kolesar and Scott Grevey had made the junket, which included a musical welcome from the Poles, a tour of the twelfth-century city of Walcz, and an infatuation with a Polish ice cream known as Lody. Neither Robbie Hodge nor any other current Garfield player had been able to afford the trip.

Robbie Hodge and Scott Grevey expressed the differences between Garfield and Taft. They shared one characteristic— both their fathers wanted them to play basketball. Beyond that, their lives were completely different, beginning with the fact that Hodge was short and Grevey tall. The Greveys were a prominent Hamilton family. Norm Grevey, Scott's father, was a successful lawyer who in the space of three days, would fly to South Carolina to see his son Brian play college ball, then up to Washington to watch Kevin with the pros, and return to Hamilton in time to be at Scott's game for Taft. He had a fourth son, only nine years old, who, he liked to say, hoped to quit junior high to turn pro as a hardship case. Norm Grevey admitted jovially, under a full-court press, that his son Scott had repeated a grade once, a widespread practice known as redshirting, which meant that Scott would be older and bigger—more attractive bait for college recruiters—by the time he played his last year of high school ball. The grade had only been repeated, Norm Grevey claimed, because of a reading problem. The effect, Don Gillespie said, was that "Scott Grevey is bored, very bored. He's old enough to graduate and he's only a junior. He just bides his time. This wastes a year of a boy's life at a moment when he is either excited by learning or gets turned off to it forever."

Robbie Hodge's father installed safes around the country for one of Hamilton's largest manufacturers, the Mosler Safe Company. An older brother of Robbie's had been in trouble with the law. Robbie himself was a nervous, inattentive student who at times seemed to have a crush on every girl at Garfield. According to Don Gillespie, Robbie Hodge's father hoped to restore his family's reputation, sullied by the older brother's juvenile delinquency, through Robbie's becoming a great basketball player. "A lot of the fathers in Hamilton try to relive their own youths, or the ones they wish they had had, through their sons," Gillespie said. "Some of them also want to make up for a lack in their lives currently. This is true in many families, not just the Hodges. Robbie is jumpy around school, and he thinks he's God's gift to women—all women. He's a great competitor—in everything."

Though he does not make any more of Garfield's early baskets, Robbie Hodge sets up his team's plays. Then Scott Grevey finds his rhythm and his eye; from ten all, Taft opens a six-point lead. Garfield has prepared itself for Andy Kolesar, its defense against him almost perfect. When Scott Grevey takes command of the Taft offense, Garfield seems to lose its bearings. Grevey has leaped past several defenders for a twisting, sinuous lay-up. A few seconds later, before the opposition can get to midcourt, Grevey steals the ball from a Garfield sophomore but is quickly surrounded. He lunges away from the basket, free of the defenders, and arches his right arm for a long, languid hook that swishes through. When Robbie Hodge has a pass picked off like a football interception, Garfield, in its own vernacular, looks out of it. Out of it, the way Garfield teenagers describe anyone who is not in it, with it, on top of it. Out of it, like their principal, who built lamps and made ham and cheese omelets in his office, like their aged chemistry teacher, who had lived only with her dogs ever since—it must have been centuries ago if it ever happened—her new husband committed suicide on their honeymoon.

Robbie Hodge is mad at himself. As if cupping the wind in his hands and causing it to shift, Hodge brings the ball down-court with a dribbling display that leaves three Tigers springing at each other instead of at him. He seems less interested in scoring than in maneuvering the ball between a defender's legs, which he does as his fans laugh. In his folding chair on the Garfield sidelines, Coach Gillespie covers his eyes. How many times has he cajoled, ordered, threatened Hodge about this? Just play straight basketball, never mind hotdog displays, we all know you know how to bounce the ball. But Hodge's tricks inspire his team and, to show his generosity, he passes off to a teammate when he has gotten most of Taft out of position. The teammate scores easily. Taft brings the ball into play, but Hodge steals it immediately and lofts himself over the defender to sink his own basket. Hodge jumps so that he appears not to be jump-ing but floating. His feet barely touch the ground before he is in the air again, on a pogo stick of ligament and tendon. When Taft misses its next shot, Hodge goes high over a six-three Tiger to take the rebound. For an instant, with everyone else frozen, watching, Hodge is a pink streak among the white and black beanpoles who populate the rest of the court. Hodge is down the court to set up a play for the tall, black Calvin Chapman who is fouled while making his lay-up. Chapman sinks his free throw, and Garfield takes its first lead when Hodge steals the ball once more and passes long to a waiting forward, who dunks it.

Scott Grevey and Sam Marcum lead Taft back in the second quarter, but the tempo is much faster than Coach McCollum likes it. "The height on this court belongs to us, Hodge has the speed," McCollum says to his starters during a time-out. "Our game is to work the ball inside to Grevey or to Kolesar if we can get him open, and let those guys run themselves out. Hodge can't keep this up, but we shouldn't be trying to run with him. Slow down and play your own game."

Taft settles into the rhythm McCollum has prescribed. A fluid teamwork with looping passes from the backcourt to the fore-court, into the corners and out to the center line again, the process continuing until someone gets free near the basket, then the swish through the net itself, almost as electronic as the red lights overhead posting two more points. Hodge misses from the outside and hits on a free throw. Tony McCoy eases off on Andy Kolesar long enough to make two baskets for Garfield. But the converse is that Kolesar himself scores three times for Taft. The game is controlled by Taft now. Taft makes the plays, Garfield only responds. The Tigers leave the court at the half with a 32–25 lead. Garfield has shown more spunk than expected, but Taft has found its pace and forced the game to fit it.

At halftime, behind the blare of two bands and the incantations of the crowd, there is the silence of anticipation. Halftime is the midpoint in a crisis, like the instant at which, when a jump ball has been thrown in the air, it is no longer rising but has not yet begun to fall. The game both imitates and escapes life better than most school activities. But some of what went on in a Hamilton classroom managed to come fairly close to real life and even closer to death.

There was John Ritchie, and there was Martin Protzman.

John Ritchie, Hamilton's first schoolteacher, arrived in 1807 from the East. He taught English grammar, Latin, and arithmetic at four dollars per student per term. Because there was not yet publicly supported education in Ohio, the Hamilton parents were supposed to pay John Ritchie themselves. Sometimes they gave him dried apples and peaches, a little grain, or corn whiskey. They rarely gave him the four dollars. Unlike many other frontier schoolteachers, John Ritchie did not take to the corn whiskey; he had come to teach. But if pioneering was hard for homesteaders, farmers, millhands, and landowners, it was harder for teachers. They were needed, but not very much. John Ritchie lived in his classroom, stuck it out for seven years, and then gave up, putting an ad in the paper that begged the parents of Hamilton to pay him what they owed him so he could return East. Still they did not pay, but John Ritchie could not afford to leave Hamilton on his own. When they arrived at school one morning in 1815, his students found Hamilton's first schoolteacher dead of starvation. He had apparently awakened in the night and lighted a last candle for himself, which was still burning. John Ritchie's bed, clothing, desk, and chair were sold at auction to pay for his burial.

Martin Protzman taught government and history at Taft High School in the 1970s. Because he felt his students should learn the connection between text and reality, and because he felt recent history should not be forgotten until it becomes safely distant, once each term Martin Protzman removed his artificial right leg and passed it around his classroom. He had left his real right leg in the Ashau Valley when he made the mistake of stepping out of his foxhole into a North Vietnamese barrage one morning in 1968. Students liked Martin Protzman because he identified with their problems and resentments; he liked them because he saw himself only a few years earlier, an indifferent student who graduated from Taft in 1964. Even with one leg, Martin Protzman loved to play golf and played so well that he won the National Amputee Golf Championship. He was equally intense about his teaching and did not mind staying late to debate a student or just listen to the perils of being sixteen. When his wife had a baby and inflation became an epidemic, Martin Protzman needed more money. He couldn't get it at Taft, and he wanted, frankly, to provide himself and his family with some of the abundance he saw around him. Shortly after the historic Bond-Issue controversy, he quit teaching and went into real estate. Martin Protzman had more options than John Ritchie.

Would the 32–25 halftime basketball score, a modest point total even for high school, have added up to 57 points for Hamilton if Taft and Garfield were only one school instead of two? That was the theory—though far more was at stake—and to some degree that was what led to the fight over the Bond Issue.

The Bond Issue came about because of birth control and all the factory jobs that left Hamilton when the South rose again in the 1960s and 1970s. In 1970 Hamilton had three thousand high school students, but ten years later the total was around twenty-two hundred and the projection was that there would soon be fewer than two thousand. Many Hamiltonians felt that the two high schools, once necessary because of the World War II baby boom, should be unified. A single school could offer far more courses and facilities than two schools with declining enrollment. In line with Hamilton's remarkable predilection for allegorical names—the smart Mayor Witt, the friendly Congressman Kindness, a neighborhood bully named Wolff, the plain-spoken managing editor Blount, an ebullient singer named Joy Rose, a yes-man named Dittoe, a contractor named Plasterer, a politician called Hack and a cashier named Miss Penny—the new superintendent of the antiquated school system was, of course, named Relic.

Dr. Peter Relic, an idealistic educationalist, was a young Ph.D. determined to modernize the schools and schooling of Hamilton. After growing up in a Slovenian neighborhood in Cleveland, Dr. Relic had done volunteer work in Peru, Germany and Turkey, and had been a school principal for Japanese and American children in Kyoto. Hamilton was his first superintendency, and if anything, his previous experience had fortified both his earnestness and his innocence. "We have a wonderful cooperation within our neighborhoods," he said, "but almost none at all between one neighborhood and another. That's why, with our loss of students, we can take the opportunity to unify the entire town by consolidating the two high schools into one. We'll be able to offer more varied courses—art, music, drama, dance are all secondary now, but they can be primary in a single comprehensive school. We can have far better teams. Hamilton used to have very, very powerful football and basketball teams on the state level; that's impossible while we have split high schools. It can be argued that pragmatically this country was built on segregation, but our ideals have always moved toward integration. Our blacks should be spread equally through the system, and one high school will do that. Blacks are locked into the Second Ward ghetto. For all practical purposes, the Supreme Court's integration decision has never been implemented in Hamilton. With a single stroke, one high school will solve all these problems."

Others in Hamilton who fully agreed with Dr. Relic's consolidation plan sensed that he was not yet in full command of the superintendency and that his constituency was dubious. A special election, nonetheless, was scheduled. The new, unified high school would cost seventeen million dollars, to be raised through a local bond issue whose fate would be decided in the special election. Once the new high school was ready, Taft and Garfield would be used as junior highs, giving the community, in effect, three new schools. Opponents said the tax bite was too large, that discipline and learning were needed far more than buildings, and that Taft and Garfield—only twenty years old— were perfectly decent high schools. It was said quietly that those against the school bond also did not want their children going to school with blacks.

A good deal of money was spent to defeat the Bond Issue by a swiftly formed group called the Butler County Taxpayers Association. They took ads in the Hamilton *Journal News* and made numerous radio appeals against the Bond Issue. The *Journal News* itself took a pro-bond stand, and its publisher, Chuck Everill, was a vigorous backer. "Hamilton is very much in need of this improvement, both for its own sake and as a symbol," Chuck Everill said privately. "This is a vote not just for a new central high school but for a solution to our racial problems and for a civic enterprise to combat the loss of pride that went along with the loss of industrial jobs. The school will give Hamilton a new image of itself, which we need badly."

Proponents tended to be the liberals, the blacks, and those who, like Chuck Everill, felt a new school would help the community's self-esteem. Their adversaries tended to be the poor whites, who felt taxed over their heads already, the elderly on fixed incomes, and fiscal conservatives, all of whom the Butler County Taxpayers Association purported to represent. The Bond Issue became a community litmus test, with overtones that were even religious. A huge woman with a severe wheeze puffed up the post office steps one day a week before the election. "With all these abortions and birth control devices," she said, "we don't need any more schools because we don't have children like we used to. The good Lord doesn't like that. Besides, Jesus is coming soon, honey, and I have emphysema." Joe Nuxhall, a Hamiltonian who in the wartime 1940s became the youngest baseball player—at fifteen—to pitch in the major leagues, saw difficulties both ways. "When they went to two schools in the fifties they divided Hamilton more than the Miami River ever did," he said. "Now they're trying to put it back together again with a seventeen-million-dollar Band-aid."

Then the Butler County Taxpayers Association, having hitherto claimed only to stand for fiscal responsibility, let its other shoe drop.

In a full-page advertisement in the *Journal News*, the Taxpayers Association warned voters that if there were only one high school, there would be "More Busing and Traffic Congestion." In case anyone did not divine the significance of the reference to busing, the ad became threatening in bold capitals: "DON'T LET THE BOOGIE MEN SCARE YOU." There it was: BOOGIE. But then it may have been the moderates who prevailed; perhaps the Association hardliners had wanted the ad to say it would be a BLACK day for Hamilton if the Bond Issue passed.

In person, at the Eaton Manor, Hamilton's only elegant restaurant, the men who ran the Taxpayers Association were not reticent. For them, the Bond Issue was a chance to ventilate a variety of concerns, not only economic but racial, sexual, and disciplinary. Bud Woltering, a local businessman with a Colonel Sanders goatee, said no industrialist would ever expand his plant in the face of a shrinking market, which was what Hamilton students were. Hack Wilson, a retired city manager who had held more local offices than anyone in Hamilton's history, liked to say that the only excuse for building a new high school was if they wanted him to come over and teach political science. With an air of provincial majesty, Hack Wilson, in a confrontation with a listener and a mirror, found it hard to choose the former, flicking frequent glances at himself the way a welterweight jabs at a sparring partner. Ray Motley, a retired radio station manager and sportscaster, was president of the Butler County Taxpayers Association and had placed the ad warning Hamiltonians about "BOOGIE MEN." "But my goodness," he said at the Eaton Manor with a perfectly straight face, "I certainly had no intention of seeming antiblack." Gordon Smith, a retired assistant county auditor, rounded out the strategy board of the Taxpayers Association as its fiscal expert.

Addressing himself in the mirror, like a candidate preparing for a national television debate, Hack Wilson said one of the biggest problems with the Bond Issue was Dr. Peter Relic's inexperience. "Let's face it," he said, "they sent a boy out to do a man's job. Some of our liberal friends, God love 'em, just don't have the hands-on experience it takes to implement their theories. It's like when they say you have to give girls the same athletic facilities as boys." The former city manager got his nickname because he was a semi-pro baseball player in 1930 during the brief and bibulous reign of a homerun-hitting Chicago Cub named Hack Wilson.

"That Title Nine stuff for equal facilities is the bull," Bud Woltering said. "Girls are being liberated from what, to what? Sure they need exercise, but physiologically speaking they are not built to stand up to us. At West Point the girls are falling like flies, flunking out every day. A girl ought to major in home economics."

"Girls can't compete with boys," Ray Motley said.

"You come across one Babe Didrikson in a lifetime," Bud Woltering said.

"If a woman is doing the same work as a man, she should get the same pay," said Gordon Smith, the former auditor.

"If a black comes in and works, actually works, he should be paid the same, too," Bud Woltering said.

"*If* he works," said Gordon Smith.

"Right, *if* he works," said Woltering.

"Why doesn't Washington practice what they preach?" Hack Wilson asked the mirror. "Is there more colored than white working for the federal government in Washington? You'd better believe it, and that's no balance."

"In Washington, D.C.," Gordon Smith said, "a black valedictorian of his high school class couldn't even get into Georgetown."

"Education has been going down here for the last fifteen years, and the slow learners, the lower economic groups, hold back the others," Ray Motley said.

"My dad was in a lower economic group," Bud Woltering said.

"Well, there are exceptions, of course," Ray Motley said. "Did you know that the blacks in the all-black schools of Mississippi have a better achievement record than they do in mixed schools? They learn better in their own environment."

"We're between a rock and a hard place on integration," Bud Woltering said. "There's too G.D. many geniuses out there, trying to see everybody getting a fair shake."

"The teachers can't control integrated classes, there's too much trouble," said Ray Motley.

"Blacks can't take the discipline," Bud Woltering said.

Hack Wilson took his eyes off the mirror and riveted them on Bud Woltering. "Don't talk to *me* about discipline. My pa was a Presbyterian minister. I did something wrong, I'd get spanked twice—once at school, again at home."

"The ACLU has a suit going right now against kids getting whipped in Ohio," Bud Woltering said. "ACLU, you know, the American Communist Lawyers Union."

"My dad used a buggy whip," Ray Motley said.

"I'd get whipped on the hand at school," Hack Wilson said, "until I couldn't open my hand. When my dad would see I had a hurt hand, he'd tell me to go upstairs and then he'd whip me with a razor strop."

"My pa used a paddle," Gordon Smith said.

"We'd have to go out and collect wooden slats," Bud Woltering said. "My dad would use the slats on us until they broke."

"My middle son says I made him spend half his life on a chair in the corner," Hack Wilson said. "But how else you gonna make 'em learn?"

Mayor Frank Witt had stayed out of the fight over the Bond Issue. He did not want to confuse the two institutions of city council and school board, and he did have doubts about the wisdom and necessity of asking the citizens of Hamilton for seventeen million dollars. But the Taxpayers Association propelled Witt into action. First, he placed his own personal ad in the paper, urging passage of the School-Bond Issue. Then he agreed to appear with Superintendent Relic at a town meeting to support a single high school. The meeting was held in the auditorium of the Hamilton branch of Miami University of Ohio.

As a rally, the meeting was more like a bridge club. In a hall that could hold over 450, thirty citizens showed up. Dr. Peter Relic, an articulate but not always effective spokesman for his own cause, went first. He was an example of the specialist who does not quite know how to organize support for his program. He made such a doctoral effort not to be patronizing that at times he even talked *beneath* the heads of his audience. To a group of parents concerned about educational opportunity, he emphasized that Hamilton athletic teams would improve dramatically with only one high school. The parents, of course, felt patronized, the very thing Dr. Relic wanted most to avoid. He was a man with a plan but no way to communicate it.

Carl Morgenstern, a highly articulate school board member, spoke next. Though disillusioned with Dr. Relic as superintendent, Morgenstern still supported the Bond Issue. He said a new central school was "the best way for Hamilton to go." Morgenstern, a prominent and highly vocal attorney who had been named the most influential citizen in Hamilton by the *Journal News*, was seldom silent on any issue. He loved verbal combat and would often dare others to take an opposing side in debate. "If everyone agrees," Morgenstern liked to say, "then someone is not thinking."

For Frank Witt, the meeting provided one of those moments that occasionally surprise a politician. The campaign waged by the Taxpayers Association, not Dr. Relic's persuasiveness, galvanized passions within Witt that he had been unaware of. As a Hamiltonian with Kentucky roots, he granted he had been a slow learner on racial equality. The mayor knew he had stayed out of a controversy that affected everyone in town. Without notes, Frank Witt mounted the podium for a speech he had no idea he was going to give until he gave it. "The new community high school is not an extravagance for the taxpayer, it is an investment in Hamilton's future," Mayor Witt said. "It can end the isolation of our neighborhoods, heal the lesions in our community. It can unite East Side and West Side, black and white, rich and poor and middle. They're telling us to watch out for boogie men; I say watch out for *them!* Watch out for those who would isolate us from each other. Watch out for those who sneak around inciting fear and race hostility. They tear the fabric of a society that needs mending. They serve ignorance, not knowledge, and knowledge is the purpose of all schools. A progressive educational system is the foundation and backbone of our youth, and our youth are the backbone of the future. I urge you to support a single, consolidated high school for the city of Hamilton." The mayor left the speaker's rostrum, not to an ovation, but to a scattered clapping of idle hands that sounded more like wind rustling through a few leaves that had escaped an autumn bonfire.

Not long after the voters rejected his Bond Issue by over three to one, Dr. Peter Relic announced he was leaving Hamilton for Washington, D.C., and a long title—deputy assistant undersecretary for education. "I couldn't turn down the opportunity, but I feel very frustrated," he said, leaving town not in triumph, but at least in candor. "I started a lot here and finished nothing."

Mayor Witt walks around to sit on the Garfield side just before the second half of the game begins. Though it is surely the right political move, he would not have bothered to make it before the Bond Issue, defeated three months earlier, so forcefully reminded him he was mayor of all Hamilton. The third quarter gets under way with Coach Marv McCollum looking around the packed, shouting gymnasium as though he were surveying a panorama of universal folly. He turns quickly back to the game. On the Garfield side, Coach Don Gillespie smiles bleakly at the scoreboard showing his team behind by seven points, then yells for Robbie Hodge to set up a play.

From 32–25 at the half, Garfield expresses itself with a single free throw by Calvin Chapman while Andy Kolesar shakes off Tony McCoy and combines with Sam Marcum to make four unanswered baskets for Taft. The score, 40–26, is well on the way to the embarrassing mismatch that the mash-nosed old steelworker, Flatiron, had predicted. Although Robbie Hodge strikes back with two quick baskets and a free throw, he is unable to set plays for his teammates, who are smothered by the taller powers from Taft. Nine points looks like a hopeless chasm that can only grow wider.

A tall, rangy black man on the Garfield side jumps down from the stands and leads a cheer. Under a low wide-brimmed Panama hat, wearing a black shirt, white tie, and a black suit with white pinstripes too thick for a banker and too narrow for the center strip on a highway, he is described by Flatiron as Hamilton's second most prominent pimp. "The top man don't show in public, nobody knows even if he's white or black." The cheer wanders a bit in the wavy mist of a Quaalude, but the crowd is familiar with the words and stays with most of them: "Aw shucks, hey now, Griffin's gettin' down. Yet and still we'll be aroun' 'cause with our pride, jump back, show you where it's at, when it comes to winnin' we're second to none, like we know that you know that we know we're Number One!"

Whatever anyone is presumed to know about Garfield, Taft controls the game. Scott Grevey delivers set shots, hooks, and jumpers as though they were in his blood, which they probably are. With Kolesar still covered by Tony McCoy, Taft's six-five center, Mike Grammel, and its six-one guard, Mike Grubbs, control the ball so well they seem to be playing catch. When Hodge or Calvin Chapman threaten to steal a pass, the game becomes keep-away. The huge Grammel is an easy target for his teammates and an impossible obstacle for Garfield. Taft simply passes the ball around until a forward, usually Scott Grevey, breaks himself open for a shot. Grammel to Grevey to Grubbs to Marcum back to Grammel to Kolesar, if he's free, and then to Grevey for his shot.

The gap seems an uncloseable twelve points when Hodge manages to intercept a Marcum pass. He laterals to Tony McCoy, who converts the turnover. The stolen ball fires Hodge and the rest of Garfield, and they step up the pace. This is Hodge's rhythm, to play at the speed of sight. It is not Taft's rhythm, and they cannot sustain it. Frustrated by Hodge, Taft begins to run hard and shoot soft. The whole team grows cold. With Taft momentarily becalmed, Hodge lifts the pace still further. Repeatedly, he spins through the Taft team, fakes, halts, then leaps for his jump shot, becoming an emblem of himself. The game is metered by his passes and shots.

In a two-man sport, such as boxing or singles tennis, it is not uncommon for one of the athletes to lead the contest in the direction most compatible with his own talents. He goes where he likes, dominating the action with his power or agility or finesse. In basketball, with ten men always on the court, it is incomparably harder for one of them to force everyone else to play his particular game. When it does happen, it is a tall man, Kareem Abdul-Jabbar or Wilt Chamberlain, who controls everyone else. For a short man to pick up the game and mold it to his own talents, as Boston's Bob Cousy once did, his hand, like a

magician's, must be quicker than any eyes but those of his teammates, who have learned what to anticipate. Robbie Hodge's
game is speed. At times earlier in the season, his hand was
indeed too quick for some of his teammates. His passes would
bounce off their chests or sail into the stands because someone
wasn't looking. Now, late in this third quarter against Taft,
the Garfield team becomes, as coaches like to say, not only quick
but fast. They run and pass and grab and lunge and shoot as
reflections of Hodge himself, and where the ball is, they are,
too.

Hodge himself is everywhere. Taft is nowhere that counts.
Shorter than any Taft player, Hodge swarms all over the Tigers
—on offense, defense, forecourt and back, out of position, stealing the ball, setting a pick, making the play. Once he even passes
the ball to himself, tricking the defender almost literally, as the
saying goes, out of his jockstrap. When McCollum sends both
Marcum and Grevey to cover Hodge, Calvin Chapman, Tony
McCoy, and a six-three sophomore named Jeff Jones collabo-
rate to score for Garfield. At the end of the third period, Chapman takes a long jumper that hits the rim and springs away. In
the rebound scramble Jeff Jones bats the ball through the hoop
at the buzzer. Taft is on top now by only four points.

"It was a drunk in a truck that hit Hodge in the Volkswagen,"
Flatiron says on the sidelines. "They say it's whiplash. I'm surprised Gillespie has left him in as long as he has."

As if on cue, Hodge begins to massage his neck in the Garfield
huddle before the start of the fourth quarter. Gillespie tells him
to get on the bench. "I'm rubbing my freakin' neck, Coach,
that's all," Hodge says.

Gillespie tells the Garfield trainer to look at Hodge's neck.
The trainer says Hodge might have a slight crick but no real
whiplash. He'll rub on some wintergreen. Turning to Hodge,
Gillespie asks, "Can I trust you, Robbie?"

"Yeah, sure, we got a shot here."

"That doesn't mean your neck's okay."

"My neck does what I tell it to, and it ain't hurt."

The last quarter begins abruptly with Hodge stealing the ball right out of Sam Marcum's hands and making an easy, fast lay-up to bring his team within two points. Grevey strikes back with a long set shot to return the spread to four points. The game stabilizes, which means Taft owns the pace. Garfield can get no closer than four points. Hodge cools off, looking tired—not hurt, just weary. His own speed has caught up with him. Taft plays ball control, shooting only when the shot is perfect. Time is on Taft's side. With two minutes left in the game, the Tigers make a free throw to go ahead by five. Hodge is fouled, but misses both shots. From the Garfield fans, in their dungarees and work clothes, comes a cheer, "Hey, no sweat, the game ain't over yet." But it looks like it is.

Taft's blonde cheerleaders give their repetitive yell again. "Geaow! Geaow! Geaow! Geaow!" The whole Taft side, flannels and cashmeres with weekend hairdos, erupts in a unison chant of "V-I-C-T-O-R-Y!"

Taft stalls dutifully for a minute and a half, letting the clock win for them, scoring no further but keeping control of their own missed shots. With thirty seconds remaining in the game, Mike Grubbs shoots for Taft and the ball caroms off the hoop against the backboard and then bounces crazily to the side. The two players nearest it are the five-nine Hodge and the six-five Mike Grammel, Taft's center. Hodge makes a soaring jump, but eight inches is too much to give away and Grammel comes down with the ball. Hodge comes down onto Grammel's elbow, which accidentally catches him underneath the arm. A harmless, momentarily painful jab, it has the effect of an injection of adrenalin. Hodge does not so much take the ball as leap it out of Mike Grammel's hands. In one motion, as if the play had been planned all season, he has hurled the ball downcourt to Calvin Chapman, who dribbles twice and puts the ball up. Chapman is fouled as he scores, and he makes the foul shot, closing the gap to 59–57 with nineteen seconds to play.

Bringing the ball down into Garfield territory, Sam Marcum juggles the ball for an instant. Tony McCoy swipes at it and suddenly there is a loose ball squiggling around the court. Garfield's Mike Hardy grabs it and throws to Hodge, who calls time out. Thirteen seconds.

Don Gillespie chooses the play in the time-out huddle. Hodge is to bounce the ball inbounds to Calvin Chapman, then break for the corner. Chapman will be guarded now by the talented Andy Kolesar, but Gillespie wants only his two best ball handlers to touch the ball. After Hodge has faked toward the corner, he is to cut inside to the key. Chapman will throw the ball near the key in the desperate hope that Hodge has managed to get there.

Like any good coach in the final seconds of a close game, Marv McCollum believes in giving his players only the most fundamental instructions. Once a game is actually under way, he dispenses with his trademark platitudes, but what he tells his team now is as obvious as his corniest slogan: "Keep the ball away from Hodge." Reading Gillespie's mind, McCollum adds that since Hodge is the best Garfield passer, he will probably throw the ball inbounds and then try to position himself to get it thrown back. He tells the six-five Grammel to make a wall above the five-nine Hodge so he will not even be able to see his teammates, much less get the ball to one of them.

A retarded boy in a wheelchair has been sitting happily near midcourt throughout the game, staring from the play up to the red lights flickering each change in the score at the top of the gym, then back to the play again. He gazes beatifically at Hodge now, only six feet away from his wheelchair, as Hodge tries to bring the ball inbounds. Does he know that Hodge has shrunk the gulf between Garfield and Taft—the East and West sides of Hamilton—to two points and thirteen seconds?

Grammel hovers over Hodge while he looks for somewhere to throw the basketball. Mike Grubbs comes over to help out Grammel. When Hodge feints to bounce the ball under them, Grubbs and Grammel are a jungle of legs. When he tries to throw over them, they are a forest of arms. The retarded boy waves to Hodge.

Urgent, possessed, Hodge catapults himself above the defenders. In the air, he stands still for what seems a full second, as though a platform had suddenly sprung up to hold him. Chapman has faked himself clear of Kolesar for an instant to receive the ball Hodge rifles to him. Surrounded, Hodge darts for the corner as Gillespie had directed. On a pivot, he cuts toward the basket. The key is so crowded he cannot get near it. Chapman looks for his own shot but there is none. By dribbling out toward midcourt, Chapman keeps possession when the traffic under the basket has made a pass to Hodge impossible. Hodge breaks away from the key, heading in the wrong direction with four seconds showing on the clock. The four seconds have neither past nor future. Now Chapman releases the ball. Now Hodge dives for the pass. Now he is smothered by Tigers. Now he fights loose, hips and elbows and a single dribble. Now, falling away from the basket thirty feet distant, he airmails the ball. Now the final buzzer brays. Now the ball smacks the rim of the basket and rebels straight into the air. Now it returns and obediently whishes itself through the net.

The gym detonates, fifteen hundred throats in peril of rupture. The town's best game in years has ended in a tie, Hamilton equaling Hamilton. The crowd owes the night to Robbie Hodge, and no one begrudges him the credit. From Garfield side comes "Hodge! Hodge! Hodge!" and the Taft side echoes. The sound builds until no words at all can be heard. It is almost like silence, the gym roaring for a performance that on Broadway gets a ten-minute curtain call and in Madrid two ears and a tail.

Hodge seems propelled not by the spirit of victory, oddly, but of excellence. Often he has performed almost alone, not ignoring his teammates the way court hogs do, but using them to express his own impulses. He wants, of course, to win, but what he plays is thirty-two minutes of court-length ballet. He draws pictures in the air; the art, to be sure, disappears every second, but the artist remains, drawing new pictures with each motion.

The overtime is just that: anticlimactic and unsuspenseful. The score stays close enough, Garfield scoring two more baskets while Taft scores three. But Mike Grammel and Scott Grevey are in charge of the game, which simply winds down like the clock itself. With two seconds to go Garfield gets the ball under its own basket. Never surrendering, Hodge yells at the teammate with the ball, "Call time out!" the way Dr. Johnson, dying with dropsy, instructed his leeches to puncture his legs and let out more water. Hodge's teammate has already flung the ball in a despairing full-court arc toward the Taft basket. The ball is stopped by a steel girder at the top of the gym when the buzzer finally ends the evening.

As the Taft and Garfield cheerleaders line up together at center court, both teams and their coaches envelop Hodge in congratulations. A Tiger and a Griffin momentarily perch Hodge on their shoulders. He blinks in embarrassment and slithers down to the floor. Don Gillespie puts his arm around Hodge as the assembled cheerleading squads send out their last yell:

> *We're from Hamilton, couldn't be prouder;*
> *If you can't hear us, we'll shout a little louder!*

IV
DELIVERENCE

Up Bobmeyer Road off the Dixie Highway, between the motels
and Hamilton's private airport, a small yellow wooden-framed
house in advanced dilapidation wore a sign: "God's House of
Deliverence, Pastor Dallis Alexander." The old house served as
the church for a movement of intense, fundamentalist Christians whose theme, however they chose to spell it, was deliverance from Satan to God. Their devotion seemed to exist
somewhere between the theaters of cruelty and the absurd, too
well meant for the former, too real for the latter.

When the hymn about the blood of the Lamb ended, Dallis
Alexander stepped to the lectern at the front of the dusty room
that took up most of the house. Benches and a few chairs faced
the lectern and were divided by an aisle. The House of Deliverence, well attended but not packed, had attracted about thirty
of its members on a rainy Wednesday night. They were in overalls and cotton prints, and more than a few had some physical
abnormality—a harelip, obesity, missing fingers, a blind eye.
Pastor Alexander was very young and wore a plaid shirt. He
was fresh-faced, sandy-haired, earnest, with wire rims framing
his glasses. Briskly, he set in motion the episode that gave the
service its axis.

"Even among those brought together by God to live in harmony, there can be affliction," Pastor Alexander said, "Jack and Rowena Clegg, there has been trouble in your home." Dallis Alexander did not ask and he was not accusatory; he simply asserted. He might have been talking about any visitation of external trouble, a burglary or a tornado.

"Drinking and beating," a high, trembling voice said from the middle of the benches on the right side of the aisle.

"Will you tell me what that means, Rowena?" Pastor Alexander asked. There was nothing challenging in his question, only tenderness and curiosity.

"He drinks . . ." Rowena Clegg sat alone except for a small baby on her lap and another inside her. She was enormous, fat as well as pregnant, and she was beginning to cry ". . . and I get beat."

Dallis Alexander watched Rowena Clegg while she sobbed and then, as though it were a spotlight, shifted his gaze to the other side of the House of Deliverence.

Jack Clegg sat, also alone, on a bench to the left of the aisle. He had chosen a seat toward the back of the room, not directly across from his wife and accuser. He was tall and lean, with the look of a young man getting old fast. Even in a sitting position he seemed permanently bent from doing heavy physical work he was not really strong enough to do. His face and the back of his neck were deeply creased, and there were three moles, dark and heavy, on his cheeks.

"What do you say, Jack?" Pastor Alexander asked pleasantly.

Jack Clegg said nothing. He looked from the pastor down to the calluses on his hands.

"It seems like it's going to take both of you to keep your household together," Pastor Alexander said. "Come now, and be delivered."

Jack and Rowena Clegg rose from their benches and shuffled toward the lectern where Pastor Alexander stood. Rowena Clegg carried her baby. Several other members of the church —friends or relatives—followed the Cleggs to the altar space at the front of the room. By the time they reached Dallis Alexander, each was flanked by enough attendants to make this a wedding.

Most of the faithful, including those who did not follow the Cleggs to the lectern, had drooping eyes and high foreheads, fat arms and thick legs, a prodigally extended family that appeared to have been inbred to preserve the trait that allowed them to load heavy things on carts and bear burdens over hilly passes. Only Jack Clegg was tall, and he was bent.

"Tell me the trouble we want to deliver you from," Pastor Alexander said.

Jack Clegg stooped lower in shame, Rowena Clegg clasped her baby and looked up.

"Tell me, Rowena," Pastor Alexander said.

There was stillness until Pastor Alexander raised his hand as if he were a conductor with a baton. Rowena Clegg began to blurt. "Friday night he didn't come home and when he come home he was off his melon and swingin'."

"Is that true, Jack?" Pastor Alexander asked.

But even if Jack Clegg had been disposed to speak, which he was not, his wife's flow had just begun. She wept as she talked. "His bottle was still with him and he roared out. I said, can I have the rest of your pay. He said, stick my pay. I said, be quiet for the neighbors. He said, stick the neighbors. He come for me and I grabbed my baby from her crib, which he made her, I'll admit that. He commenced to beat on both of us till I screamed and she screamed. He hit me some more and some more, and I was afraid for my baby and the one I'm carrying. He drank a big lot and put his bottle down and pulled my baby out of my arms and held her over the stove."

Now, as Rowena Clegg tried to catch her breath, her husband uttered one line in the direction of his feet. "I wan't fixin' to hurt Ulalume, I just wanted you to shet."

"We come and hushed him then," said a squat older man with a grizzled chin. He stood in back of Jack Clegg. "It wan't no trouble."

Dallis Alexander raised both his arms high and stood on his

tiptoes. He could only have gone higher if he had taken wing, though he was still not as tall as Jack Clegg stooped. "Praise Him!" Dallis Alexander thundered. "Praise the living Lord!"

Rowena Clegg, huge and pregnant, with her baby in her arms, began to shake.

"All praise be to the Lord!" Pastor Alexander boomed again, still louder, and Rowena Clegg shook harder. She stopped shaking for an instant, turned around and put her baby down on the lap of a friend in the front bench. Then she approached closer to Dallis Alexander's lectern.

Except for mumbling at his feet, Jack Clegg was silent, but he, too, shuffled closer to Pastor Alexander. More self-conscious than his wife, his shame seemed mingled with some desire to bolt. He glanced at the door behind him as if it, not Pastor Alexander, were his means of deliverance. Pastor Alexander's attention was on Rowena Clegg.

He shoved his hand against her forehead and pressed down hard. She trembled. As Pastor Alexander mentioned each of the Trinity, Rowena Clegg's abundant body shook more violently until it seemed she had been struck by some wrathful disaster in nature, an earthquake or lightning. "Praise all, in the name of the Father, yes, and in the name of the Son, that's right, and in the name of the Holy Ghost! Hear me!" Rowena Clegg wailed and shrieked. She almost fell from shaking so hard.

In a corner of the church a few teenagers played with a collection basket. They paid no attention to what was happening at the altar. They used the small basket as though it were a hat or a ball or a frisbee, now wearing it on their heads and mugging beneath it, now throwing it to each other, now sailing it across the brief expanse of the House of Deliverence.

"I command the devil to go out!" When Pastor Alexander shouted at Rowena Clegg, he was still pressing her forehead. She heaved and fell down, issuing a great moan. On the floor she still shook and shuddered. The pastor was serene. Jack Clegg stared at his downed wife, humiliated, triumphant. He

looked up at Pastor Alexander, who had just accomplished what
he, her own husband, had not been able to do—get Rowena
Clegg on the ground in total submission. The pastor wanted to
be sure. "Again, I command the devil to leave! Now!"

In his practice of repairing domestic relations through exorcism, Dallis Alexander had not forgotten who the principal miscreant was. But it was not the pastor's way to force a parishioner
to his knees who was not so inclined, and Jack Clegg was not. In
a test of wills with a doubter, especially a drinking and wife-
battering doubter, Pastor Alexander could only lose. If Jesus
could sponge all sin unto Himself for the sake of mankind,
surely a wife could absorb some of it for her husband. "Rowena
took on the devil for both of you, Jack," the pastor said. "Do
you understand that, Jack?"

Could Rowena have beaten Satan for both of them? Could
she have shaken and trembled and wailed the devil away from
the whole family? Jack Clegg began to mumble, and the words
that came out were "Lord" and "forgive." He struggled a moment, seeming to search, then added "never, never," as if to
ward off both the devil and John Barleycorn, who in the House
of Deliverence were identical.

"Rise up, Rowena. Stand near, Jack," said Dallis Alexander.
"Friends, we have seen the devil leave this couple, but he'll be
back. He always is. Now, Rowena and Jack, join hands."

Rowena Clegg was wringing wet when she clasped her husband's hand. Jack Clegg was subdued and dry, drier, perhaps,
than he had been in months. They stood together, facing their
judge.

"When that devil comes back, Jack and Rowena, and he will,
when he comes back into your home, REBUKE HIM! You must
REBUKE HIM! You must have nothing to do with him but to
REBUKE HIM! You can do it. When he starts to happen in
your home you both join hands, as you are now, and you pray
and you pray, and you send that old boy off down the road. We
don't want him, we don't need him, and we won't have him!"

Chastened, cleansed, Jack and Rowena Clegg retreated from

the altar. Rowena Clegg reclaimed her baby from her friend in the front row and marched proudly to her old bench. Jack Clegg followed, still not sitting beside his wife, but taking a bench only two rows back of her on the same side of the aisle. Rowena Clegg looked the more purified, her husband the more mortified, though it was not clear whether he looked this way because of his bout with the devil or because he had had to watch his wife shriek and moan and fall over in a public place. But Rowena Clegg was beatific, hugely beatific, as she rocked her baby against her bosom.

"All right now, we hope we've brought help to some people," Pastor Alexander said. "Is there anyone else? Anyone else right now for deliverance?"

Jack Clegg looked at the door in back, appearing to measure the distance to it. Could he get out before the young pastor bellowed at him again? Should he ask his wife to come now? Could they get home in time for "The Waltons"? But an elderly man just in front of him had risen.

"My best friend has cancer, Pastor Dallis. He may not get deliverance in time. Can we pray to the Lord for my friend, because he has had the cancer two years and it's a lot worse. Oh God, pray for him, can't we, Pastor?" The elderly man sat down.

"Of course we can. We will right now." Dallis Alexander closed his eyes and cast them upward, but his spirit seemed still to belong in the exorcism of the Jack Cleggs. "Let us pray."

Pastor Alexander prayed silently, eyes shut, moving only his lips. Rowena Clegg stood up, cradling her baby, and walked to the center aisle. When Jack Clegg joined her, she handed the baby to him. Together, quietly, they stole toward the rear door.

V

IN COURT

At nine in the morning, in the courtroom on the third floor of the City Building, the judge rapped the legal retinue of lawyers and bailiffs and witnesses to silence as an officer ushered in the first defendant, a skinny nineteen-year-old blond boy originally from Hamilton, now living in Cincinnati. The judge spoke idly, with neither kindness nor harshness.

"Let's see, you're accused of stealing an eighty-nine-dollar lawn mower, is that right?" the judge asked.

"Yes sir, that's what it is." The boy's face was riddled with acne, and he wore a gray prisoner's uniform, having been brought over from the jail.

"Do you have counsel?"

"How's that, sir?"

"A lawyer. Do you have a lawyer?"

"My mother says I don't need one, sir, and I can't afford one."

"You're entitled to a lawyer. Do you want the court to appoint one?"

"No, sir, that won't be necessary."

"Are you ready to plead to the charge then?"

"Yes, Your Honor, I am. I took it. The only thing I come back from Cincinnati for was to see my mother and take the lawn mower from the lady down the street."

"You're pleading guilty then?"

"I'm pleading guilty. The only thing I took it for, Your Honor, was I wanted to sell it. I wasn't going to use it or anything. I was just going to sell it."

The boy was fined fifty dollars and court costs, given thirty days in jail, with the rest of a six-month sentence suspended. This was his third offense. He reacted with no surprise, but only scratched his acne as he left the courtroom to return to jail.

The boy was not humiliated, hanging his head in shame for being caught in a caper after which a son of the middle class might seriously entertain suicide or at least lighting out for Alaska. Then there would be a tearful reunion with forgiving parents, and the father would say, "Just remember, son, we're behind you all the way. This isn't the end of the world. As a matter of fact, I've never told you this, Mom knows about it, I took a car once myself when I was a kid . . ." Then they would all be brought closer, admitting offenses and feelings they had never mentioned before. A soap opera that could continue ten or twelve days on any daytime serial or one thoroughgoing hour of nighttime. But in the family this boy was from, nobody even bothered to throw a beer can at him after he got caught with the lawn mower.

Unlike the House of Deliverence, the justice dispensed in the courtroom was veiled and unemotional. That did not make it *in*justice. It did make this a more abstract way of dealing with a social offense. The same kind of people, left out or behind the inexorable march of the middle class, came before this judge as before Dallis Alexander. They came for very nearly the same causes—wife-beating, petty theft, breaking into a neighbor's home. Often they had backgrounds similar to those of Pastor Alexander's parishioners, coming from the hills and hollows of Kentucky and Tennessee. The principal difference was that in the House of Deliverence the neighborhood, the subculture, was dealing with its own problems, whereas in the courtroom the problems had been referred to the larger community for institutional disposal. What the church handled irrationally and emotionally, the court was settling rationally, coolly, and without, in all senses of the word, interest.

The lawyers chatted and told jokes as they waited for defendants to be brought in. Except for the deputy prosecutor, who joked along with the rest, they were all for the defense and all court-appointed. The judge, the lawyers, the prosecutor—the machinery of justice—were self-evidently from one class, and the defendants were all from another. It was not that the middle and lower classes could not communicate in this courtroom; it seemed, rather, that they simply had nothing to say to each other.

The elderly white-haired judge, Wendell Parks, was in a dismissive mood—not that he would dismiss the cases, but that an air of the perfunctory hung over the proceedings. Nothing in court was as serious or dramatic as the issue of freedom versus prison would seem to warrant. Everyone—lawyers, judge, most of the defendants—had been here too many times before. It did not matter what Judge Wendell Parks said to a defendant. His lectures were not listened to, so he seldom gave them. When there was active counsel the bargain had either been struck prior to the opening of court or the crimes themselves left very little latitude for the punishment he was able to mete out. Judge Parks had long since learned that becoming indignant, showing rage or compassion or just puzzlement would lead only to ulcers, frequent reversals by a higher court, and early retirement. Whatever else it was, remaining on a judicial bench in Hamilton was better than becoming a prune on a park bench in Sarasota or Scottsdale.

In the single instance where it was a young man's first time in court, Judge Parks brightened considerably. He listened eagerly to the tale of a stolen ten-speed bicycle, gave a little sermon on the need to work for what you get, and sent the boy on his way with a cheering rendition of the Golden Rule, adding, "Now buck up and don't let me see you in here again." He might almost have been Coach McCollum reprimanding an erring forward.

Though this was not juvenile but criminal court, the judge qualified as an authority figure for youth just as surely as the teachers at Taft and Garfield. His tenure in their lives was far briefer, of course, but his impact was immediate and lasting. What he decided, unless overturned, would control the next several years of a young life.

Curiously, the lawn mower case did not die. Later in the morning, another boy was also charged in the theft, and he came to court, not in a prisoner's uniform, but as a civilian with a court-appointed lawyer. While waiting for the judge to call them, the lawyer asked the boy, as blond as his alleged confederate who had gotten thirty days, what his connection with the case was. The boy said he didn't know. "You weren't even a witness to the crime?" "No." When the judge asked how the boy would plead, the lawyer answered not guilty. The woman who owned the lawn mower was brought in, and she testified she saw nothing. "All I know is my eighty-nine-dollar lawn mower is gone." A witness to the crime was produced, a respectful, lower-middle-class, clear-complexioned boy who minded his own business and already saw how he fit into things. He identified the new defendant as one of the two thieves, the other being the boy who got the thirty days. The witness looked as laundered and credible as his fresh, checked shirt. The defense lawyer asked him, "Did you say anything to them? Did you try to chase them? Did you talk about them to anyone else?" to all of which the witness answered, "No, sir." The court-appointed lawyer, confronted with a witness he had not expected, a case he had not prepared for, and a client who had probably lied to him, asked for a postponement. He added that the defendant intended to maintain his plea of not guilty and ask for a jury trial. As the judge continued the case, the defendant gave the finger to the witness.

A thirty-five-year-old man, short and wiry with beady eyes,

pled guilty immediately to drunken driving. His attorney said he was a good man with a good job and he had never been arrested before. Mr. Poates, the defendant, admitted to flunking the breathalizer test, the attorney said, and will never do this again. The arresting officer took the stand. "Defendant Poates was also in possession of a concealed weapon," he said. "When I arrested Mr. Poates and a male companion, I locked them in the patrol car and went back to Mr. Poates' vehicle. I saw a bulge under the floor mat, and when I looked I found a thirty-two caliber pistol." Even if no one else was interested, the officer wanted to make certain the concealed weapon was unconcealed in court. If Mr. Poates and his friend had been belligerent rather than docile drunks, they might, on the point of arrest, have pulled their pistol from its hiding place and begun firing.

The defense lawyer asked where the driver's license and registration were from. "His driver's license was from Florida, and Kentucky was the registration on the car," the officer said. Since the defendant lived in Florida and Trenton, Ohio, and his passenger lived in Kentucky, they were not Hamilton's problem. The defense lawyer asked if the officer had determined who owned the revolver. "I asked them both," the officer said. "They denied ownership."

The passenger was summoned, a fidgeting man who took the stand as if mounting a scaffold. His name was D'Abney, and he had the small mouth and pinched features that characterized much of the laity in the House of Deliverence. At the moment, these features were gathered in worry. "God's truth, Your Honor, I was too drunk to drive, so I was a passenger in Mr. Poates' car. Me and him was both intoxicated beyond our limit." Poates and D'Abney were looking very contrite, chastened boys who happened to be in their late thirties. D'Abney was excused from the witness stand to rejoin his wife, who was also small-featured, and his little girl, who was tiny-featured and who began rubbing her father's knees as soon as he sat down next to her in the spectator section. It could not be readily established whom the gun belonged to, no crime had been committed with

it, and the defendant and his passenger were both out-of-town-
ers, so Judge Parks told them to go away. "Get back to where
you came from and keep out of Hamilton."

A case of wife beating drew from Judge Parks a quick ten-
dollar fine. As soon as the judge had disposed of them, a skinny
man and a fat woman walked out through the door marked
"Cashier—Fines and Costs." Passing through this door after
judgment meant a defendant had been found guilty but would
not go to prison, that his or her offense was redeemable
through money rather than time. Standing in line to pay the ten
dollars, the husband and the wife he had beaten were a prophecy of the Jack Cleggs half a decade later, when they would
have passed beyond the point of seeking divine rather than
legal intercession.

Divinity and the law were also staked against each other in
the session's most baffling case. Only a celestial subpoena would
have helped the court determine whether the death in question
was attributable to crime or to the simple, ineluctable hand of
God. Shuffling to the docket as if his legs were manacled,
though they were only clothed in gray jail overalls, a young
black man refused to look at his parents, a proud couple in their
sixties who had dressed as they might for church. The young
man stared instead at an old white man, who stared back. They
nodded at each other, not in greeting but in recognition, certainly not in friendship but not in hostility either.

"Charles Hibbard, Jr. Breaking and entering, attempted burglary with a complication," Judge Parks read from the charges
in front of him. "Is there a Regis Walls present?"

The elderly white man stepped forward, standing almost beside the prisoner. "Your Honor?"

"You're the plaintiff and the principal witness for the prosecution. This is not the trial yet, only a hearing. Can you tell me
what happened?"

"My wife and I were asleep in our bedroom," Regis Walls
began. "We heard a racket in the living room which woke us up
and my wife says to me, 'Lord, Regis, get that man out of there.'

She could only mumble since her first stroke, but I could make out her words. I went into the living room and I found this fellow, Mr. Hibbard. I could barely see him in the dark, his outline was dim, but I can tell by the way he is standing here now it was him. This Mr. Hibbard. He just stood there. I asked him what he was doing in my home, we're old and don't have but our Social Security. He said just two words to me."

" 'No light.' " Charles Hibbard quoted himself without looking up.

"They was the two words, that's all," Regis Walls continued. " 'No light.' Then he made a telephone call, or he tried to, but I guess he got no answer. He didn't take anything. He came into my house through a window which he broke, but he didn't disturb anything else."

"Did your wife see him?" Judge Parks asked.

"She was blind after that first stroke two years ago. When Mr. Hibbard finished the telephone call he was trying to make, I showed him the door and said, 'Get going.' But then he looked at me queerly like he didn't want to go."

"They was chasing me," Charles Hibbard said.

"That's what he told me, 'They're chasing me.' I told him I got a very sick wife and he had to leave. I opened the front door for him, and out he went. I called the police, and I understand they picked him up later on speeding. When I went back into the bedroom I told my wife I'd got rid of the fellow, Mr. Hibbard here. She said, 'Lord, Regis, I don't know what would happen to me if something happened to you.' She was shaking real bad. She meant the blindness and all. We went back to sleep, but she woke me an hour later and said, 'I'm going, Regis.' It was a heart attack. The next Tuesday we put her out at Greenwood. It takes them three months there to get the headstone ready."

"All right, there's more to this," Judge Parks said. "Son, just take the breaking and entering. How do you plead?"

Charles Hibbard kept his head down; he made no sound.

"He broke into the house, Your Honor." Charles Hibbard's

father had approached the bench, a portly, distinguished supplicant.

"Are you his lawyer?" Judge Parks asked.

"I'm his father."

"I asked the defendant how he pleads, not his relatives."

"We can't afford a lawyer, Your Honor," Charles Hibbard, Sr., said.

"The court will appoint a lawyer."

"I beg your pardon, Your Honor," Charles Hibbard, Sr., said, "but all we have here is a broken window."

"I'm not sure," Judge Parks said. "It's true he didn't take anything from Mr. Walls' home. But the breaking and entering might have contributed to Mrs. Walls' death. I'm going to send him back on ten thousand dollars bond and turn the case over to the grand jury."

As Charles Hibbard, Jr., was led from the courtroom, Charles Hibbard, Sr., approached Regis Walls and stuck out his hand. Regis Walls took it. "He was a good boy right up through the ninth grade," Charles Hibbard, Sr., said.

VI

COPS

Sergeant Chuck Furman worked at Champion Paper, where his father had always worked, and then he hung out a while before he joined the Police Department. He liked keeping in shape, meeting all kinds of people. In a sense, he liked also to give a kind of performance.

On nights when he patrolled Hamilton, Sergeant Furman began his rounds at eight o'clock sharp. After thirteen years on the force, he was nobody to mess with. Even his hair was tough, close-cropped with the premature salt and pepper coloration that emphasized a steel wool quality in its owner. His careful musculature inflated his sergeant's uniform, suggesting individual attention to lats, delts, and pecs. He moved with the combination of thickness and litheness that recalls Marine NCO's with a lot of time in grade. Jogging would be a soft, almost mental activity, compared with the gym workouts, handball, and boxing that honed Sergeant Furman. If there were trouble on the block, Chuck Furman would be the man to have around only if one could contrive to be on his side.

Whenever he rode around nocturnal Hamilton, pitch dark except for streetlight pinspots, it was immediately apparent to

Chuck Furman that the biggest misconception about police work is that most of it is routine. It perhaps becomes regularized for members of the department; walking and working by the numbers, patrolling according to municipal grid coordinates, does become a matter of repetition. But it is a routine to disguise danger, to provide a shield of order against the dread of the unexpected they would all feel if they were not so busy filling out everything in triplicate. And it is hardly a matter of routine to chase speeding cars, catch armed robbers, confront prostitutes, pimps, cocaine dealers, bunko artists, gamblers, burglars, killers. It is hardly routine to meet a colleague at night in a deserted parking lot to sign an accident report, as Chuck Furman did at 8:11, or to call the hospital to see if last night's stabbing had "made the fatality list," as Furman did at 8:13. The police get used to being on society's front lines—whether they are seen as guardians of the public peace or as the establishment's shock troops—but they would be scared all the time without the general concurrence to call their work routine.

"Uptown," Sergeant Furman said, "is usually dead at night. The trouble we have is in the bar section, that's the area near the tracks, and the colored section. There's not supposed to be a colored section anymore, and we're not supposed to call it colored, but it's there in the Second Ward. Whites don't move in unless they're worse than poor, and blacks hardly ever move out.

"I graduated from high school up in Oxford, but I came to Hamilton to find work. After they laid me off from Champion I did some electronics. It was intricate but boring. I wanted the activity, the adventure, and the security, so I took the test and came into the department. My wife and I have just the one daughter but we're expecting."

8:19. A radio call directed Furman to the corner of Ludlow and Seventh streets—the heart of the bar section, as he called it. What the radio described as "a white youth" was weaving around under a street lamp, not quite losing his footing while making menacing gestures in the direction of pedestrians who looked like any other Americans on skid row. The lady with tufts of hair on her chin and no front teeth, the grizzled old-timer with sad eyes and a fixed smile, the red-eyed black man drinking from a pint bottle in a paper bag. The young man who was making the commotion stumbled away from the corner into the shadows as the squad car approached. Out of the car onto the curb, Furman moved swiftly without any appearance of hurry or suddenness. The boy, tall and thin, gave one lurch down the sidewalk but stopped abruptly as Sergeant Furman came abreast of him. Furman did not touch him. He asked the boy his name.

"James Rodney Eichelhorn, Officer," the boy said with exaggerated precision, pulling himself up to his gangly height and swaying only slightly.

"Are you drunk, James Rodney?" Furman stood next to Eichelhorn with his hands at his sides.

"No sir. I'm hoping to be. But I ain't yet."

Back in the squad car, moving through the bar section past flop houses and shacks with tarpaper roofs, corner places where Ripple sold at forty-five cents a shot, Sergeant Furman explained that he saw no point in picking up James Rodney Eichelhorn. "It's a discretionary matter. If someone is definitely disturbing the peace, you pick him up and let him spend the night in the tank. If he's not really bothering anyone, there isn't much point in making the people of Hamilton pay for his lodging. Of course, there's a double standard here. As disheveled as he is, if Eichelhorn were doing this on the West Side in a residential neighborhood, you'd hustle him right out of there. Over here, among his fellow bums, it doesn't much matter."

What looked like a threatening encounter to an amateur was the most ordinary procedure for a policeman. With Eichelhorn waving a bottle and jerking around uncontrollably on the sidewalk, a civilian imagination had no trouble conjuring a gun in his pocket. He might, at the least, whip out a knife when Furman began to question him. Headlines reeled—"Another Cop Shot," "Drunk Assails Cop, Is Killed," "Cop Knifed on East

Side," "Cop, Drunk Dead in Skid Row Melee"—the confrontation a perfect set-up for violence. Even allowing for bad television and cheap journalism, the paradox of police life is that such situations are both normal *and* ripe with furious potential. Policemen can be trigger-happy; so can civilians, and for those who are, a blue uniform is the lightning rod to catch their hostility.

8:38. Chuck Furman drove past a combination store and warehouse with a long green sign proclaiming "Sammy's Used Appliances." Furman slowed the car, watchful but not tense. When describing suspects, he could talk like a print-out. "The proprietor," he said, looking for a light in the warehouse, "is a known fence. Sammy receives stolen property from blacks and sells it, but we haven't been able to apprehend him yet. Three young black males stole some CB radios to sell to Sammy. We caught them before they could complete the action. Each of the thieves is drawing public assistance. Now they have asked to be tried separately, so the taxpayers will have to bear the cost of three separate trials for three obvious crooks on welfare. It must be remembered, of course, that no one ever said democracy, freedom, and their safeguards were not expensive." Just beneath his proper surface, sometimes not beneath it at all, Furman had the resentment of the police for those who give them most trouble, the bitterness of all constabularies toward the underclass from whom they are sworn to protect the upper classes. He leaned toward his radio.

The radio crackled, at 8:54, that on Dayton Street there had been a brother-sister fight. This came over in casual tones. The dispatcher, like an announcer at a very dull boxing match, went on to describe a brother hitting his sister with a belt. "It looked like he was going to get more serious when the neighbor called us, but one of our cars has arrived, and the situation seems to be under control."

Furman cruised toward the West Side and a more prosperous neighborhood, a pilot in search of better weather.

8:57. The radio again, with a report on a "hit-skip," which is

Hamiltonian for a hit-and-run car accident. The intrusion from the dashboard reminded Furman to call in his coordinates to the dispatcher. Passing the headquarters of the Citizens Bank downtown, he said policemen cannot live on their salaries. "We all moonlight. There's no way not to." Most of Furman's moonlighting was for a local bank. "I repossess cars and other property on bad loans. Pay's good, and it's usually easy work." To Furman, repossession of poor people's goods for a bank was not enlisting himself in the service of one side in a class war, as a European might see the same duty; it was simply protecting, and thereby identifying with, the valid interests of Hamilton's essence, the owners of property.

"Moonlighting," Furman said, "is not illegal. It's only frowned upon; it's not corrupt, it's necessary. In the old days, the department left lots to be desired. We all know about Hamilton's reputation in the thirties as Little Chicago."

On the street named for Hamilton's own patron saint, John Woods (though the city fathers knocked off the s), there were once eight whorehouses. All of them paid protection to the police. The most famous prostitutes were a pair known as Sallie Bunce and Puss Slo-Go. The most celebrated and least arrested proprietor was named Madam Flo, from whose house a tunnel led directly to one of Hamilton's banks. Other Middle Western towns were also called Little Chicago, but only Hamilton was the hideout for John Dillinger. The police were so scared of him—his weapons, as well as his reputation, far exceeded theirs—they wanted no part of him, not even to be paid off. In 1980, the husband of a retired piano teacher still recalled proudly that his wife had once played in a local speakeasy for Dillinger. Criminals and murderers were hardly the only participants in Hamiltonian vice. "Would you believe it?" asked the host of a large West Side party, as though about to divulge that his son's high school physics teacher had won the Nobel Prize. "Tyrone Power got laid on Wood Street!"

One of Sergeant Furman's colleagues on the force, Jackie Flannery, a policewoman whose bawdy sense of humor led her to collect brothel stories, relished the vision of a customer who wound up at the bottom of a privy. "It was a fat jewelry salesman who was afraid to leave his gems anywhere but tucked into his own clothing," Jackie Flannery liked to recall. "He weighed in at over three hundred pounds, and one night when he went to the john in an outhouse back of the whorehouse, he fell through. They had to call the Fire Department to get him out with a winch because he was in crap up to his neck. They never could get his jewels out, which just perished in the shit. In those days, college girls used to come down to help out in the whorehouses on their holidays. One particular customer had to have a bouncer throw him out of the house in order to ejaculate. He'd give ten dollars to the bouncer first, then the bouncer would throw him out. That would get his rocks off. An old retired prostitute told me another customer would take her into a room, whip out a hairbrush, and brush her pubic hairs with it, and that's how he would come off. And priests, you know, they were good customers too," Jackie Flannery would add with a triumphant Irish twinkle. "The great house of Madam Flo had a stainless steel kitchen in the days when no one else in town but the Becketts could afford one. Sex in America is a wonderful thing, never doubt it, and it pays so well."

Some of the Hamilton quality were actually as shocked by the red-light district as they professed to be, but a number of those in the first families opposed sumptuary legislation, laws designed to regulate personal habits. The problem was that as long as the rest of the country insisted on curbing sex, gambling, and (for a time) liquor, there could be no protected whorehouses, bookmakers, or speakeasies without payoffs to the police. Hence corruption. "During Prohibition," said Jim Blount, a local historian as well as managing editor of the *Journal-News*, "policemen on duty would come into my father's luncheonette and drink in the back. They would push a secret buzzer that signaled my father when they wanted a fresh round of free drinks. My father didn't like it, but it was the price of staying in business. One day a policeman came in with his whole family and asked my father to feed them all free. My father refused. They argued, but finally the cop had to pay. The next week, that same cop brought in a whole team of inspectors who cited my father for serving liquor to minors and closed him up for thirty days. Every bar was hooked up to a bookie joint, or to a beer and juke box operation, and most of them to slot machines. Later on in Prohibition, when whiskey running became common, my father would send one envelope with cash in it every week to the chief of police, and another to the cop on the beat."

But the police were no more corrupt than those they served; in some ways, they were only playing follow the leader. "You went along," said Jim Blount, "with what the old families wanted. They were hand in hand with the criminal element. The first families had businesses that used mob suppliers, so they worked together that way. Then, if a small grocery didn't allow policy slips and slot machines, a bank wouldn't give it credit when it wanted to expand. The banks were controlled by the first families. So was the city council, with the power to decide which enterprises to favor and which to deny permits." Faces on the city council changed, of course, and Mayor Witt did not even know most of those who had been council members in the Little Chicago days. But Hamilton's largest banks, the First National and Citizens, remained in the control of the Fitton and Rentschler families who had owned them for generations. Dick Fitton and Tom Rentschler were each blessed with total recall where the misdeeds of the other were concerned, and a bemused amnesia regarding his own bank. "If those shenanigans did go on in the old days," Tom Rentschler said smilingly, "then I guess I'd have to confess it was the other guys that did them, not us."

The corruption of the old days was hardly unreflected in the new. Aside from the convicted sheriff who was imprisoned in the 1970s, the banks themselves were accused of immorally blocking progress. They would, it was charged, refuse to lend money to blacks and Kentuckians who wanted to start small businesses or move out of their blighted neighborhoods. The banks, according to this allegation, were engaged in a corrupt smugness, denying the American dream to those for whom it had not yet come true. "As a matter of fact, we do make loans to marginal low-income families and to risky new businesses," Tom Rentschler answered, "but we don't claim to be social reformers. Basically, a bank is a money store, and we sell to those who can afford to buy. Show me a store that operates differently, and I'll show you someone who's on his way out of business."

As much as it is drawn to romance, Hamilton loves its legends of corruption, especially those containing both romance and corruption. One of Chuck Furman's superiors, Lieutenant Henry Smith, known as Smitty, a cop with a wide girth and a wider smile, reminisced about corruption with nostalgia for a time he had never known directly. When he met his friends, the Irwins and the Duersches, at a huge Protestant-Jewish wedding, they were consumed with the illicit derring-do that was so much a part of Hamiltonian mythology. Philip Irwin and Emily Duersch, who would not have dreamed of breaking a law themselves, spoke of John Dillinger as though he had been canonized or was at least Clark Gable. His movements between Hamilton, Indiana, and Chicago were described as stations of the cross.

Smitty: "I've been on the Police Department twenty-seven years, but my dad was in private enterprise as an electrician for the Capone syndicate. They had him on the dog-track tour. The dogs were legitimate themselves and my dad was never in any trouble, but he worked for the syndicate which laundered its money through the tracks. Dad pioneered in innovations and circuit-breakers with the little mechanical rabbits that run around the track. He could have made a fortune if he'd patented his ideas, but the syndicate treated him well."

Philip Irwin: "Dillinger, you see, had a babe stashed down in the Second Ward. Nothing new, Mad Anthony Wayne had his mistress here in the 1790s. Dillinger wasn't a local boy himself, but he came up here on weekends. One day he drove into my filling station. He asked me, 'You got an *Inquirer?*' meaning the

Cincinnati paper. I gave it to him while I filled his tank. He goes straight to the stock page, pulls a lot of stolen stocks out of his pocket right there in his car, and he starts to compare them with what's on the stock market page in the *Inquirer*. I knew it was him, of course, but I was young and full of vinegar so I asks him, 'Say, bub, where do you live?' He looks at me cool and says, 'D Street.' That's over on the West Side in one of the best neighborhoods. I knew he was lying, but what was I supposed to do? The cops here would drink with all the gangsters. They might just as well. I mean what could they do with their little service revolvers against the kind of artillery Dillinger and them had?

"We had a fellow named Murphy, a mob man from Cincinnati, come up and stay here in the Grand Hotel. Prohibition liquor from Murphy's gang was being hijacked in Hamilton on its way from Cincinnati to Chicago. Well, Murphy was murdered by Bob Zwick and Turkey Joe Jacobs at the corner of Sixth and Heaton. Zwick and Jacobs were the big-time for Hamilton, and they were mixed up with some of the best people. So Murphy's body was laid out on a slab in the morgue, and lines of people came around to see it. I mean we had nothing else to do in those days so we went and viewed Murphy's body, both my wife, Birdie, and me. Murphy was lying there almost cut in two with bullets. Every hole had cotton stuffed in it, and he had cotton all over his body. The very next Saturday night, Turkey Joe and Bob Zwick were having a chicken dinner at the old Symmes Tavern, not the one there now. When they came out, a green sedan pulled up and let them have it. Turkey Joe Jacobs goes right down, killed instantly. Zwick jumps on the running board of a passing car, rides three blocks, and jumps off—one of his fingers is shot off and he's grazed in the head. He goes in a house, tells the lady he's been in a car wreck, and calls himself a cab. The taxi takes him downtown to the Second Ward where he's got this girl by the name of Dago Rose. Dago Rose drives him down to Newport, Kentucky, where they kidnap a doctor to fix Zwick up. Nothing was heard of him for five years until finally a cop in Toledo shoots it out with him, captures him, and sends him to the pen."

Emily Deursch: "I only saw Dillinger once. I was in college, and he came into a restaurant as I was walking out. I looked at him real close, and we passed right by each other. This chill went through me. I just kept right on going. You don't want to mess with him. I knew who it was and I was afraid. Of course, you knew it was him, he was the most famous man around. He had just escaped from prison, but he wasn't in any hurry walking into that restaurant. People around here wouldn't touch him and he knew that. He had his dinner in that restaurant, and it was two days after that he went over to Indiana. And then from Indiana he went on up to Chicago where he got it out in front of that movie theatre. Poor soul, that was the end of him."

The pride so many Hamiltonians take in the infernal aspects of their town's history is testimony to the enduring power of evil to fascinate. Disobedience in an adult is far more menacing than in a child, but it still enthralls. In a community where the rule of reason and civility has been enthroned for almost two centuries, attention is compelled by the untamed quality of wildness (like the "wild child" in France), by the irrational, by raw and wanton acts beyond control of the authorities. Fantasies of acting on impulse cannot, apparently, be entirely erased by the call to goodness. The law-abiding Hamiltonian would not willingly trade places with a felon, but the felon reminds him of a freedom that is sacrificed by civilization, of an earlier stage of social evolution prior to the coronation of order and the Internal Revenue Service. It is not easy to find a Hamiltonian who is ashamed of Dillinger, the whorehouses, or the fact that the town was so famously corrupt it was placed off-limits to the Navy during World War II.

Sergeant Chuck Furman was stopped in traffic at 10:22. What irritated him was that on the deserted night street were only two cars, one traveling in each direction, and the drivers, recognizing one another, stopped their machines for a chat. It irritated Furman more that even when he pulled the squad car to within inches of the Thunderbird blocking him, then turned on the rotating roof light, neither car budged. Furman got out to talk to the drivers. The two vehicles had nuzzled so close that Furman had to wedge himself sideways between them, looking awkward for the only time all evening, in order to speak to the drivers.

"Do you gentlemen know you're blocking a police car as well as anyone else who may want to pass?"

"That's cool, Officer Furman, we're about done," said the black driver of the Thunderbird, demonstrating some scholarship regarding the one-hundred-fourteen member Hamilton Police Department. He wore a white hat with a small fish embroidered onto the brim.

"Well, well, well," said Chuck Furman, recalling television shows that had been in reruns over a decade, "Sunshine Sodderbine. I thought we ran your hide out of here in '74."

"I done my time, Officer Furman, except all my good behavior got me out a tad early."

"It's *Sergeant* Furman now. What are you doing back in town?"

"I knew the Police Department would recognize your value in putting dudes like me away. You have my sincere congratulations, Officer Furman. I come back because this is my home, man, this is my town. Where else I got to go?"

"Move it out, Sunshine."

Sunshine Sodderbine stuck his hand out the window, palm up, toward his friend in the other car. "I catch you later, my man." The other driver grazed Sodderbine's hand with his own, waited for Sodderbine to do the same to him, and was laughing by the time he gunned his car away. "Now look, Officer Furman, you real positive you don't want me to wait while you call in my name and license plate and see if they got anything on me?"

"Good night, Sunshine."

"That's what I like about you, Officer Furman, you always give a dude a break." And he was gone.

The police dispatcher checked with his computer, which predictably had nothing on either Sodderbine or his Thunderbird. "We've brought in old Sunshine," Sergeant Furman said, "for everything. Bad checks, stolen cars, breaking and entering, fraud, forgery, bookmaking. He's nonviolent. We get convictions on him, but he's a sweet talker with the parole board. He always gets out. There's lots worse than Sunshine."

10:41. Another car needed information. "Give me a rundown on Gerald Tempey, a.k.a. Hobo," the officer in the other squad car asked headquarters. Chuck Furman snatched at his microphone like a contestant on a quiz show. "Hobo Tempey is a pusher and he traffics in stolen property," Furman said rapidly, beating the computer at headquarters easily. "The trouble is, he's also an informant. Tread lightly if he's minding his own business." Furman put the microphone back on its hook. "Hobo's problem is he brags when he helps us solve a case. He won't last long as an informant. The importance of informants in police work is often denied, but a lot of times they make the case for us, piece by piece, letting us know who is involved, where something is hidden, which gang is mad at whom." Furman liked the intimate relationship that often existed in Hamilton between policemen and lawbreakers. Each knew more about the other than either knew about anybody else in society. It was not hard for policemen and those they chased to imagine trading places.

10:44. In the ghetto of the Second Ward, Furman stopped a fight between three young black men. It was an uneven match since two of the young men were sitting on the third, bouncing his head against the pavement. Furman took the third man, who was not badly hurt but was drunk, to his home across the street.

"The fellow in the wheelchair over there," said Furman, back in the car and pointing to a middle-aged man smoking a pipe on his porch, "was shot by someone who broke into his home to burglarize it. He was trying to protect his wife and daughter upstairs. He'll never walk again. Two doors down, in the light green house, a man stabbed his wife twenty-one times while the two kids divided their attention between a TV show and their parents."

10:49. A burglar alarm went off in a jewelry store on the edge of the ghetto. No one was in the store, its windows were unbroken, its lock secure. Furman shut off the alarm.

Every cop had his war stories, and Furman did not think his were distinguished by anything more than his own occasional sense of irony.

When Furman worked on the James Ruppert case, a notorious local murder of eleven relatives by a deranged young man on Easter Sunday, he found two ironies that conflicted, which put them into the category of rumor. One story had it that James Ruppert's motive was to collect the life insurance on his mother, brother, sister-in-law, and eight nieces and nephews. The other was that Ruppert simply wanted to wipe out his whole family, including himself. After finishing off all the others, he suddenly remembered that he was a Catholic, which meant he was forbidden to commit suicide. Thinking about this so exhausted Ruppert that he had to take a nap in the same room with seven of his demised kin before he called the police. "You can't get hardened to that kind of thing," said Furman, who was the second officer on the scene, "or else you won't be a good policeman anymore. The flashback to those corpses still turns my stomach."

When he was assigned to investigate the case of a woman who was stabbed sixty times by her lover, the Oedipal implications gave Furman bad dreams for months. "The guy was making it," Furman said, "with both a mother and her daughter. The daughter held the mother for him while he stabbed her."

Just the week before, Furman was called in the day after a husband and wife had gone into a small, downtown bar. They had sat and talked for five hours, always in low tones, not arguing, never raising their voices. She, drinking a little bit. He, drinking more, but not getting drunk, and certainly not becoming raucous or in any way troublesome. At the end of all these hours, the husband rose abruptly from his seat, pulled a gun, shot his wife dead, and returned to a seat opposite her. Sitting, he then finished the job with a bullet that whipped in one of his ears and out the other. The police issued an instructive statement that the couple were rumored to be having marital difficulties. "She had," Furman said, "been running around on him."

As a young policeman Furman had sometimes put himself into positions he would never get into again. "In a bar fight once," he said, "I waded right in and tried to separate everybody, maybe seven, eight guys all going at each other. One of them stuck a gun in my stomach. I should have backed off and tried to calm these guys down, but just as a reflex, I pulled a judo throw on the man with the gun. Threw him right over my shoulder. I fractured his face, actually broke the headbone. I was wrong. The fellow was fifty-six years old, and all I needed to do was disarm him, which wouldn't have been too hard. I shouldn't have gone into the fight, and I shouldn't have busted the guy's head. They didn't think he'd make it, but he pulled through."

Furman's favorite caper involved a series of muggings downtown. People were saying Hamilton wasn't safe after dark anymore. Furman and his partner got permission to pose as drunks. Some of their fellow officers thought it was wrong and undignified for policemen to dress and act like bums. Others opposed any cop behaving at any time as a decoy.

The first two nights, Furman and his buddy weaved around town, pretending to drink from pint bottles and sagging against buildings. No one attacked them, though the enjoyment of their roles kept them from getting bored. The third night, two bruisers began following them and the partner ducked into a bar, leaving Furman an easy target. He wandered into an alley and let himself be trapped at the dead end. The muggers pulled knives and told Furman to hand over his money. Acting very drunk, Furman said he had none. One of the muggers said Furman was lying and he hated liars. He got Furman up against a cyclone fence, about to stab him. "He had me pinned so good I couldn't even reach for my service revolver," Furman recalled. "I saw myself as a potential fatality." Latinizing death into fatality took away some of its sting. It did for Furman what by-the-numbers did, put a layer of protection between him and terror.

Just in time, a little slower than planned, Furman's buddy came running up the alley waving his gun and yelling for the muggers to freeze. One did, but the other took off. While the partner guarded the first one, Furman went after the second. "That was my best chase," he recalled. "The guy ran up one street, down another, and flew around a corner. I stayed with him, but wasn't gaining. I finally fired warning shots in the air, which you're not supposed to do. The regulations say that if you're going to fire a shot, you aim to hit somebody. So the warning shots are not SOP, but that's how I caught him."

What Chuck Furman loved about the caper was that he got to act out a role, the role became dangerous, he caught his man, and for once he was able to break one of the myriad Police Department regulations he lived by.

11:09. On the respectable West Side, on a lower middle-class residential street, Furman cruised by a group of teenagers drinking beer and singing loudly. Girls as well as boys. "Hey kids!" Furman had to yell to get their attention even though he gave his roof light a couple of quick rotations. "We don't drink outside in public, and we don't make that kind of noise at this time of night. You want to knock it off, or would you like to give me some ID's to show you're old enough for the beer?" "Right, man." "Sorry, Officer." "See you around, sir." The kids split for several homes.

"They don't mean anything," Furman said. "The tall one's brother took a car once, though."

11:11. "All cars on the West Side! All cars in the neighborhood of K Street!" For once the radio did not crackle but lofted the highest fidelity into the night. "Report a shooting involving two white males at 2132 North K Street. Suspect alleged leaving scene in auto, conflicting description, late model. Victim is on K Street. Possible fatality."

VII

MURDER

In the middle of K Street, in front of his house, a young man lay dying. He said to an even younger man who had rushed to help him, "Don't touch me, I'm hurt bad." A third man strolled away. Earlier, when it had looked as though there was going to be trouble, the dying man—then whole—had called the police to complain about his brother-in-law. Within ten minutes of his call for help, the police had arrived; seeing the gravity of the situation they called for reinforcements, and within ten more minutes one of their photographers was taking pictures of the young man's soon-to-be-lifeless body. Within twelve hours of his call, an autopsy was being performed on his cadaver.

Billy Krug and Ned Wortees had been waiting for each other almost from birth. One was a bully, the other a slow but volcanic burner; both were lifelong losers, deep losers, the one who got pushed around against his meager will, the other who liked to do the pushing. When they finally met, their relationship was marked not so much by hostility, though that was abundantly there, as by a kind of psychic countdown. While Billy Krug was reckoned a town ruffian, Ned Wortees was just a shrub of a man. To others, if not to themselves, it seemed they both lay in wait all their lives, unknowing, until they met and hated. Then they bided their time until circumstance and temperament combined to provide the opportunity for one to dispatch the other.

As a boy, which at twenty he had long since ceased to be, Billy Krug liked swimming best of all. His mother Irma thought he could stay under water all day, and his sister Marilyn thought he acted as though he was born in water and wanted to keep on living in it. By the time he was ten Billy could beat both his older brothers to the end of the Y pool. He could stay under longer than either, too, though one of them caught him sneaking a breath through a straw once and whipped him for it.

The three brothers liked fun. What they called fun was mischief to some, plain meanness to others. No place could hold the Krug boys, not home or school or a job. When Billy was thirteen, his father died of cancer after thirty-five years in maintenance for Champion Paper. Irma Krug set her face against the past and worked wearily to maintain a household. She mended clothes until she could settle in as a lunchroom cashier. Nothing went right with her sons. Her three daughters were fine, Marilyn the brightest, but the two older boys were ungovernable until they moved away. Reports back to Hamilton were not good. At home, her youngest son Billy started to get into trouble. "It beats me," Irma Krug reflected later with a stare of marble. "Except for one English grandmother, they were from good German stock on both sides."

Pranks, Billy called what he did. Hubcaps, a firecracker in a classroom, doughnuts from the supermarket when he didn't feel like waiting in line, stuff like that. Maybe an edge of the tormentor in some of it, taking little kids' bikes, setting fire to a neighbor's swing. It turned meaner when he snatched an old lady's handbag, more practical when he discovered that with a little more effort you could take not only the hubcap but the tire it was attached to. A cottage industry, The Midnight Auto Supply, was born.

A much older sister married early and had two sons only a few years younger than Billy. Billy and his nephews, Ken and

Art Claflin, adored each other, and the Claflin boys knew only his kindness. "Candy and toys, all the time," Ken Claflin said. "When we were little and he was bigger, he never came to see us without a present. After he went away it was just the same. We wouldn't hear nothing for weeks, then he'd show up at the door with a squirt gun or some package, and he'd just toss it to us, and we'd jump all over him and wrestle him down. No matter what happened, there he'd be in your doorway with a bunch of damn balloons."

The trouble got more serious. When other kids were gingerly trying pot, Billy was heavily into hash. The teachers knew about some of it at Taft High School even when Billy was a sophomore, but they didn't know how to stop it. Billy was at Taft because his family, though working people, lived on the prosperous West Side where the Champion factory was located. A couple of years after his father died, Billy's Midnight Auto Supply began fencing accessories that other kids took and turned over to them, from hood ornaments to car stereos. The police had little difficulty hearing about the cottage industry, and Chuck Furman arrested Billy Krug for receiving stolen property. Billy got off with probation, but The Midnight Auto Supply was over. To help out at home, Billy got a job in a bicycle repair shop, though he had no bike himself.

Arriving at Taft a few years after Billy, his nephew Ken Claflin and Ken's girlfriend, Maria Amberson, found two kinds of weather at the high school, sunny and threatening. The first was for the students going on to college, the second for everyone else. Ken Claflin was a tough, handsome kid who lived, like his Uncle Billy, on a respectable tree-lined street with medium-sized frame houses. At the upper end of Ken's street were a number of higher priced homes, in one of which a Champion executive lived. The street sloped toward the river, and at Ken's end the houses tended to be occupied by two families, three at times, and the screen doors had not been recently repaired. The furniture had the odor of a generation of babies and several generations of pets. In Ken Claflin's living room, almost exactly like Billy Krug's a couple of blocks away, the two overstuffed chairs were oozing their stuffing, and the divan had sagged. There were no shelves for books. Two pictures, a color family photograph and a bright painting of a New England autumn, were all the walls held. The impression was of a home that was permanently temporary, that the Claflins were always planning to go somewhere better the next year or fix the place up, but had never quite gotten around to either.

Ken Claflin liked to wear a bullet on a thin chain around his neck, and he favored a belt whose copper buckle was sculpted with a cannabis plant. His girlfriend, Maria Amberson, was a neighborhood beauty whose delicate features managed to express both fear and defiance at the same time. After all the violence was over, Ken and Maria shared an afternoon with Billy's older sister Marilyn, who had also gone to Taft High School.

What was remarkable about the three was the degree to which all of them—Maria and Ken still in their teens, Marilyn in her midtwenties—expressed class consciousness, even anger. "By the time you get to Taft it's pretty much decided who's who," Marilyn said, behind glasses and sad eyes that disguised, but did not obliterate, the fact that she, too, was defiant. "They go to Wilson Junior High and we go to Harding. They come to Taft and flaunt what they have. They go to Europe in the summer. They wear better clothes. They drive flashy cars their folks have bought them for their sixteenth birthdays. They're snooty to the rest of us, yet they didn't earn it themselves. Even if they make money they don't really earn it, because they start with cushy jobs their dads get for them."

"Taft has the prominent families with the doctors and the lawyers among its parents," Maria said. "The girls act like they don't know you if you're not one of them. You don't have their clothes, you're not in their college-prep classes, and you better not go out with their brothers. They let you know you're on an ash heap. Not one of my ten best friends is going to college."

"Not one of my *twenty-five* best friends at Taft went to college," Ken said. "The only guys I even knew who also knew the college-bound kids were those who played on athletic teams with them. I worked afternoons and Saturdays in Elroy Kogel's bakery making rolls and bread and wedding cakes. On Friday nights I'd drink nine or ten glasses of water before I went to bed since no alarm clock could wake me up but my bladder could do it. I'd wake up at three-thirty needing to go to the bathroom and that would get me to the bakery by four A.M. With that kind of schedule I couldn't associate with the kids going on to college and they wouldn't be interested in me. It was the same with my Uncle Billy. When Billy went to Taft, some of the most prominent families in Hamilton had kids there. He knew who the Rentschlers, the Becketts, and the Greveys were, but they didn't even know he existed. Not that we ever cared."

With one term left to graduate, Billy dropped out of Taft. If he couldn't swim or play ball, he wasn't much interested in school. He also got the feeling the cops were looking at everything he did. By this time, his oldest brother Henry had moved south, been picked up for stealing a radio, and was in jail. Billy's middle brother, Stephen Krug, was living in Toledo, so Billy went to stay with him. There was more to do in Toledo than Hamilton, more girls, and more prospects for a job. Billy had made up his mind to stay there when one Sunday Stephen went out alone on his motorcycle and got hit by a truck. Everyone assured Billy that Stephen never felt a thing.

His mother wanted him home so Billy came back to Hamilton, but he didn't feel like hanging around home for long either. With the Vietnam War almost lost, Billy joined the army. Irma Krug would have been against it if there was any chance of her youngest son's going to Vietnam right after his brother's death, but under the circumstances she thought the army might do Billy some good. To his own surprise, Billy loved basic training. The army shaped him up, made him feel he belonged somewhere. He wrote Marilyn he used to think he was tough, but now he knew guys who were teaching him what tough really was. Maybe he would stay in the army. Unlike school they didn't seem to mind if you had a little fun now and then. Marilyn wrote Billy back that she was getting married soon.

Henry Krug was released from prison a bitter man. His term had been too long for stealing a radio, he had been beaten by the guards and raped by an inmate. Drifting around Nashville, Henry found work in a paper factory. He was angry and unhappy, but he had a job Irma Krug hoped he would keep. Maybe her son would settle down and be like his father, who had spent all those years with Champion Paper in Hamilton. Irma Krug was glad when Henry invited Billy to come down and visit him on a three-day pass.

The weekend began beautifully, Billy said later, with the brothers going out for mucho beer on Friday night. They found a pair of girls, singing sisters as it happened, who thought the combination of beer, grass, and sex was great enough to write a song about. Very late, in an after-hours bar, the girls introduced the boys to a gambler who asked if they would like to play cards the following night. Henry and Billy said they'd think about it and made a date to see the girls again anyway.

Saturday, Henry and Billy argued about whether to go in the card game. Henry wanted to—why not give it a try, what can we lose?—but Billy thought it wasn't a good idea to put his uniform, which he was very proud of, in the same room with a lot of poker chips. They finally decided Billy would pick up the girls and take them to a movie, Henry would play cards for a few hours, then they would all meet in the after-hours bar. Billy and the girls went to a drive-in and saw—inevitably—*Nashville*. They waited for so long in the after-hours bar that Billy figured Henry must be doing very well since he knew his brother had had only a few dollars to start with and couldn't have lasted long unless he was winning.

At four A.M., with everybody getting bored and drunk, the same gambler they had met the night before came into the bar and told Billy he had come directly from the hospital but it was no use. Henry had been shot to death in the card game. When

Henry caught another player cheating, the gambler had tried to intervene and throw them both out. Henry told the cheater he wanted his money back, and the cheater told Henry to kiss his ass. Before Henry could attack or defend, the cheater simply rose from the table, Saturday Night Special in hand, and plugged Henry twice in the abdomen. While the others scattered, the gambler called the police and stayed with Henry. Henry was alive, the gambler said, in the ambulance, but he went out fast as soon as they reached the hospital.

Billy Krug went back to the army, still only eighteen, convinced he would not live to be twenty-one. He got reckless. The rules that had protected him and made him feel safe were now just obstacles to mad pleasure. Marilyn wrote him that they both still had a lot to live for. Billy did not answer. He went AWOL, and the army gave him another chance. He was insubordinate, and the army simply gave him a month's latrine duty. He beat up a smaller, weaker recruit, and he lost his private's stripe. His CO thought Billy should see the chaplain. Billy talked about the deaths of his brothers, and the chaplain talked about the challenge for Billy to live differently. Everybody had trouble, the chaplain said, but trouble didn't have to defeat you if you took it as an opportunity for improvement. Billy pulled himself out of it—no one knew how, not even the chaplain—and spent five blameless months, at the end of which he got his private's stripe back.

Marilyn asked Billy to come home for her wedding. She could hardly believe it, she told Billy, after the sadness they had been through with Stephen and Henry, but she was on her way to being a happily married woman. Her fiancé was gentle and caring. He was so generous he reminded her of Billy. He wasn't just out for what he could get on the first or even the sixth date. He had had some trouble—who hadn't?—but he was straightened out now, with a good job for an electrical contractor.

Though he didn't tell her so right away, Ned Wortees was actually on parole when he met Marilyn Krug. He was almost ten years older than her brother Billy, and his record was that

much longer. He had deserted from the Marine Corps and
served time in the stockade before they gave him a dishonorable
discharge. Chuck Furman had arrested him once in Hamilton,
as he had Billy Krug, for auto larceny, which meant a late model
Chevelle. He had been in an Illinois penitentiary for another
car theft and then had been arrested for parole violation. Afterward he had done six months for assault and battery. He didn't
taunt people the way Billy Krug did, but if he got rubbed he
could get mean. He was on the short side of medium, whereas
Billy was strapping. Marilyn liked Ned's lack of pretense, not
swaggering like so many she knew. Though he'd never had time
to develop much humor, Ned had a twinkle to him that Marilyn
liked, too. He could have fun without taking advantage, unlike
a lot of fellows she had grown up with. When Marilyn met Ned
he was soft as a puppy, hungry for a fresh start.

Billy Krug danced home for the wedding in his proud uniform. From first sight, he and Ned Wortees never spent an easy
moment together. The family said later that what flowed like
water at the wedding was not champagne but bad blood. Not
that any blows were struck. Billy wanted Marilyn to have the
best time she could, and he wasn't about to do anything to wreck
the weekend. But Ned seemed to resent the uniform and even
the physique of his brother-in-law. Though he wasn't going to
say anything, Billy looked at Ned the way he would at a runt.
During the reception they glared at each other. When it was
time to get back to his base, Billy tried a lame joke. He shook
hands with Ned and told him to be nice to Marilyn or the big
bad Billy-bully would get him. Ned said anytime you want to
try, and Billy left quickly.

Though he was not really short, Ned never felt good around
people who found him small. He would begin by being uneasy
around them and end by hating them. Sometimes he would
hate just the person he assumed was his tormentor, sometimes
everyone. He had been so mad he wanted to crush every skull
he saw, even a mother wheeling a baby carriage, even the baby
in the carriage. People whispered about Ned, he was sure of

that. You guys think I'm puny and sad and no good, he had thought. Okay, there's nothing to whisper about if I come right out and shout. Here's how sad and puny I am: Pow, Bam, Squish! Forget it. No problem.

Yet Ned could control himself and he could be patient. He believed the speech they gave when people began their prison terms. Don't serve time; let time serve you. He studied electrical engineering, he got a degree, he came back to Hamilton full of resolve. It worked. Ned got his good job doing construction wiring, and he met Marilyn.

After he started going with Marilyn, Ned's sister, Ellen Gandy, thought he was calmer and nicer than he had ever been. Ned had his new beginning, and Marilyn was helping him make the most of it. Ellen herself had introduced Ned to his first wife, but she was hardly to blame for what happened, especially since the introduction had occurred when Ned and his future wife were in the third grade. That was the year their father had left their mother and headed south. Ned seemed to take it harder than Ellen, and he folded up at school. The only times he unfolded were when other boys would tease him, and then Ned would throw things and everyone would get into trouble. Rae, the little girl Ellen introduced Ned to, was odd and sheltering, a lonely girl who liked stray animals. From the third grade on, Ned and Rae were together off and on. Ned would still get into trouble, and his mother, who could not control him, would ask his father to come get him or at least let her send him south. The father was newly settled and married in Florida, and his Hamilton family no longer concerned him.

Eventually, Ned and Rae married and had a son. Now Rae sheltered the son. Ned would hold himself in, but he was not happy in the relationship anymore. He would be in trouble elsewhere, sometimes with the police, but he would still keep it in at home. This made him kinder than many other men Rae knew, though Ned often seemed pent-up, about to erupt. When Ned finally burst, what flowed was the skittish, unprompted rage of a weak king. Arbitrary and tyrannical, Ned thought his wife looked at another man one day in their neighborhood, and he ran her down in the family car. He ran over Rae repeatedly, back and forth, back and forth, while she screamed until she lost consciousness. He only stopped, Ned told a prison psychiatrist, when he figured she was dead. That would teach her to flirt. Minus a leg but still miraculously alive, Rae divorced Ned.

Marilyn Krug did not, of course, know the details of the break-up of Ned's first marriage when she agreed to become Marilyn Wortees. Ned told Marilyn only that he had been married, divorced, and had had problems with the law that were now over. He cherished Marilyn and was sweet and grateful to her. She found herself caring about him even if, she later reflected, she was not really in love. He gave Marilyn a respect she craved and had never before had from anyone outside her family.

Yet his anger would come suddenly, especially when he drank, which meant more often in summer, less in winter. Ned would get mad at funny little things, like Marilyn's putting the eggs in the wrong section of the refrigerator. They could not afford their own home so they lived downstairs from Marilyn's mother. Although Irma Krug let them alone, Ned was hardly the kind of man whose pride could afford the price of living with his mother-in-law. Yet that would not be what he got mad about. He would get mad because Marilyn left the eggs on the bottom shelf instead of at the top of the refrigerator. Then there was his brother-in-law.

Billy Krug, a born tease, saw that Ned Wortees was the easiest mark he had ever run into. He would come home on leave and kiss his sister and mother, then shake hands with Ned while holding a mock-electric buzzer in the palm of his hand. Nothing vicious, just pranks. Ned bristled, tried to chuckle, hating it.

A few months after Marilyn's wedding, Billy no longer wanted to stay in the army. He had thought it was his home, the one situation that could ever shape him up, maybe he would become a lifer. But once he had proved he could handle it, the army was dull. Now, with fun waiting on the outside and endless drudgery on the inside, Billy let his friends know he was nervous in the service. A jeep was hot-wired one Saturday night and still was not back in the motor pool by Sunday afternoon. The first sergeant asked Billy, who was working at the motor pool, if he knew where it was. Billy took the question as an accusation and denied it hotly. On Sunday evening, the jeep was found wrapped around a tree near the rifle range. Billy's closest army friend admitted having driven it, but he had no access to the motor pool. Again the top kick asked Billy if he knew anything about the jeep. Although Billy's punch missed the first sergeant, by the following Thursday he was being processed out on an undesirable discharge. Not as bad as Ned Wortees' dishonorable, but close.

Installing ducts for an air-conditioning system, Ned wrenched his back. He missed some work and was in too much pain to have sex for several weeks. When Marilyn asked him why he would not see a doctor, he thought she was getting impatient. Maybe she was, a little, but she said she was just concerned for his health. "I'd better not catch you running around on me," Ned said.

Marilyn's nephew, Ken Claflin, came over with Maria Amberson one night. While Marilyn and Maria went out for pizza, Ned and Ken played cards. They drank some beer, kidded each other, and talked about girls. Dealt a few hands of gin rummy, no money involved. Just sitting around, Ken had a good time, almost as much fun as if his Uncle Billy had been home. They went out to buy more beer, and Ned paid for it. He even let Ken drive his car, his prized red Monte Carlo. They came back home and stayed up almost all night talking. Finally Ken and Maria, like a grown-up couple though they were only seventeen and sixteen, thanked Ned and Marilyn and left. Ned would be his good buddy, Ken told Maria. He would introduce him to the electrical contractor, who might have a summer job for Ken that would beat getting up at four A.M. to go to the bakery. The next morning, Ned woke up and told Marilyn he never wanted to lay eyes again on that son of a bitch, Ken Claflin.

Billy came home from the army no hero with his undesirable, though no disgrace either. He had stuck it out for over a year. He strutted into a family homecoming dinner, and Ned didn't like it that Billy got all the attention. The undesirable discharge did not make Billy a first-round draft choice on the Hamilton job market, but he got along. Two weeks at a filling station, odd jobs he was a little old for, like mowing lawns, skylarking his way from one month to the next. Marilyn did not like Billy asking their mother for money, but Irma Krug usually found something in her purse. He turned twenty and began to go with a girl named Dolores. Though she was three years younger than he was, Dolores settled Billy a bit, and he started to think about a future he could control instead of the other way around. At thirty, his brother-in-law Ned, never mind what Billy thought of him, had come through some hard stuff and still had a good job. Billy should be able to beat that with his eyes shut. He talked about a correspondence course in TV repair or some kind of selling. He could be real good with people.

Billy rarely ran into Ned. When he saw his brother-in-law coming, each knew enough to look the other way. It seemed to Marilyn that Ned resented a younger, stronger version of himself. For his part, Billy seemed to resent her marriage to Ned. At a birthday party in their home for one of the Claflin boys, Ned criticized Marilyn for not having the place neat enough. After some vodka and a few beers, he wouldn't let the subject drop. Billy finally told Ned to leave his sister alone. Ned pulled a knife. Everyone but Billy jumped up from the table in shock. Marilyn glared at her husband, then at her brother, then back to Ned again. Billy sat calmly and said, "You better be ready to do a good job with that, Ned, because if you don't I'll crush you." Marilyn stared Ned down. "Something got into me," Ned said at last, putting the knife away. "I don't know what." But he collected guns.

Billy got serious about Dolores. Dolores's mother figured she could spot bad news a couple of neighborhoods away and told her to drop Billy. The relationship cemented quickly after that.

One day, putting away Dolores's laundry, her mother found some birth control pills among her underwear. That confirmed her worst fears about Billy. She called Dolores in and ordered her to stop seeing Billy immediately. Then she marched into the bathroom, pills in hand, and flushed them away. Within three weeks Dolores was pregnant. Billy wasn't sorry; he wanted to stay with this girl. Six weeks later, in a February freeze, they were married. Marilyn liked Dolores but was sure this was not the right way to start out in life, a shotgun wedding for a marriage made not in Heaven but literally in a toilet.

From his experience in the Midnight Auto Supply, Billy had become a decent mechanic. He got lobster shift work in a twenty-four-hour garage on the Erie highway that leads to Cincinnati, no great job but not food stamps either. Dolores and he got their own place, their own car. The trouble was, going to work at midnight meant he did not see much of Dolores, who was trying to finish school before the baby was born. Billy still hung out with his friends, especially a chili cook named Homer. Homer had gone to school with Billy and was now eager to leave Hamilton and go west.

In spring, Ned took Marilyn to a stock-car race. It was a hot Saturday and Ned had a fair amount to drink during the races. On the way home a car swerved in front of them, almost causing an accident. Ned had to cut and brake suddenly, and he came back swearing the way most other drivers would. But the swearing was not enough. Ned had to follow the car for miles and miles. Finally, the discourteous driver pulled up in front of his home, turned off his motor, and emerged from his car with a shotgun. Ned said he was sorry, he had thought the man was an old friend of his and merely had followed him to say hello.

Warren Claflin, Ken's father, came over to see the Wortees that night. An easygoing, bespectacled switchman for the telephone company, Warren Claflin was one of Marilyn's favorite relatives. She told him about following the car all the way home. Warren Claflin began giving Ned Wortees some rather mild advice to the effect that his temper could get him in trouble if he did not figure out a way to keep it down. Still mad at the driver who had swerved in front of him and, no doubt, at himself for caving in so quickly in front of Marilyn when the shotgun was produced, Ned Wortees picked up a heavy ashtray and hit Warren Claflin with it so hard the ashtray broke. Blood fountained from Warren Claflin's head and neck, soaking both men, but Ned Wortees was not satisfied. He went for a rifle and pointed it at Warren Claflin. It misfired. He hit Warren Claflin with the butt until he was almost unconscious. Then, remorseful, Ned Wortees loaded Warren Claflin into Claflin's own car and drove him home. The police happened to find Ned Wortees walking back to his and Marilyn's house drenched in blood, though without a scratch on him. He told them he had been in a fight, and the police demanded to see the party of the second part. Warren Claflin, out of loyalty to Marilyn, refused to press charges. He told the police there had been a family spat, that was all.

The next morning, his sons Ken and Art, together with Billy Krug, all said they were going to separate Ned Wortees from what was left of his senses. Warren Claflin told them they would do nothing of the kind. Instead, Ken would go over to the Wortees' home and ask for his father's glasses, which had fallen off when the ashtray hit him. From then on, they would have nothing to do with Ned Wortees. Billy Krug begged to be allowed to take care of Ned Wortees all by himself. Warren Claflin said no, and Marilyn said her brother mustn't beat up on her husband. Billy promised to do what his big sister wanted, but why did she stay with such a damn worm?

When Ken went for the glasses, Ned Wortees opened the door a crack, shoved them out, and closed the door again.

Marilyn left Ned the next week. She moved upstairs to her mother's. Ned cried and pleaded with her to come back. She had a good job as a bookkeeper and didn't feel she needed to be tied to a violent husband. Ned wept some more and said he was sorry for everything, and everything would be different if Marilyn would only come back downstairs. When he agreed to go to a marriage counselor, Marilyn agreed to move back in with him. They went twice to the marriage counselor, who said Ned had feelings of rejection and inadequacy as a man. After the second time Ned walked out and said he didn't need that shit anymore.

Dolores Krug, Billy's pregnant wife, was now accepted back into the ranks of humanity by her mother. Billy was spending more time with his nephews, the Claflin boys, and his friend Homer, the chili cook, than he was with Dolores. He said he loved her, but he didn't know how to keep her happy and when he was laid off by the garage, he was no longer supporting her. He couldn't even pay the rent on their apartment. Dolores's mother saw her opening. Dolores had done the right thing in marrying Billy, and the baby would have his father's name, but enough was enough, Dolores should come home. She did.

Billy was morose. He borrowed money from his mother to pay the rent, but Dolores would not return. It was no fun being heavily pregnant in summer, and her mother at least had air conditioning. Someday she might get together again with Billy, but he had a few things to prove first. Otherwise, her mother was right about him.

Now Marilyn had somewhere to go besides up the stairs to Irma Krug. Ned had begun to complain about her in bed, hitting her once when he could not get an erection. Leaving her furniture, television set, and appliances with Ned, Marilyn moved over to Billy's paid-up apartment. This time begging did not budge her. She went to a lawyer for a separation agreement and got a court order forbidding Ned to move any of her belongings out of their home. Ned was furious, but there was nothing he could do. Billy's friend Homer moved in with Marilyn and him, so the two men provided Marilyn with a reasonable amount of protection.

Billy wanted to do more than protect his sister. He wanted to pay her husband back for his rages and mistreatment of Marilyn. He also wanted to have some fun. One day he and Ken Claflin poured talcum powder all over Ned's red Monte Carlo, turning it a dead orange. Another time they sneaked into Ned's downstairs apartment while he was at work and mixed ground-up razor blades into his toothpaste. Ned's fuse burned a little shorter.

Dolores had left Billy in May after only three months of marriage, but in July Billy was still mooning over her. He wished he could get her away from her mother for a little while. Dolores would not come see Billy, and her mother would not let him come see her. Marilyn and Homer both told Billy to forget Dolores, start over, he was only twenty. Start over? Billy asked. My brothers are dead, my wife's left me, and everyone in town looks at me and sees a loser. That's the point, Homer said, everyone in town. You go west, man. We'll go west in August, to California. Billy was trying to get Dolores off his mind, and he didn't care too much what they did out there. Like earlier Hamiltonians in the last two centuries, they had no plans, they would just head out. They would screw around, they said, until they found some place they liked, and they would have a ball, get work, take off, settle down, start over again. In California, in August.

Television is often accused of wreaking social havoc, of causing more crime than the Mafia. If only because, unlike the Mafia, it has no will of its own, television is undoubtedly innocent of most of the strongest charges laid before its lidless eye. Surely in the case of Billy Krug versus Ned Wortees, the tinder had long been present. They had never liked one another, neither was averse to violence, and both had frequently found themselves on the wrong side of the law. Yet it would be hard to imagine a crime to which television was more intimately connected—as a machine, a possession, a medium, and as a bearer of messages.

Early in the morning of July 13, Irma Krug's television set broke. Like many Hamilton widows of modest means, she took in sewing. Television was her way of humming to herself, of daydreaming, while she mended and stitched. When her set stopped suddenly near the end of "Not For Women Only," she was bereft of daytime, of the beloved soaps that took her from seams to hems to buttonholes. Marilyn stopped by on her way to work, bringing Irma a ripped winter coat belonging to the wife of the head accountant at her bookkeeping firm. The coat would need reweaving, an Irma Krug specialty. Since Ned had left already for his own job, Irma sent her daughter down to his apartment to bring up the television set there. Ned had left the door open when he went to work. The television was Marilyn's anyway; she had bought it before her marriage.

What Marilyn saw downstairs both frightened and angered her. Empty and half-empty beer cans littered the floor and lay in the seats of chairs. Cigarette butts had been ground into the wall to extinguish them. Some of her belongings had been piled into suitcases that stood by the door; their only china had been stuffed into a cardboard box in the kitchen. Was Ned planning to skip out with everything they owned? Then the scary part: Nestling on the living room couch, as though put to bed there, were Ned's guns. She knew he had them, but had never seen them all together. Three rifles, a shotgun, and a pistol. Marilyn grabbed the television set and lugged it upstairs.

All day she worried about losing her things if Ned left town. At lunchtime she went over to the supermarket to pick up some cardboard boxes of her own in case she needed to make a preemptive first strike to keep her possessions. Marilyn decided to confront Ned that evening. With his temper, and the weather as steamy as it was, it would be a good idea to have Billy and Homer around in case Ned was drunk and abusive. She asked them to meet her at the Krug house on K Street at six o'clock.

After work Marilyn went first to see Ned's married sister, Ellen Gandy. The sisters-in-law had remained friends even after Marilyn had left Ned. Marilyn wanted to avoid a scene with Ned if she could. Ellen said she didn't think Ned was getting ready to go anywhere. Their father was in town from Florida for a rare visit back to Hamilton, and Ellen was having a barbecue that evening for him. Ned was coming over, and Ellen promised to ask him what his plans were.

Billy and Homer were not yet there when Marilyn reached her mother's. She called the Claflin boys who lived only a few blocks away, and they said they'd be right over. Ned arrived home, tired from work, hot from a July day that stretched out like a prison sentence, to find the television set gone. He screamed upstairs that he wanted it back. Marilyn, refusing to open the door, screamed back that he couldn't have it, it was hers. Ned had no bathroom downstairs and asked if he could at least come in to clean up before he went out for dinner. Nothing doing, said Marilyn. Ned swore some and went back downstairs. Even though he couldn't wash, he changed his shirt and pants and headed over to his sister's house, this time locking the door to the apartment.

Ned was sullen at the barbecue Ellen gave for their father and his present wife. When Ellen's husband, a truck driver often on the road but home for the evening, asked Ned what was wrong, he said Marilyn was. She took their TV, she wouldn't talk to him face to face, she had her mother and the rest of her family turned against him, and yet, damn, he still wished she'd come back to him. "That's the thing about women, Ned," Joe Gandy said, "you can't live with 'em and you can't live without 'em." Ned asked if Joe would like to see his new pistol, which was out in his glove compartment.

Billy Krug and the Claflin boys, arriving at 2132 North K, were told by Marilyn how angry Ned was. Ken Claflin had brought along Maria, who suggested there could be trouble if they hung around waiting for Ned to come home. Why didn't they all, including Mrs. Krug, go over to the Claflins' for the night? "Nope," Billy said, "then Ned takes everything in that apartment, breaks into this one and does the same, and beats it before morning." "Right," Marilyn said. "Let's get a U-Haul and take my stuff out of there. We'll store it at the Claflins'."

They called several more friends to help them, and Ken Claflin had a U-Haul there in less than half an hour. Ned had gotten a new lock for his door, so Marilyn broke a window to let them into Ned's apartment. Within minutes they were carrying out the refrigerator, the washer, the living room couch, and everything else. They took the rifles and shotgun that had been on the couch, but Marilyn didn't notice that the pistol wasn't there. None of them liked Ned anyway, and they got mean. They took Ned's beer out of the refrigerator and passed it around. They took his clothes out of the closet and loaded them in boxes and took them to the U-Haul. They laughed and drank more beer while they dismantled the bed. Billy said Ned would have nothing to sleep on when he got home, but what the hell, after all he'd done to Marilyn. They carried the chairs and tables out to the U-Haul, and then Billy remembered he had an old crossbow upstairs. He brought it down, cocked it with an arrow in it, and had Ken bring a chair back from the U-Haul. Setting his contraption in the chair, Billy ran a string from the bow to the door so that when Ned came home, the crossbow would shoot an arrow at him. What a kick.

Quickly, they drove over to the Claflins' and unloaded everything into the garage. The beer had made the night steamier. Everyone was edgy. Ken and Maria had an argument. She accused him of looking too long at another girl that afternoon. He denied it, but she left angrily. The rest of the party returned the U-Haul and drove back to the Krug home to await Ned. Marilyn knew they had provoked him—it hadn't been necessary to take his things as well as hers—and she was afraid he would destroy her mother's entire house if they were not there to protect it.

They went upstairs at 2132 North K and waited. The one item from the Worteeses' household they had not moved over to the Claflins' was Ned's beer. They passed around some more of it now.

At Ellen's, when they finished the ribs, Ned's father asked his son how he was getting along. Ned reckoned not too good. He was in a poor mood. His wife and her rotten brother put him between a rock and a hard place. Asa Wortees never did know what to say to his son, and his son always looked to him to say something. Well, he was leaving tomorrow to go home. It was safe to ask Ned over when over was a thousand miles away. "Come on down to Fort Myers sometime. Trailer park's just a spit from the Gulf. It's the life."

Ned said he was tired and hot. The Gandys did not have air conditioning, but Ellen asked if Ned wanted to go inside and lie down. He could at least rest. No, Ned wanted to go home. Anyway, he would feel better in his car.

The lights were blazing upstairs as Ned arrived home. Someone was watching out the upstairs window. A signal was given, and everyone was quiet as Ned walked into his downstairs apartment. He could not hear them, but he knew they were there. They could hear him, and even after all the beer, they tensed, wondering how he would react.

Ned opened the door to his apartment and heard an object fall to the floor. It was the cocked crossbow, which failed to snap its arrow and was merely pulled off the chair by the string attached to the door handle. When he turned on the lights, he saw that everything he owned was gone. He had not had much. Never had had much. But he had what he had, and everything was gone. No bed, chairs, clothes. Everything that told him he had been married to Marilyn was also gone. There was not even enough left to swear about. Anyway, they were all upstairs waiting for him to blow, so he wouldn't do that. They were waiting to laugh, so he wouldn't give them anything to laugh at. He heard the goddamn television set Marilyn had taken upstairs that morning. He could fix that anyway.

Ned walked downstairs into the basement and pulled out all the fuses that lighted the upstairs portion of the house. Now it was they who swore. Billy and Marilyn, Ken and Art Claflin, Billy's friend Homer, and Irma Krug. Everyone was yelling. In the dark, but yelling.

If they would take all his things, Ned figured, what might they do next? He walked out to his Monte Carlo, almost bumping into a contrite Maria Amberson on the lawn. She had come over to make up with Ken. Like two animals of different species who neither prey upon each other nor have any similar tastes, Ned and Maria passed silently and warily.

In the street, Ned raised the hood on his Monte Carlo, took off the distributor cap and put it in his pocket. Now, at least, they could not hot-wire his car. That was one thing they could not take. He opened his glove compartment and took out the .38 he had showed Joe Gandy. That was another thing.

Upstairs, Irma Krug called the police. Her estranged son-in-law had turned off her electricity. It was hot and dark. She couldn't use her air conditioner, and she couldn't play her TV. Would the police come right over? The dispatcher took her address, but said the police cannot intervene in domestic disputes, the best thing was to buy some more fuses in the morning.

Downstairs, Ned Wortees also called the police. His wife had taken all his furniture, even the bed he slept in. The dispatcher noted the identical address and repeated the explanation about the police and domesticity.

The police department tape recorder preserved the dispatcher's remark to the patrolman who had just brought him coffee. "Looks like they don't like each other out on K Street. Isn't that your neighborhood, Shaw?"

Upstairs, Ken told Maria everything between them was cool. There might be trouble with Ned, though, and she better get out of there. Maria went out and sat in Ken's car. Ken said he would be down soon if nothing happened.

Downstairs, Ned walked next door to his neighbor's house. The neighbor, a carpenter named Dan Pender, had never liked Billy Krug since Billy had trick-or-treated his windows one Halloween with real paint that would not come off. That made Dan Pender a natural ally of Ned's. Pender felt sorry for Ned. The guy had had bad breaks since his old man split on him when he was a kid. He was trying to turn it all around, but now his wife and her brother were giving him nothing but a hard way to go. He had been out when the Krugs had done their job with the U-Haul, but Pender was furious when Ned told him about it. Billy was no good, just like his brothers. Once old Charlie Krug died, the family had gone to hell. He had seen it coming. Why didn't Ned come on in and watch some TV?

Dan Pender gave Ned a beer, and since it was baseball's mid-summer night, they sat to watch the two dream teams from each league play the All-Star game. It was coming from a western city, which meant it started late in Ohio, and by the third inning it was no game at all. Two American League pitchers could not find the plate with radar, and the score was quickly eight to one. Ned was distracted, Pender was bored. If only television had delivered them a tight game, which would at least have held Ned's attention, there might have been no further trouble. Ned used Pender's phone to call the Gandys. He told his sister what Marilyn's family had done in his apartment. "She's taken everything I own." He was in tears. Ellen said she and Joe would come over with a camera and take photographs of the gutted apartment. The pictures would show that Marilyn had violated the court order she herself had obtained.

Dan Pender gave Ned another beer and suggested, since the All-Star game was so boring, that they sit outside on the front porch. Dully, Ned followed Pender outside and sat down. Next door, in front of his own house, two cats were fighting.

Upstairs, the family was getting tired of sitting around in the dark. The moment for a confrontation had come and gone. Ned had not exploded and tried to tear the place apart or burn it down. He had simply turned off the lights. Now he was over at Dan Pender's, maybe lining up support for an assault on the upstairs apartment. Pender was not the kind of man who looked for a battle, but it was true he had no use for Billy Krug. As much as they had baited Ned, and as much as Ned hated them, Billy saw everybody losing if there was a fight. He decided to place another call to the police. He told the dispatcher there was bad trouble with his brother-in-law, and the police had better come over or else he and his friends would handle the problem themselves. The dispatcher, noting that this was the third call from 2132 North K, told Billy he would send a car over, but the officers could not come inside to settle a family argument. Billy would have to go downstairs to the street to meet them, and then they would see what they could do.

Billy went downstairs to wait for the police.

Ned, sitting on Dan Pender's porch, saw Billy come outside. Billy stooped on his front lawn to break up the fight between the two cats.

Billy noticed Ned with Dan Pender as they watched him. He turned away.

On Dan Pender's porch, Pender asked Ned if he would like to spend the night. He could use the living room couch. Ned said he wanted to be in his own home, even if nothing was left. He would sleep on the floor. Pender said think about it.

"You took all my shit," Ned said to Billy across the narrow lawn between Pender's house and the Krugs'.

"You beat up on my sister," Billy said.

"It's done," Ned said. "She asked for it."

He got up from Pender's porch and moved toward the downstairs door of the Krug house. He had to walk past his brother-in-law.

Upstairs, Ken Claflin said he was going downstairs to wait for the police with Billy. Irma went to the window. Marilyn went to the bathroom.

On the lawn, each brother-in-law watched the other coming toward him. They almost made it past one another, Billy to look for the squad car, Ned to spend the night in his gutted room. But they got too close on the lawn.

It was not the middle-class moment of American legend, the unavoidable crisis when one member of a nice family turns exasperatedly to another. Hey fella, let's agree to disagree, huh? Right-o, better not see each other, somebody might get his hair mussed. That moment is civilized, cooked, this one was raw. Separately, Ned Wortees and Billy Krug were two torrents of anger and contempt; together, a dam about to burst.

When his sister's husband was even with him, almost past him, Billy sprung his fist at the side of Ned's cheek. If it had connected accurately, the police, having already been summoned by three members of the family including both of the combatants, would have scored the fight a knockout instead of a murder. But the punch landed up on Ned's head and only dizzied him.

Ned spun at Billy with his right hand bringing the .38 out of his back pocket. Billy turned away but had no time to duck or run. Ned's first shot hit him in the back of the neck. His second one missed. Billy stumbled toward the street. He leaned against Dan Pender's parked car as Ned followed him. Billy slumped to a crouch in the street.

"Goddammit, don't hit my Caddy," Dan Pender said from his porch.

Ned was standing near where Billy had fallen.

Billy rotated his wounded body and came on his knees to Ned. "Please, Ned, don't shoot me again," Billy said.

Ken Claflin had reached the lawn and was hiding behind a tree. Maria watched from Ken's car.

Ned shot three more times. Two of the bullets hit Billy and knocked him the rest of the way down onto K Street. Ned walked calmly toward his own car, completing an errand, his wrath spent with his bullets.

Ken Claflin caught up to his uncle, who lay in the street. "Don't touch me, I'm hurt bad," were Billy Krug's last words as his killer's red Monte Carlo turned off K Street for parts unknown.

The police whom he had called stood over Billy just before he died.

Late that night, Dolores's mother said, "I'm glad the son of a bitch is dead. This will eliminate all her problems."

The autopsy described Billy Krug as "a normally developed, well nourished, young adult Caucasian male measuring 70½ inches in length and having an estimated weight of 170 lbs." All three bullets had entered from behind. Fifteen hundred millilitres of blood were found in one lung, and one thousand millilitres were in the stomach. Billy's pancreas was light tan and lobular, his young prostate gland "unremarkable." His liver, weighing thirteen hundred fifty grams, was smooth, glistening, and red-gray, that of a youth with his whole future in front of him.

VIII

TRIAL

"We'll fucking get you for this, you son of a bitch!" Ken Claflin yelled at Ned Wortees. Deftly, because he was skilled enough as a mechanic to break down and reassemble any car he had ever driven, and swiftly, because it was dawning on him that he had better make tracks for the county line, Ned was replacing the distributor cap underneath the hood of his red Monte Carlo. As he drove off toward one end of K Street, the first police car was turning onto the street at its other end.

Marilyn Wortees came downstairs with her mother and rushed into the street to Billy. Maria joined Ken standing above the body. By the time the police car halted, everyone who lived in the surrounding houses was camped in the street. Even if the street had been empty instead of thronged and impassable, the officers in the squad car would have had to stop to see if anything could be done for Billy Krug. That gave Ned Wortees the margin he needed.

Numb, Irma Krug stared blankly at the form of her third son to be killed violently. An hour earlier, her household, however bothersome, had consisted of herself, a son, a daughter, and a son-in-law. Now it was half that size. She heard the men in the squad car radio for help, help she knew would be too late to stop her son from dying and her son-in-law from escaping. Still, K Street was sealed off in a couple of minutes.

When Ellen Gandy reached K Street, she screamed. Her husband Joe had driven her over with a camera to take the pictures her brother Ned wanted of the apartment emptied by the Krugs. As soon as she saw the street blocked off by the police, before she was told there had been a shooting, Ellen surmised Ned had shot Marilyn. She waited in the car while Joe got out to investigate. In the movie of her mind, there had been a terrible fight, both of them yelling and throwing things at each other. He would have shouted she was a bitch for taking all his stuff and he couldn't stand her family. She would have shrieked that he could not make it as a provider or a lover either. He would have gone crazy and shot her. The movie ended only when Joe came back to the car and told Ellen what had really happened.

Irma Krug, oblivious to the police, was taking it in. Her eyes, less sad than Marilyn's, gave the impression of being made of an alabaster so impenetrable that no feelings could pass through them in either direction. Yet they were not without expression. They communicated denial and stoicism, a combination that gave Irma Krug, for all the grief that was starting to crash over her, an enormous power. These eyes sent messages that appeared to say: This isn't happening and It doesn't matter, messages that clashed like two armies vowing to take no prisoners. The police photographer, when he was through with his camera, said he was sorry but he had to ask Irma a couple of questions. Without waiting, she began to talk. "He was an ordinary boy. Wanted a good time. Not much different from any of them." Irma Krug turned and went inside to begin preparations for the burial of her third and last son.

At first, Ned Wortees took side streets. No avenues, no highways. No Interstate until he was below Cincinnati. Then it occurred to him that as long as he obeyed speed limits, he was safer on a crowded Interstate than on back roads. He joined up with I–75 and kept going.

Down through Kentucky, Tennessee, and a side trip off into North Carolina. He didn't know why he was headed south except he got started in that direction. Ned heard himself described on the radio as "the object of a nationwide manhunt." He ate at Steak 'n Shakes, slept at Ramada Inns, and wheeled on south in zig-zag lines. Cave City, Kentucky; Sweetwater, Tennessee; Cherokee, North Carolina. The crooked route was partly to keep from getting bored, partly to throw police off his trail, partly because, even as far down as Buford, Georgia, he still was not sure where he was going.

Ned was nervous and figured he must be looking in the rearview mirror a thousand times an hour. His stomach hurt and he slept poorly. At times even the object of a nationwide manhunt has to relax; he went to a frontierland amusement park. It helped a little, but when he heard simulated gunshots for a stagecoach robbery, he doubled over in pain. Outside Metter, Georgia, a highway patrolman flagged him down. Ned assumed it was all over and was somewhat relieved. The cop only wanted to warn him that one of his rear wheels was wobbling. Even more relieved, Ned had it fixed in the next town.

He was over into Florida before he knew that was where he was going. He stayed at a Ramada Inn in Yulee. He saw on his map Fort Myers was way down, far below St. Petersburg. He would never make it. He was almost out of cash and was using his American Express card. That meant using his real name, and that meant the Hamilton police would be only two or three days behind him at most. For that matter, what did he hope for in Fort Myers? His father's house would be staked out like it was radioactive. Still, that last night in Hamilton, his father actually did invite him down. They had both always acted as if Asa had something Ned wanted, and neither knew what it was. After what happened, Ned could not even call his father up. Maybe Asa wouldn't want to hear from his son the killer anyway. Whatever gas station phone booth he used, in whatever part of the country, the police would have it surrounded in two minutes. It gave him a chuckle—what a menace the fucking cops were.

"Red Dog" Don Gabbard was assigned to solve the murder of

Billy Krug. Since there was no question about the identity of the killer, Detective Gabbard did not have to follow leads, only a trail. The all-points did not turn up so much as a questionable motel receipt for over a week. Some genius in Cairo, Illinois, a town where Ned Wortees had once been imprisoned, stopped an orange Thunderbird, but no one spotted a red Monte Carlo.

Gabbard went around and questioned everyone, but either no one knew anything or, knowing, was not saying. At first it occurred to Gabbard that the Claflin boys might be saving Wortees for themselves, but he decided their attention span was not long enough. They were mischievous, not vengeful.

Then he talked to Wortees' boss, the electrical contractor. Junior Wheelock was a huge man who spat cigar juice like a deputy sheriff in Mississippi. He liked Ned Wortees, said he was a good worker. He had promoted him a few weeks ago from lineman to troubleshooter. If that sounded like a joke now, since shooting was what got Wortees in trouble, Junior Wheelock couldn't help it. Gabbard didn't think anything connected with shooting was a joke. Old Charlie Krug was a hell of a man, Wheelock went on. He wished he could say the same for his boys. The Krug family gave Wortees a rough time from the git go. Between Marilyn wanting more money, her mother thinking he should have a better job, and Billy putting dog shit on his windshield or whatever the hell he did, Ned was a tuna thrown in with a school of barracuda. He wouldn't say Billy Krug deserved to die, the Lord wasn't sharing that decision with anybody just yet, but the Krugs did a good amount of rubbing Ned Wortees raw.

Wheelock got to his point. Wortees had phoned him twice since leaving Hamilton. Wheelock couldn't care less where the poor bastard was calling from, and he wouldn't tell Gabbard if he knew. But he did know a frightened man when he heard one, and Ned Wortees was looking for help. Wheelock said that before Wortees could tell where he was, he had refused to send him any money, and he had advised Wortees strongly to turn himself in. Gabbard left Wheelock believing the second part anyway.

Among the detectives on the force, Don Gabbard was known as Red Dog more as a joke than an accolade. He did not earn the designation by being overly aggressive or mean—he was a straight arrow, a slightly younger Chuck Furman—but simply because he had red hair and kept after a case doggedly until it was solved. In the absence of any discernible trail from Ned Wortees, as inconspicuous in flight as he had been, unhappily, in his own family, Red Dog had little to do but wait. While he waited, giving descriptions of Ned Wortees to the FBI and police all over the country, he got angry, not for the first time, at what he saw as two of society's impediments to police work.

First, there was the whole mess that guy Miranda caused. Confessed to a crime before he had been told he had a right to an attorney. Then he changed his mind and took it all the way to the Supreme Court, which ruled that every arrested suspect has to be advised by every arresting officer that he has a right to counsel and a right to remain silent. So if someone picks up Ned Wortees in, say, an attempted robbery and Wortees feels like coming clean suddenly about the whole Krug business, the cop has to interrupt him in midsentence and read him Miranda. Then, if he has any sense, Wortees stops and thinks, Hey, maybe I can beat this rap after all, why don't I shut up till I see what my lawyer says? The irony of the whole thing was that Miranda himself, rights and all, got stabbed to death in a card game. He wrote no will, but he left a legacy to every cop in America. Talking to the suspect is out, get hard physical evidence and witnesses or forget about a conviction.

Second, there was the telephone. Gabbard couldn't even get an authorization to tap Marilyn Wortees' phone. Wife of a known killer, and Gabbard had to sit around until she got a call from her husband and decided to tell the Hamilton police about it. Junior Wheelock didn't want his phone tapped either, and he had had two calls from Wortees to which he admitted. Maybe if Gabbard got the chief of police to give him permission and took several days off to go to court, he could get a judge to issue a court order for a tap. But even in a murder case you have to fight so hard to get a tap order it was generally not worth the

trouble. There was Marilyn Wortees, going to and from her job
as a bookkeeper, likely getting calls every night from a killer.
She hadn't told Gabbard much when he talked to her. Irma
Krug said her daughter was leery. They still loved each other
was what Red Dog Gabbard figured. That was how it usually
was in these domestic cases. Arrest the wife, the husband threat-
ens to kill you. Arrest the husband, even after he had beaten
her till her face looks like a watermelon, and the wife screams
you're taking her man away. You couldn't win in domestics.

The second time Gabbard went to see Marilyn, though, she
wasn't leery anymore. She broke down almost as soon as they
started to talk. Love Ned? How could such a smart-looking
detective even ask that question? She hated him. He murdered her brother. Before that he beat her up. Before that he
insulted her mother and all her friends. Before that he drank.
She hated herself for marrying him. She hated herself more for
asking her brother Billy to move the furniture out of the apartment, for egging Billy on to bait Ned, to fight her own battles.
Most of all she hated herself for not warning Billy that somewhere in that downstairs apartment there should have been a
pistol, and if there wasn't, Ned undoubtedly had it on him. She
hadn't lost a husband in all this, she had gained her freedom.
What she had lost was her last brother, and it was her own fault.
"It's a shame, Mrs. Wortees," Red Dog Gabbard said, "but blaming yourself won't bring him back. We all have our bad days
after a tragedy."

Back at the station, Gabbard had a message from American
Express. Motel receipts had come in from the Ramadas in For-
syth, Georgia, and Yulee, Florida.

The object of a nationwide manhunt tooled around in Florida
for three days before he knew he had nowhere to go. It was too
hot to think, he was in the right place at the wrong time. After
picking up some change in a crap game in Gainesville, Ned
headed north. A different, slightly westerly route—I–65 instead of I–75—took him through Alabama. A furnace in July.

In Selma, the man at the Holiday Inn looked heavily at Ned

as he registered. Did he recognize him? Maybe they had posters
out. "Say, Buddy, if you're not doing anything later, maybe we
could catch a movie uptown?" Ned traveled on.

He bought a six-pack and put it on the seat next to him. The
first can killed the thirst, the second made it easier to drive, the
third turned his sweat almost to rain, the fourth made it harder
to drive. He finished the six-pack in about eighty miles and
bought another. When it got dark, he picked up a burger and
some French fries. The burger was sawdust and he threw it
away. He pulled off into a field and slept in the car. Using the
American Express had been a bad idea, they'd have little push-
pins on a map by now. That Selma thing happened to him too
often. Queers seemed to think he was cute, or maybe just man-
ageable. Marilyn was probably with some guy already. She could
go to hell.

In the morning he phoned from a gas station, but there was
no answer. It was Saturday, so she wasn't at work. He didn't
want to call the number upstairs and risk getting his mother-in-
law. If Marilyn hadn't moved back into the apartment downstairs, she might be with some friend. Some new friend. Before
he left the gas station, he borrowed a hose and washed his car.

The two warm cans left from the second six-pack made a stale
breakfast. He had thirty-two dollars cash besides the American
Express. If he bought gas at places where they would take his
card, he could still go for a few more days. He hadn't touched
the .38 since the night he left Hamilton. It was probably burning
up in the glove compartment like he was in the driver's seat.
One of these country general-store filling stations wouldn't be
any big deal to knock over. Yet he didn't like violent crimes.
They wouldn't believe that in Hamilton, but it was true. Anyway, these country folks kept rifles all over the place.

He had people in Kentucky. If he could get to them. Nice
enough, a second cousin who had been in Vietnam and his
daddy who farmed and mined. How many times removed did
your cousin have to be before the police would not bother to
stake him out?

Back through Tennessee, keeping well clear of Knoxville because he had been through it on the way down and almost got into a fight in a bar.

His Kentucky relatives did not have a phone; he would have to drive right up to their farmhouse. He got to Bowling Green, a happy town. These people didn't know what tough was, dressed up and wearing glasses, driving new Fairlanes. They would want to get rid of someone like him fast. Better not chance the cousin.

When it rained and he had to shut the car windows, he stank so much he couldn't stand it. He went into a lake, but he didn't dare stay in one place long enough to wash his clothes and wait for them to dry.

Up into Indiana—Greensburg. He bought a pair of Wrangler brand jeans and a Mohawk Banlon blue shirt. At least the smell was gone, along with all but four dollars and sixty-five cents. He took a right and headed east back into Ohio.

He wide-berthed Hamilton and kept on east until he was almost to West Virginia. Everything was hard there, and he didn't know anyone in the whole state. When he fixed a flat tire, he got a grease mark on the Mohawk shirt. The highway was getting him, and he wasn't looking in the rearview any less.

He pulled off into a rest area and finished his last can of beer. A whole family was peeing. It was nice there, a haven from the eighty-mile-an-hour terrors of the Interstate. He walked over to the telephone booth, looked at the emergency numbers on it, and dialed, no coin needed. A voice said sheriff's office. "My name is Nedrick Bean Wortees," Ned said. "I shot a man over in Hamilton—Butler County. I'm in the Windy Hill rest area in a red Monte Carlo, which I have kept clean the whole time."

When Red Dog Gabbard drove the one hundred seventy-five miles to pick up Ned Wortees from the Noble County Jail and return him to Hamilton, he found his prisoner almost jovial, though reticent on the subject of his in-laws. On the way back to Hamilton, Wortees talked about his trip south and his job as an electrician. He would not mention the case. That was Miranda,

Gabbard figured. The sheriff who scooped Wortees out of the rest area had read him Miranda, and it was a rare prisoner who did not clam up after he heard Miranda. Wortees was looking to his defense.

As Ned Wortees watched the hay and wheat fields wave by, and the farmers' pick-ups, what he was looking to was his life in stir. He hadn't done all that badly on the inside before. If outside meant the Krug family, the hell with it. He didn't want to think about them, talk about them, deal with them, ever again.

When they drew near Hamilton, Ned saw a place he had always enjoyed. "Old LeSourdesville Lake. Took me many a bass out of there," Ned said.

"Likewise," Red Dog said. "You'd go up there after school and a couple of hours later you'd come home with dinner."

"*After* school? What about during school?"

"Right. Playing hookey at LeSourdesville."

"One day I spotted the truant officer there," Ned said. "So I hid in the bushes and was about to run for it until I seen him reach into his pocket and pull out some worms. Then he brought out this fold-up pole he had with him, and I knew we was all right."

"Ha ha, many's the time," Red Dog said.

Surrounded by pictures of himself with F. Lee Bailey and James Cagney, watched by a lion cub photographed for the inscription, "I'd rather live one day as a lion than one hundred years as a lamb," buoyed by a plaque triumphantly identifying him as a "Dale Carnegie Instructor," Hugh David Holbrock prepared his defense of Ned Wortees. He liked action and he loved trying cases, performing in front of a jury. He stayed with Lee Bailey when Lee tried a case in Cleveland, and he went all the way to California to watch Lee during the Patty Hearst trial. As for Cagney, Jimmy was a very, very close personal friend who also happened to collect horse-drawn carriages, as did Holbrock, a past president of the American Carriage Association.

Holbrock, at fifty, had white hair and soft, pliable features.

Normally, he kept his eyelids about one-quarter closed until he decided to transfix a listener, or a jury, at which point his eyes would spring into a full glare. This was a face that would do anything its owner wanted at any time: show grave concern, impress a judge or jury with lethal seriousness, flower into a beatific smile, heckle with mirthless laughter, or ooze limitless compassion. "I'm not in this to make a dollar," he would say. "I'm in this to see justice done." He would pause to let that sink in.

"Why did the first settlement come to Yorktown in 1607?" (He would say Yorktown rather than Jamestown, perhaps making a genuine mistake, possibly only to plant a seed of doubt.) "They came to be free. Free of the English, where you're guilty until proven innocent. They had a new idea that you'd be innocent, innocent always until proven guilty, and judged so by twelve of your peers." (Wait a minute, the idea of a jury of peers *came* from England, didn't it? Are you really guilty in England until proven innocent? Wasn't that the Napoleonic Code? More doubt.) "The Founding Fathers, they, too, wanted freedom. Freedom of thought and of publishing. Freedom from search and seizure. Not freedom if you had money, if you had property, or if you were mentally competent. But freedom for all. Not that you were equally endowed from birth with intelligence and money, they didn't believe that. But you had the right to equal treatment. That's what they believed, and that's what I believe.

"I've been practicing law since 1953. That's how many years?" (Thirty-something, no twenty-something, anyway a whole generation, and we're in the hands of a veteran, reliable, case-hardened humanitarian.) "I have always wanted my clients, and all Americans, regardless of whether they have money, to be walking around free, unless twelve of their peers after due deliberation decide that beyond a reasonable doubt, notice I said *reasonable* doubt, they did something that should prevent their walking around.

"I don't believe all that for the dollar it gets me. It often gets me no dollar at all. Someday I'm going to be judged by Somebody a lot tougher than any jury I've faced, and I want to be able to come into His court with the cleanest hands possible. I want Him to judge me by the worth of what I've done here, not by how much money I made, not by how many clients I represented. Then I won't have to tremble. Then I'll know I can rest the case of Hugh D. Holbrock."

That was it, then. Hugh Holbrock needed to impress people, but he did not need them to believe him. Doubt was all he needed. The prosecution needed credibility, the defense only needed to set people to wondering. Was it Jamestown or Yorktown? Does the English system say you are guilty until proven innocent? How many years since 1953? How could that witness have made a positive identification when he was scared to death at the time of the burglary? Could an honest man remember whom he had dinner with even a week ago Wednesday, much less the hair color of an assailant whom he saw once for a few seconds fourteen months ago? Uncertainty, contestability, skepticism, unresolved questions, confusion, vagueness, puzzlement, disbelief. As a potter used clay, wheel, kiln, and glaze in an endless series of relationships, the copious species of doubt were the tools of Hugh Holbrock's trade.

A big trial, like a World Series, would draw amateurs. The everyday case would attract only the hard core. Like baseball fans enjoying the exploits of Cy Young, Napoleon Lajoie, and other ancient players long gone before they were born, Hamilton's courthouse adherents liked to chew on the cases of old. This flock of pensioners would shift their cuds of tobacco from one cheek to the other and ask the bailiffs when a case would begin, or if they knew when the jailed former sheriff would come up for parole. One would chuckle over something that happened thirty years ago while another complained that no one works very hard any more. Among them, the murder buffs formed a clique of their own, like those who would examine only strikeout records in baseball's past. They liked to recall who was the first murderer from Hamilton to be electrocuted.

Alfred Andrew Knapp killed four women in 1894 and 1895

but was not caught. He remained quiet, the proprietor of his small ice business until after the turn of the century. Seized again by the urge in 1902, Knapp strangled his wife in bed. He got a shoe store to give him a wooden packing box and borrowed a team of horses. Still, he could not lift the packing box onto the wagon, so he got several passers-by to help him. He hauled the crate down to the Miami River and threw it. It floated, and Knapp went to the electric chair in 1904.

Several of the courthouse devotees carried the case of a Hamilton barber named Charles King in their own memories. One night, a few weeks before Christmas in 1929, King turned on the gas in the family home and killed his wife and four children. He left a suicide note and disappeared. When he was found a year later, he accused his despondent wife of having done herself in along with the poor children. He claimed the suicide note was not in his handwriting and that he himself was "innocent of the entire affair." A fifth child, whom he had been unable to find when he gassed the rest, turned up to testify against the barber, who was executed in 1931.

The favorite case of the murder buffs, indeed of all courthouse hangers-on, was the Ruppert rampage of 1975, still fresh in everyone's memory. Even though James Ruppert gave himself up after killing his eleven relatives and so was never at large, curfews were made earlier for every teenager and locks were changed all over town. Hugh Holbrock had defended Ruppert with a plea of insanity, which a three-judge panel had rejected. Vowing not to rest until he got Ruppert out of prison and into a hospital, Holbrock got Ruppert's conviction overturned in 1978 on a technicality. Three years later Ruppert was still awaiting retrial. Holbrock's general prominence and his particular defense of Ruppert made any murder case he tried a Hamilton event.

FIRST DAY

The murder was in summer, the trial in the middle of a sub-zero winter. In February the wind knifed off the frozen Miami

River, forcing the lizard-skinned old men who had lain about the yard in July into a lower courthouse floor, where it was necessary to look at least half-busy.

The Victorian courthouse had four floors, each ornately different. The windows at the top were shaped like portholes; the lower floors had gracefully arched oval windows of increasing size. All four sides of the courthouse had broad steps leading up to majestically columned entrances, ornamentally Corinthian. Two of the entrances were often blocked by deferred renovation attempts. When the building was dedicated in 1886, the dean of the Hamilton bar, Thomas Millikin, judged that "the structure is commodious, is well-heated and ventilated but is not well arranged and adapted to the purposes for which it was erected. Its architecture is a half century behind the age." Millikin looked to the earlier federal Georgian courthouse as the true mother of justice in Hamilton. The official dedication of the new Victorian courthouse described it as "the finest structure this county ever built, public or private." Both this characterization and Millikin's remain accurate almost a century later. Like a lover with a deformity, the building manages to be both beautiful and ugly at once.

Dressed in herringbone, with pleasing and trustworthy, if not quite handsome, features, Deputy Prosecutor James Schnell opened the case against Nedrick Wortees. He had been educated by Jesuits and taken his law degree at the University of Cincinnati. Still finding his way with juries—a useful, not entirely disingenuous posture—Schnell had tried fewer than half a dozen murder cases. He announced that the defendant, "with plan and design did cause the death of William Krug." He was going for murder one, now called aggravated murder in Ohio. Second degree had been simplified to plain murder, and third degree was known as voluntary manslaughter.

Initially, the defense plea was "not guilty by reason of insanity."

Ned Wortees had on a dark blue leisure suit with thin white piping around the pockets. He continued to wear it throughout the trial. In the six months he had been in prison, his moustache had grown fuller. His light brown hair had been permitted to creep about two inches below his earlobes on the sides and well over his collar in back, approaching a pageboy length that enabled the defendant to look both neat and approximately four years out of style. His full lips contrasted with his small, watchful eyes, and his round, fleshy chin was saved from weakness by its determined set. Next to Wortees, separating him from the prosecution, sat Red Dog Gabbard with his dark red hair and light red face. Although they had traveled together as custodian and prisoner, Gabbard's ride back to Hamilton with Wortees had been, ironically, almost carefree for both of them. Gabbard sat at the counsel table as an aide to Prosecutor Schnell and therefore could not be called upon to testify.

Hugh Holbrock was joined in the defense by his law partner, Joe Bressler. Tall and dark, with sideburns just beginning—and only in bright light—to show the faintest gray, Bressler had worked his way to a prosperity he took some pains to show. His black alligator shoes, green silk suit, long 1960s sideburns, and thin moustache gave him a reputation as the Mississippi riverboat gambler among Hamilton's defense lawyers. Holbrock himself affected glasses fitted with long straps so that the lenses could droop to his chest when he was not using them. The bags under his eyes made him look tired; it would be a hard-hearted juror who could remain unsympathetic to such badges of care.

The judge excused two well-dressed prospective jurors, one because he could not take enough time off from his business, the other because he knew Joe Bressler. A third left with a toothache, and a fourth was excused after he said he "knew the boy that was killed's big brother, who was also killed." A fifth left when Holbrock and Bressler had him excused for confessing to believe the commandment, "Thou Shalt not Kill." A sixth juror said he knew a Marilyn Wortees but he was not sure it was the same one as the defendant's wife. The judge directed his bailiff to bring Marilyn Krug Wortees forth for identification.

Marilyn came in, newly blonde and scared, wearing a red waist-coat, white blouse, and carrying a brown leather purse. She and Ned exchanged a quick, flinty glare. The juror said it was not the same Wortees, and Marilyn was led out again.

Arguments about seating jurors took most of the day. In mid-afternoon, Holbrock told the prospects who remained, "The State of Ohio has to prove every element of this crime 'beyond a reasonable doubt.' We don't have to prove anything. All we have to do is sow the seed of that reasonable doubt in your minds." Since Holbrock was having his colleague Joe Bressler deliver the opening argument after the jury was fully selected, he took the opportunity before all twelve were chosen to sow all the seeds he could. "Now the prosecution is like a man in a footrace," Holbrock continued, his glasses hanging down to his chest, bumping amiably against his Countess Mara tie. "He may be in the lead and get all the way to the finish line—almost. He may get to within an inch of the end and then collapse. Doesn't quite make it. This is the prosecution's case. They may look to you to be convincing—convincing almost. But that isn't enough. I want you to look at the defendant and imagine him wearing a bright red cloak with neon signs all over it that say, 'PRE-SUMED INNOCENT, PRESUMED INNOCENT, PRESUMED INNOCENT.' These signs flash continually until something else is proved and until it is proved beyond a reasonable doubt."

Jim Schnell asked if the details of the murder would bother any of the jurors so much they would not be able to agree to a guilty verdict for fear of vengeance from the defendant or his friends. He was sowing his own seeds. Joe Bressler, belying his riverboat appearance, was the pleasantest and most reasonable of the three lawyers, leading the jury carefully along whatever path his argument took. He had, however, a tendency to apol-ogize occasionally. "I'm so sorry," he said to the almost-complete jury near the end of the first day, "if I communicate poorly. I mean well, but once in a while I'll use a technical term as though you naturally understand it. I don't know your job, and you don't know mine, and you're not supposed to. I hope you won't hold it against my client if I make a mistake, as I am all too prone to do," he concluded, ending his brief foray into magnanimous modesty, a territory usually occupied unashamedly by his partner, Hugh Holbrock.

Wortees pulled hard on his cigarette during a recess. Soft and earnest—though silent—in the jury's presence, he seemed fierce and calculating in the deserted courtroom. He looked outside. The wind was whipping a blizzard against the courthouse windows. When Holbrock leaned toward him and told a joke about the number of psychiatrists needed to change a lightbulb, Wortees smiled until there were crinkles around his eyes. He stopped abruptly as the bailiff approached. "It's too hot in here," he complained. Anything outside was better than anything inside.

The bailiff, Fritz Remgen, held the match for Wortees' next cigarette. At seventy-six, he had seen hundreds of prisoners shuffle in and out of court. No matter what they did, he told his friends, no matter what they were *accused* of doing, you ought to be nice to them because this might be the last daylight they'd see for a long time. Fritz Remgen was surprised when Ned Wortees stood up. Sitting, the prisoner looked normal. His face had the pallor they all got after several months in the clink, plus a little acne near his chin. Otherwise he looked like anybody else. But when he stood up he became short. So his torso was all right, but he had sawed-off legs. That must bother him plenty, no help when you're locked up either.

An Elk for forty-seven years, Fritz Remgen was past president of the Elks National Bowling Association. "My real name is Urban," he told Wortees, "but people throughout the Midwest call me Fritz." He had been a hanger-on at the courthouse, a legal buff like the others, when they made him bailiff fifteen years earlier, but now it was his job to keep order in the court and to pass along tidbits to the other buffs. It was a point of honor with him to make friends with the defendants. Trial after trial, year after year, the rest of the faces in the courtroom did not change. The defendants were always new, always helpless.

Plus they were interesting, if they were accused of a biggie. The less they said, the more mysterious they became.

Fritz Remgen looked at Ned Wortees and saw a man with a history he could only guess at, motives he could not even imagine.

Ned Wortees looked at Fritz Remgen and saw an American flag in his lapel, a sport coat and slacks that were both gray but did not match at all.

As a way of finding out about others, mainly defendants, Fritz would tell them about himself. It didn't always work, especially if they had already seen him dozing while their fates were being argued, but Fritz felt closer to people when they knew something about him, and since he was hearing their own pasts unraveled before him in court, it seemed only fair to share a little.

He had always stayed a bachelor. His three sisters liked to look after him, though one of them got married herself. He left home only once. In the 1940s he was too old for the war, but everyone else was having adventures and Fritz wanted to do something. He and his friend Klingle did some serious drinking one night and Klingle more or less kidnapped Fritz to go up to Willow Run to work for Ford. Klingle had his family there because he had started for Ford the year before, so Fritz lived with the Klingles. It was just like he was one of them.

On the job at Willow Run, Fritz was a machinery fixer for a foreman named Scarlett. He was a funny boss, a very nice one but a funny one. At night he would go out with you and have a great time and be all buddies, and then the next morning in the shop he wouldn't know you. All business, like he was one of old Henry's vice presidents or something. But then, late in the afternoon, Scarlett would be your brother again, with a heart as big as the tanks they were assembling.

After almost a year, Fritz came back for the weekend to see his mother and three sisters. He ran into a manager from the Baldwin-Lima-Hamilton Corporation on the Elks' golf course. The executive asked Fritz to come home for good and work at Baldwin-Lima. Fritz missed his sisters, but he had to tell the

executive that he was making good money at Ford. They didn't
pay a white man's wage down in Hamilton. The executive said
he would match whatever check Fritz had in his pocket right
now from Ford. Fritz came back and worked for Baldwin-Lima
until they left town in the sixties. After that he got the bailiff's
job to go along with his pension.

Bowling every night before he went home to his sisters, Fritz
topped out at around two hundred. Right now in his seventies,
he could still hit between one sixty-five and one seventy-five. He
didn't go so much anymore. He liked his judge, and he liked
telling everyone to rise when the judge swept in wearing his
black robe. He never got tired of saying, "Hear ye, Hear ye.
Court of Common Pleas, Butler County, Arthur J. Fiehrer presiding, now in session."

It was four in the afternoon by the time the final juror was
selected, and Judge Fiehrer saw no point in starting arguments
at that time of day. The last thing a jury heard in the afternoon
tended to go stale overnight. He adjourned until nine A.M.

In his chambers, the judge shed his judicial manner along
with his black robe. "Wortees is overindicted," he said. "Charging him with murder one, or aggravated murder as we now call
it, is too high. The case sounds just above manslaughter to me.
Of course, I don't know all the facts myself and we'll have to
hear them unfold in court. The prosecution knows he has a
record as long as your arm, so the charge of aggravation may
be to scare the jury into putting him away for a good while. The
defense has offered to plead guilty to manslaughter, which the
prosecution rejected. The trouble is, if the defense proves insanity, Wortees could get sent to the hospital at Lima and be out
by Easter. That would be one month's keep for killing your
brother-in-law."

Arthur Fiehrer was a portly, genial judge who liked to use the
wastebasket in his chambers as a spittoon. Befitting his profession, the judge's face was owlish and aging gracefully. He had a
straight, thin mouth that sagged a little at the corners, rising
easily when he laughed, which was seldom in court, often in his

chambers. His hair, though it had receded on both sides, was still dark and parted in the middle as in old-fashioned photographs of early Rotarians. Among members of the Hamilton bar, he was regarded not as scholarly but as extremely fair—fair to the point of admitting when he himself made a mistake that could easily have been covered. During the afternoon's examination of prospective jurors, which had dragged on tediously, Jim Schnell had objected to a question asked by Hugh Holbrock. Judge Fiehrer could have overruled or sustained the objection without explanation. Instead, he simply admitted he had not been listening. "Ladies and gentlemen of the jury," Hugh Holbrock had said, "we have a magnificent human being here for our judge, and I will now restate my question."

As a lawyer, Fiehrer had done probate work. He had also been in public life for many years, both on the city council and as a one-term mayor. For the past sixteen years he had been a judge. His older brother, retired now, had once been Hamilton's most efficient prosecutor. "Every defendant was afraid of him. He used to send people to the chair here just like you were getting someone a plane ticket," Judge Fiehrer recalled fondly.

SECOND DAY

Judge Fiehrer summoned a bus as the court convened to take the jurors to the Krug home. The bus wound across the river to the West Side and made its cumbersome way down the narrow, residential K Street to number 2132. Behind the bus, in a heavily guarded patrol car, Ned Wortees returned to the scene of the crime for the first time since he had shot his brother-in-law. He sat in the back seat, handcuffed, wordless and expressionless. His chief guard, Deputy Sheriff Gus De Natale, joked with the driver about an arraignment the week before when an accused child molester had tried to jump out a courthouse window. De Natale told the driver he would work the weekend for a patrolman whose father had just died.

At his old home on K Street, Wortees stayed in the car while the jury walked from the Krug lawn to the porch of Dan Pender, the neighbor whom Wortees had been visiting the night of the killing. Silently, they paced back toward the Krug front door, where Wortees had been heading when he had his final confrontation with Billy Krug. The night of the boring All-Star game in July, the adjacent yards had been green and lush; each now wore its fringe of snow. Like a schoolmaster, Judge Fiehrer guided his charges once more around the premises. The jurors stared at the Krug front door as though it would tell them the whole meaning of the case if only it would open. Then they filed onto the bus again.

Back in court, a vocational training class of senior girls from Garfield High School was in attendance. They watched Ned Wortees at the counsel table with fascination and their teacher with disdain. The teacher, Joy Cohen, was a handsome, animated brunette with a son in the senior class at Taft. Mrs. Cohen explained that they were about to see American justice in action, but none of the fourteen girls was listening. They stared at the back of Ned Wortees' head, whispering, sucking in their breath whenever he turned to the side so they could see part of his face.

In his opening for the prosecution, Jim Schnell said he would show that the defendant, Nedrick Bean Wortees, murdered his brother-in-law, William Krug, "with prior calculation and design." As Schnell rehearsed the crime, he stressed, of course, the culpability of the prisoner at the bar. He did so, however, not with prosecutorial zeal, which might build sympathy for the accused, but with a casual recitation structured to make the case into an open-and-shut murder. "This marriage between Marilyn and Nedrick Wortees was not exactly made in heaven." When Schnell had finished a casual account of the marriage and subsequent breakup of the Worteeses, he dramatized the crime itself in staccato detail. "The two brothers-in-law met on a small strip of ground between the Pender and Krug houses. Krug, angry at the cut-off of electricity, threw a punch at Wortees.

Wortees pulled a revolver and fired twice. Wounded, Krug went to the street where he fell to his knees and pleaded for his life. Yet Wortees shot again and again. Not once or twice, but five shots in all. Wortees left the scene immediately, his victim as good as dead, and fled the state. When you have heard the evidence you'll see that Nedrick Wortees is guilty as charged of aggravated murder."

Ned Wortees listened and watched impassively. He could have been watching the television set Marilyn had taken. He looked neither bored nor personally involved. That morning before court, he had told his sister, Ellen Gandy, he knew he was in a mess, but he still felt the Krugs had gotten him into it. The whole family—Marilyn, her mother, the Claflin boys, Billy himself—had given him nothing but trouble. Even now, he was mad at all of them. Damn right he had exploded. Who wouldn't? It was inevitable.

"Ten seconds," Joe Bressler said, opening for the defense. "Ten seconds is all it took from beginning to end, for something to happen that never should have happened. Let's watch that second hand up there on the wall." Bressler was silent as the second hand descended from the three to the five on the court-room clock. "We call this 'The Case of the Last Straw.' The straw that broke Ned Wortees' back. Let's see how Ned was pushed, pushed to the brink and beyond. His wife, Marilyn, his brother-in-law William Krug, other in-laws by the name of Claflin—they took Mr. Wortees' furniture, beer, guns, everything he had accumulated in the time he had been married. Ned Wortees was even afraid they would steal his car so he took off the distributor cap. Planning a quick getaway? Hardly. 'Prior calculation and design,' says the state. 'A plan and a scheme to kill.' We'll see.

"Ned Wortees refused Dan Pender's offer of a bed to sleep in because he wanted to be in his own home. Leaves his friend's porch and starts to his door, just a few steps away, just a few feet between Pender's house and Wortees'. But Krug ambushes him with a sucker punch in the back of his head. Bam!" Bressler punched his right fist into his left palm, making a loud clap. "As hard as he can. Wortees is staggered, dizzy. He wheels and fires five times fast, quick, rapidly. All in ten seconds. He walks to his car and puts the distributor cap back on. Prior calculation and design? He drives away, leaves the state. Two weeks later he comes back and gives himself up. For ten seconds all control and reason are lost. The other man pushed Ned over the edge. He didn't commit any aggravated murder. The victim brought it on. He facilitated it, egged Ned on until Ned was no longer in control of himself. Simply a reflex action that took only ten seconds after he was sucker-punched from behind. This is no Perry Mason whodunit. We don't need experts taking up your time telling us which gun fired the shots and who was holding it. We know all that, we admit all that. We say this shooting was no aggravated murder, no murder at all, but the act of a man who was temporarily not in control of himself due to repeated provocation on the part of the victim and the victim's family. When you have heard the evidence, we are confident you'll come back with a just verdict. Thanks."

The prosecution called its witnesses.

A half-dozen police officers testified to what no one disputed —that they found Billy Krug near death of gunshot wounds on the street in front of his house—but the parade of uniforms might impress the jury. Desk officers from the police station recounted the phone calls for help from the Krugs, but not from Ned Wortees. Holbrock asked the police to describe the call Ned Wortees made to complain that all his furniture had been stolen. No officer remembered such a call. Holbrock asked if they had listened to the police tape recording of all incoming calls. The officers admitted it was always destroyed at the end of each month, and their preparation for trial had begun almost six months after the killing.

Holbrock was indignant. "Once again, ladies and gentlemen of the jury, we have a tape gap. We have selective memory. They remember the victim's call but not the defendant's. Even after what they describe as a murder, they destroy the tape.

They admit Billy Krug warned them that if the police didn't get out there to K Street, he and his friends would handle the problem themselves, yet they can't seem to recall Ned Wortees telling them he had been robbed out of house and home."

Like Bressler in his opening for the defense, Holbrock was drawing a picture of a besieged and bereft Wortees, attacked by his own family, abandoned by the police. He specialized in turning the question of criminality into a social issue. When was an act a crime, he wanted the jury to ponder, and when was it a physical response to conditions created by others? He was not precisely claiming self-defense against Billy Krug's provocation, though that was part of it. Inferentially, Holbrock was arguing for the existence in the central nervous system of a mechanism called naturally into play by environmental forces that demand an individual adapt his behavior in order to avoid extinction. Here in the docket, then, was not a criminal but a survivor.

When Judge Fiehrer declared the luncheon recess, Wortees was taken out by his guard, Gus De Natale. The prisoner's hands were free in front of the jury—otherwise they could hardly presume him innocent—but De Natale had to handcuff him whenever they left the courtroom. They became, if not friends, easy companions. De Natale gave him a cigarette now and lighted it for him. They ate together twice a day during the trial. When a man has been in trouble as much of his life as Ned Wortees, he becomes more familiar with the constabulary than he ever expected to. Cops who hated their work or were on a power trip were the toughest. Those who let you alone or liked their jobs were the easiest to get along with. De Natale loved his work.

As a deputy sheriff, Gus De Natale found himself guarding many prisoners, which he did not mind since he met more interesting people that way. He had always wanted to be a policeman when he was growing up in Brooklyn. He was raised in Bedford Stuyvesant while it was still dangerous for blacks, and when it became dangerous for whites, the De Natales moved out to Sheepshead Bay. Though he was at Saipan, Guam, the

Philippines, and Okinawa for the navy in World War II, De Natale was too light and too short for the New York City Police Department.

He came out to Hamilton to visit a navy buddy and met his future wife. After they married, they returned to Brooklyn, where De Natale drove a truck, but he still dreamed about becoming some kind of cop. Ned Wortees had to respect someone who wanted to do his job as much as De Natale did, even if it was putting away people like himself. Sitting behind the wheel of a truck, De Natale put on a couple of dozen pounds, but he worked out and stayed fit. When he began to go bald, he grew a thick moustache and bought a hairpiece with the subtlety and consistency of a broom. Still wanting to be a cop when he was almost a middle-aged fireplug, De Natale made his move. "I'll always love Brooklyn," De Natale told Wortees, "but I had to get out when things got too rough. My kid would get in a fight at school and there would be fifteen or twenty coloreds waiting outside our house that night. One afternoon a colored boy knocked on our door and wanted to visit my thirteen-year-old daughter. I said, 'That's it,' and we came out here. I've never been sorry."

The girls from Garfield were agitated at lunch, and Joy Cohen had trouble controlling them. Economically, socially and culturally, Mrs. Cohen was so far removed from them it was not easy for the teacher and students to relate to each other on any level. She was a professional whose husband had a prospering scrap metal business. Among Debbie, Pam, Holly, Jenny, Dondra, Mia Lou, Carlene, and the rest, there was no girl whose parents had ever bought a new car or owned the house they lived in. Black and white and teacher, blue-collar Christians and upwardly mobile Jew, fragments of caste and class in Hamilton were all over the lunchroom. Mrs. Cohen wanted to renovate the old courthouse. The girls could not have cared less. She liked the Hamilton Philharmonic and hoped they would come with her to a concert. They wanted to hear The Who at Riverfront Coliseum in Cincinnati. She wanted them to pay attention to their schoolwork, as she had done growing up in the Bronx. They wanted her to help them get jobs. They were furious at the way the trial was going.

"The cops are so stupid," Holly said.

"Right," said Mia Lou. "If they had come to the house after the first call nothing would have happened. This is all their fault."

"Aggravated murder is too high a charge. This should just be manslaughter," Debbie said.

"This reminds me of the gun laws," Mrs. Cohen said. "If we had the kind of gun control we should, this could never have happened. It would just have been a big fist fight."

"You ever heard of cutting?" Mia Lou asked. "Wortees could have used a blade."

"My family knows the Bresslers," Mrs. Cohen said, trying to fill the girls in on courtroom sidelights. "Joe Bressler met his wife while he was stationed in the army down south. Joe's wife worked in his mother's beauty parlor to help put Joe through law school."

"Did you call Frisch's Big Boy for me like you said?" Carlene asked. Some of the girls were unemployed. Others worked after school at Leshner's Textiles, Citizens Bank, McDonalds, Frisch's, and Fair Acres Center for the Mentally Retarded.

Mrs. Cohen had barely stood to go to the ladies' room when the girls began to complain bitterly about her. "Do you believe what a witch and a half she is?" Jenny asked. "She gave me five demerits the other day just because I asked if I could skip next Friday to go to my girlfriend's shower."

"It's a total bummer to be in class with her," said Dondra. "She called me defiant for saying the principal was a dork to make pizza in his office."

"She's mean. She wants to break all of us down and get us to cry," Jenny said. "Then she can pat us on the head and say, 'What's the matter, dear?' "

" 'Dear' sucks," Mia Lou said.

Returning, Mrs. Cohen asked if the girls were getting an insight into the judicial system.

"It's not what you know, it's who you know," Mia Lou said. "If
your name is Rentschler or Beckett you can bust up your
daddy's car and run down thirty-six pedestrians and get your
license suspended for two-and-a-half weeks. You grab yourself
a little change off a shelf if you're Eddie Ebersole, and you're in
detention for five years."

"Eddie Ebersole beat up a seventy-seven-year-old widow to
get that change," Mrs. Cohen said.

"His father is a drunk and his mother never paid any attention," Jenny said. "What else you want him to do? He had a few
drugs, he needed some more, now he's in maximum security.
What *real* choice did he have, Mrs. Cohen?"

"What about the seventy-seven-year-old victim? Did he have
to hit her?"

"Yeah," said Jenny, "he had to hit her."

"I like the trial," Pam said. "Wortees is good-looking, but he's
got spooky, beady eyes. He looks like he could do stuff to you."

"The lawyers are neat," Debbie said. "They're like on TV
when the jury's there. Then right afterward, during the break,
they get real chummy and laugh with each other."

"I'd like to be a lawyer," Pam said. "That's a life for you. But
when I'm home I'd rather watch TV. I don't know how long it's
been since I picked up a book I didn't have to."

As he was led back into court by Gus DeNatale, Wortees
talked to his sister, Ellen Gandy. Despite his handcuffs, he
looked relaxed and full after lunch. Ellen looked thin and
scared, furtive even in the presence of her own freedom. She
resembled a small bird whose eyes flick constantly, always on
the lookout for danger. When DeNatale took Ned over to the
counsel table, Ellen wept a little, but she did that furtively, too.

Spryly and eagerly, her hair dyed from gray back to light
brown for the trial, Irma Krug mounted the stand. She looked
much younger than she had in the summer when Billy was

killed. Then her hair had been almost white, and every feature had seemed withered. At the trial, in a bright turquoise suit, her newly brown hair parted across the front and swept forward into girlish bangs that hung to her glasses, Mrs. Krug was in comely disguise. Only her mouth showed what it cost to bury three sons. Her lips were held so stiff and tight they made a brutal slice across the bottom of her face. Yet the mouth was not expressionless. It seemed to hold within it some permanent citrus so many times more sour than a lemon that the lips themselves were uncertain whether to form into a pucker or shriek.

"I am the mother of Krug and the mother-in-law of Wortees," Irma Krug said to identify herself. As a witness for the prosecution, she told Jim Schnell about the trouble in the Worteeses' marriage and Marilyn's removal of the television set from Ned's apartment. She did not flinch when she came to the gore.

Schnell: What happened when Wortees shut off the lights?

Krug: After Billy called the police and walked downstairs to wait for them, I went to the window where I did not see anything. I heard firecrackers, I *thought* that's what they were. Then I heard Billy say, like he was asking for a glass of water, "Please don't shoot me again, Ned." I still couldn't see him, and I didn't even realize he was hurt yet.

Schnell: Did you hear anything more?

Krug: I heard some more firecrackers and a groan from Billy and this time I knew they weren't firecrackers.

Schnell: What did you do then?

Krug: I called the police again. I went downstairs and saw blood, a trail of dripping wet blood from the yard to the street. I saw Billy lying in the street and Ned's car going around the corner.

Schnell (holding up a photograph): Is this the body of your son, Billy Krug, lying in the middle of K Street?

Holbrock: Your Honor, we stipulate that it is. We further stipulate that he was killed by a gun fired by Nedrick Wortees. What possible need is there to make this poor woman relive her agony which proves nothing about my client or his relationship to the deceased?

Krug: That is the body of my son.

Hugh Holbrock's strategy was to soften Irma for the cross-examination, during which he wanted to establish that Ned Wortees was more the victim of Krug family bullying than Billy Krug was of Wortees' bullets. Yet he was also genuinely sympathetic to a widow who had lost her three sons. His colleagues in the Hamilton bar found Holbrock to be a man of more moveable parts than a Tinkertoy. In addition to acquiring antique carriages and meeting James Cagney at conventions for collectors, Holbrock had once been an amateur magician. ("Exactly what all of us should have done who were going to face juries almost every day of our lives," said the attorney Carl Morgenstern, an occasional adversary of Holbrock.) During World War II he had been lightweight boxing champion of the U.S. Navy Amphibious Corps. He was a showman who loved sleight of hand, a fighter who loved the arena.

The kind of practice he had, Holbrock took all comers, and the comers defined significant aspects of the relationship between the individual and authority in Hamilton. According to court buffs, in his last two cases before defending Ned Wortees, Holbrock broke even. He won a judgment of $163,000 in a product liability suit where a tire spun off a car into a pedestrian. He lost to Champion Paper in a debt default case. Holbrock had admitted his client owed money to Champion. He granted that as the largest manufacturer in Hamilton, Champion's value to the town's economy could hardly be overestimated. No one liked to go up against Champion. Ten years earlier, the corporation had moved its headquarters out of Hamilton, first to New York City, then to Stamford, Connecticut. By the late 1970s, key decisions that affected the economic future of Hamilton were made in Stamford, and the surest way to terrify Mayor Witt, the Rotary, and every businessman and union member in town was to start a rumor that Champion planned to close its giant paper mill. Still, Holbrock argued that

Champion could afford to wait on the debt at hand, whereas paying immediately would bankrupt the defendant, a small paper supplier. The jury decided to make Holbrock's client pay.

Whenever he had to grope for words in front of a jury, or wanted to appear to be doing so, Holbrock would eat a brand of humble pie particularly rich in sucrose. "I'm afraid my vocabulary isn't as big as that of lawyers who went to Harvard. No sir, I went to night school myself." He had, for a fact, worked to get every cent and degree and possession he owned, but he had not precisely pulled himself out of a gutter. The Holbrocks had operated a shoe store in Hamilton for almost a century. The store belonged to Hugh's uncle, however, not his father. His father only worked there. As a child, Hugh lived in the best neighborhood surrounded by the leading families of Hamilton —Rentschlers, Fittons, Becketts. Yet the Holbrocks themselves were always scraping, keeping up an appearance that denied the head of the house sold shoes for his brother. Hugh Holbrock grew up a poor boy on a rich street.

His courtroom colleagues and opponents agreed Holbrock was a sharp attorney who had somewhere picked up the idea that juries voted for performance as though they were selecting an Oscar winner. "Hugh bangs his hand down hard and gets his voice to tremble because Edward Bennett Williams and Lee Bailey do that," Carl Morgenstern said. "Yet he is a fine lawyer and a truly decent man."

Working Irma Krug like a fish he could not quite land, Holbrock managed to establish that Ned Wortees had been thoroughly provoked before he got his finger on the trigger.

Holbrock: Where did your daughter get the television set she brought upstairs?

Krug: From downstairs but . . .

Holbrock: Just answer the question, please Mrs. Krug.

Krug: Could you repeat it, please?

Holbrock: Where did your daughter get the television set she brought upstairs?

Krug: She bought it at Elder-Beerman before she and Ned were married.

Holbrock: After she left her husband, did your daughter Marilyn move out and ask you not to tell her husband where she had gone?

Krug: Yes.

Holbrock: When she came back and took the television set on July 13, was Ned Wortees upset?

Krug: Right. He was very upset.

Holbrock: So after he was already upset about the television set you got your son and other relatives to move his furniture out?

Krug: He was very threatening. We thought he might . . .

Holbrock: Answer the question. Knowing he was upset about the television set, you moved his furniture out, right?

Krug: Right.

Holbrock: How long did all this take?

Krug: I'd say from about 6:00 to 7:30.

Holbrock: So in an hour and a half you moved all the belongings Mr. and Mrs. Nedrick Wortees had accumulated in several years of marriage out of their apartment. I wish I knew such efficient movers, but can you tell me why you left a cocked crossbow in the Wortees apartment when you left?

Krug: I don't know anything about that.

Holbrock: Why did your son come over to your house on the night of July 13?

Krug: Marilyn and I asked him to be with us.

Holbrock: In case there was any trouble?

Krug: I just wanted him there.

Holbrock: To move out everything Ned Wortees owned and wait for him to blow up. Will you tell me why you didn't just leave the man a bed to sleep in?

Krug: It wasn't up to me. I was helping my daughter.

Holbrock: Where was your son Billy going to sleep that night?

Krug: On the floor upstairs in our apartment in case Ned tried anything.

At this point the girls from Garfield emitted a collective "Ooh." Dondra said, "That's neat. That means they *were* expecting trouble."

"Go Robbie Hodge. Holbrock just dribbled right around her and sank his shot," Mia Lou said.

Kenneth Claflin, Billy Krug's nephew and Irma Krug's grandson, appeared in a white shirt, tie, and three-piece gray suit. He could have been about to usher at a friend's wedding. At seventeen he was regarded by his neighbors, without great affection, as the prank king of Hamilton. He could count on his fingers the number of times he had worn a suit, but Ken made a good impression. He had small, neat features and wavy brown hair. Perhaps his eyes shifted about the room a bit warily, but no one expected a teenager to feel at home in court.

Schnell had Ken tell his version of the night of July 13 so as to emphasize Billy's begging for his life and Ned's response with the lethal fusillade. Ken, it turned out, thought the first shots, before Billy's plea, were firecrackers, too. "Actually, I thought Billy was playing some kind of trick. Then I saw him stagger forward and fall. I was behind a tree, but my legs gave out when I saw that. After I heard the fifth shot there was silence and I got up and went to Billy in the street. He tells me not to try to move him, he's very bad. Then he can't say any more. He just stops. I holler at Wortees and at the same time I'm trying to help Billy, patting him on the face to bring him around. I look up and see Wortees' Monte Carlo going off."

Bressler, on cross-examination, emphasized that Claflin and Billy Krug had been drinking beer, that they knew they were enraging Ned Wortees when they took his furniture.

Bressler: You and your uncle and aunt and grandmother all knew he'd be upset when he got back and found his apartment stripped, and there had to be trouble.

Claflin: That depends what you mean by trouble.

Bressler: How many beers did you have?

Claflin: I don't know.

Bressler: Yet Ned Wortees tried not to cause any trouble. All he did was to walk down into the basement and turn off the electricity. He didn't attack anyone, he didn't slug anyone, he didn't speak to you even after you stuck his bed in your garage —not for anyone else to sleep in, but just so *he* wouldn't be able to sleep in it. You got your girlfriend out of the way by telling her Wortees was hopping mad—yet Wortees himself caused no trouble. Meanwhile, Billy Krug calls up the police and tells them, "You better get someone over here right away or I'll take care of this problem myself!" Right, Mr. Claflin?

Claflin: Billy was mad but not mean the way you're talking.

Bressler: Then, after Krug sucker-punched Ned Wortees in the back of the neck, and Ned finally found it necessary to defend himself, you screamed at Wortees, "You son of a bitch, we'll kill you for this." Right?

Claflin: I don't remember.

To the girls from Garfield, Ken Claflin and Maria Amberson, who testified next, were a golden couple. Maria, in a flowered blouse and light blue jumper, was self-assured and pretty as a bride, which was, indeed, the way she almost thought of herself. She described Ken as being "my boyfriend in July, now my fiancé." "All right, Maria," Carlene said. "Go, Babe," said Mia Lou.

From Maria's vantage point, the killing unfolded cinematically. "I'm outside waiting for Ken," she told Prosecutor Schnell, "when suddenly Ned comes out and smokes a cigarette and looks real mad. I only met him once to play cards, but you can see he's upset. He puts out the cigarette with his foot and stomps back inside. Ken comes downstairs and tells me to go sit in the car because there might be trouble. I obey Ken, and I sit in this green Pinto with his brother. I hear these shots and go running toward the house. I see Billy and Kenny. Billy is on his back. Ken, he's in shock. He seems to be trying to help Billy. I never saw Wortees again until now. I just saw his red Monte Carlo go around the corner and disappear."

Massaging familiar ground for the cumulative effect of re-emphasis, Holbrock asked Maria Amberson how everyone knew Wortees would be so mad.

Amberson: I guess you'd be mad too if you came home and found you had no furniture.

Holbrock: Exactly. Weren't you trying to make him mad, wasn't that the purpose of taking the furniture?

Amberson: We were protecting Marilyn's stuff, and we were ready to protect Marilyn because he had threatened her many times.

Schnell (on redirect): Did you hear Billy Krug plead for his life before Ned Wortees pumped the last, deadly shots into him?

Amberson: No sir. I heard shots. I saw Billy down and Ned Wortees leaving. That's all.

The Garfield girls were ecstatic. They said Maria was terrific for standing off both sides and sticking to her own version. Judge Fiehrer stopped the trial to thank her when her testimony was over. She seemed to be trying to help neither prosecution nor defense, but to give a forthright and spontaneous rendering of the night's events. Holbrock's cross-examination had made aggravated murder seem remote, even a rather ludicrous charge. When Carlene and Mia Lou rushed into the hall to congratulate her, they found Maria crying. Not for Billy, she said, she had done all she was going to for him, but just for her nerves. She had been scared to death on the stand and was so relieved, thrilled, that it was over.

The Krugs' next-door neighbor, Dan Pender, testified to the bad blood between Ned Wortees, whom he liked, and Billy Krug, whom he did not, but added that it would not have been spilled except for the tedium of the All-Star game. "The National League got so far ahead so early, Ned and I just went out on the porch and that's when the trouble started. At first, even when I saw the gun, I thought Ned was playing. I saw Billy stumble, I didn't think right then he was hit." Pender, a prosecution witness, did not recall yelling at Ned Wortees to avoid shooting Pender's Cadillac while he dispatched his brother-in-law, but it was clear he did not prize his relationship with Billy Krug. On cross-examination, he even accepted the "sucker punch" characterization that Holbrock and Bressler were fond of.

Bressler: Right before he was sucker-punched from behind, Ned was going into his own home to go to sleep?

Pender: Yup, just like that. Ned was minding his own business.

Bressler: Had you had problems with Krug?

Schnell: Objection. Irrelevant.

Judge Fiehrer: Sustained.

Bressler: You knew Krug and Ned were having trouble?

Pender: I knew they were not corresponding well. I never thought it would come to this. Billy and his buddies were harassing Ned.

Bressler: And you heard Ned complain about raising a ruckus and pranks like ground-up razor blades in his toothpaste?

Pender: Right. It seemed to be getting worse.

Bressler: So Ned had every chance in the world, and a lot of reasons, to go after Billy Krug, but he didn't. Not until the sucker punch. Thank you, Mr. Pender. No further questions.

With Dan Pender ending the second day of the trial, Holbrock and Bressler were making the state's own witnesses look weak. Pender had virtually turned into a defense witness. The case was resolving itself into an impulsive killing brought on by repeated provocation from both the victim and his family. As Gus De Natale led him away for the day, Ned Wortees cracked a grin at his sister Ellen, who never stopped looking scared.

But as they milled downstairs in the courthouse that evening, the talk among the trial buffs was that Wortees' principal line of defense, temporary insanity, was not going to hold. Everyone already knew the prosecution's psychiatrist had found Wortees disturbed but sane. Now, according to courthouse speculation, the forensic psychologist hired by the defense, who had been expected to say Wortees was in a pathological state when he pulled the trigger, had decided he could not stand up under prosecution questioning. He had apparently concluded, after reviewing the testimony and the available psychiatric data on Wortees, that the shooting, far from being insane, was quite possibly the most direct expression of Ned Wortees' rage he had ever permitted himself. The expression took a grievously anti-social and deplorable form, but Ned knew what he was doing. All the testimony pointed to the deliberate act of a man who, though provoked, knew what he did and what the consequences would be. The shooting had not become hazy; to the contrary, it was the clearest moment of Ned Wortees' existence. As a matter of fact, the psychologist was said to feel, Ned was still angry.

There, according to the informed conjectures of the trial buffs, went the insanity plea. Neither shrink would testify.

THIRD DAY

Sad-eyed in her beige slacks and blouse, before thirty-eight spectators who, sensing the conclusion was near, seemed a virtual multitude in comparison with the handfuls of previous days, Marilyn Wortees testified to the dissolution of her marriage to Ned Wortees. The fight over the television set on July 13 was only a replay of so many they had had before. Though she would not cry, Marilyn began to quiver as she told of Ned's anger over the missing TV and of her response that he had taken a great deal from her family, including four hundred dollars worth of meat they kept in a basement freezer and expected to last at least a year. Ned had screamed that he ate the meat himself and that if any was missing, her brother Billy probably took it. "He hated my brother Billy," Marilyn said quietly.

Most of the furniture was hers, she claimed, just as the meat had been hers and her mother's. She was afraid of what Ned might do next, which led her to move the Wortees' belongings out of the downstairs apartment.

Marilyn said the night had been tense, and she shook tensely describing it. Schnell made Marilyn identify a photograph of her brother's bullet-ripped body. She flinched and looked away, affirming that it was a picture of Billy.

Holbrock, cross-examining, told Marilyn the defense had long since admitted the picture, and others, were of Billy Krug, and he had no idea why the prosecution would put her through the agony of again witnessing her dead brother. Looking at him warily but squarely, Marilyn thanked her husband's attorney for his sympathy.

Holbrock: You were in the bathroom during the shooting, so you didn't actually see it?

Marilyn Wortees: I just thought I heard some pops.

Holbrock: When you filed for divorce you got a restraining order preventing Ned Wortees from disposing or secreting your property. Do you understand the word 'secrete' means hide?

Wortees: Of course.

Holbrock: Despite the fact, then, of your getting this restraining order preventing your husband from disposing of any of your joint property during the divorce proceedings, you had virtually everything in the house taken away so he had no access to it.

Wortees: Right.

Holbrock: So even though you got a restraining order you were the first person to violate it.

Schnell: Objection. The restraining order, if one exists, is not before this court, and the witness has no legal training enabling her to tell what constitutes a violation.

Judge Fiehrer: Sustained.

But Marilyn had shuddered herself into large sobs.

Holbrock: I know this is difficult, Mrs. Wortees. I have not intended to draw tears. May I ask why you are crying?

Schnell: Objection. Why Mrs. Wortees is crying is not an issue before this court.

Judge Fiehrer: Overruled. It may have some bearing. You may answer, if you know, Mrs. Wortees.

Wortees: I have remorse. I should not have taken the furniture away, and I should have told Billy that Ned was likely to carry a gun and could be violent when he was angry. I knew about Ned and how much he hated Billy and me. This is my fault.

Holbrock: No further questions. The defense is almost ready to rest its case on the prosecution's own witnesses.

Schnell: Marilyn Wortees may feel pain and some responsibility for the disastrous events of July 13, but she pulled no trigger.

Judge Fiehrer: The jury will decide the case, not opposing counsel.

When the trial was turned over to the defense, Holbrock and Bressler presented a single, inconclusive witness. A neighbor of the Krugs' testified to seeing Marilyn and Billy remove objects from Wortees' apartment before July 13, as well as to watching the whole cavalcade of furniture, bedding, and clothing on the evening of the killing itself. The neighbor, a pleasant, moon-faced young mother named Martha Kemble, was credible but added nothing to what had already been put in the record until she described hearing the shots themselves. At that point, the killing, as with Maria Amberson, Dan Pender, and the other witnesses, became her personal home movie.

Kemble: I was putting my boys to bed when I heard the shots. There was a BANG, and a pause, then four more shots fast, BANGBANGBANGBANG. The whole thing took about four seconds.

Bressler: May I direct the jury's attention to the second hand on the clock while you repeat the sequence, Mrs. Kemble?

Kemble: It sort of went BANG, pause, BANGBANGBANG-BANG. Maybe it all took five seconds.

Bressler: That fast. Just five seconds, all in the heat of passion, of anger in response to being sucker-punched. What happened next?

Kemble: I looked out my screen door and several people were hiding behind a van. Someone said, "Damn you SOB, Wortees. We'll get you. Dan Pender, we'll get you, too." I ran up to my boys' room to see they were okay. They were already asleep.

Then I came back and watched out the screen door until they took Billy away.

As the defense rested after its lone witness, Ned Wortees sat in silence, having agreed not to take the stand. The wrath he still felt toward the man he had killed, and even more toward Marilyn, would have surfaced, and could only hurt his cause. Although anger was a cardinal point in the defense contention that the killing was impulsive and unplanned, a display of it would only frighten the jury into wanting Wortees put away for as long as legally possible. Beneath his moustache he looked ready to storm. Behind him, among the spectators, his sister Ellen sat looking full of fear, the other side of the Wortees family coin. Ellen accepted, Ned rejected, the life they had had to lead. The stories she told herself in order to survive all ended in disaster if she tried to change anything. The ones Ned had told himself before he killed Billy Krug were full of hope, with flashing visions of escape and freedom. He was always one lucky break from a different destiny.

Yet Ned did not quite believe the stories. He could never actually complete the escape. He would get his new start, job, or wife, then he would crumble at the second or third sign of adversity. Billy Krug had been one sign too many.

During the brief recess before Judge Fiehrer's charge to the jury, the dead man's people sat to the right of the aisle in the spectator section of the courtroom, while his killer's sat on the left, a satanic replay of the Krug-Wortees wedding three years earlier. No one on the left said a single word to anyone on the right. It was Wortees' family that was most bitter. Marilyn had tried several times since Billy's death to speak to Ellen Gandy; Ellen refused to acknowledge her. The Krug family hated Ned Wortees for killing Billy and wanted the state to take every possible vengeance, but they held no grudge against his relatives. The Wortees family, to the contrary, attributed to the Krug family all Ned Wortees' present problems. They had always known Ned was dangerous when vexed, but they felt the Krugs had literally sat up nights figuring out ways to vex him.

"Ned was getting his act together, he was going to come live with us," Ellen Gandy whispered to a friend on the spectator bench. "The Krugs pushed him into this thing every inch of the way."

From the town's point of view, both Billy Krug and Ned Wortees were bad ones. Wortees, the ex-con who was always turning over a new leaf and finding maggots on the underside. Billy Krug, born to mischief, bored with his life and not knowing what to do with it. He would screw around, seldom meaning definite harm but not knowing what else to do. School disappointed him. Work and marriage disappointed him. Impatient and dissatisfied with himself, Billy could not resist probing the weaknesses of others.

These two men, Hamiltonians felt, were born to collide. Put them in the same family, the moody, worried self-doubter and the mischievous taunter, add a sister/wife whom they both loved, and they became an inevitable catastrophe. Billy exploiting Ned's insecurities, Ned steaming away at Billy until his boiler burst. Two of life's losers finding each other, losing everything.

Judge Fiehrer told the jury their function was to decide the merits of the evidence and the credibility of witnesses. "You should take into account the appearance, manner, accuracy, reasonableness, intelligence, interest, and bias, if any." The judge then defined the three possible guilty verdicts. "If you find the defendant formed a prior design and calculation to kill, you may find him guilty of aggravated murder. If he did not have a plan but did have a specific intent to kill, he is guilty of murder. You must find he had a conscious object of producing specific results. If the killing was done on momentary impulse but without prior plan or specific intent, you may find him guilty of voluntary manslaughter." At ten minutes past four on the third day of the trial, after the foreman requested further definition of the three possible guilty verdicts, the jury retired.

Immediately, the courtroom was transformed. Where it had been solemn as a church, it was now a legal hive buzzing with shoptalk. Joe Bressler sat in the witness chair and talked about forensic psychiatry and sex offenders with a couple of lawyers who had wandered into the room. Hugh Holbrock asked several spectators whose courtroom manner they had preferred among the three lawyers. After all but one said they preferred his manner, Holbrock said to them, "You see, I read the lives of the great persuaders—Percy Foreman, F. Lee Bailey, Bishop Sheen, Norman Vincent Peale. If their methods made them successful, they'll be successful for me, too. That's what the public wants. Not just a show but a show to win your point, get your case across."

Holbrock was asked if he was nervous about the verdict. "You bet I am. The day my adrenalin stops flowing before a verdict, I'll pack it in. When I hear the buzzer sound that tells us they've reached a verdict, it's like the bell ringing for a fighter. Which, of course, I used to be in World War II."

Jim Schnell said he was not nervous before a verdict. "No sir, a friend of mine throws up before he faces a jury, but the day I can't relax in front of them I'll give it up and do something else." Schnell and Bressler discussed whether it was necessary to establish, as Schnell had forgotten to do, that the Krug-Wortees killing had occurred in Hamilton, Ohio, rather than in some unspecified locale.

In his chambers, spitting into his wastebasket, Judge Fiehrer told his secretary he had virtually directed a verdict of voluntary manslaughter. "Wortees was nowhere near aggravated murder, as the prosecution charged. The trouble with a lot of indictments, they take into account a man's past record." He unfolded the Hamilton *Journal News* to pass the rest of the afternoon until the verdict.

At six-thirty, with the jury still out, Prosecutor Schnell and defense attorneys Holbrock and Bressler left the courtroom and repaired together for dinner to the Hamilton City Club, an institution that neither the defendant nor his victim nor anyone in either of their families nor anyone they ever knew or even directly worked for could have gotten into.

The buzzer indicating a verdict sounded in the courtroom at nine-thirty. The lawyers were back from dinner. "Okay, I'll admit it," Jim Schnell said. "I hear that buzzer and my juices are flowing." Ned Wortees was returned to court and sat impassively in the same chair he had occupied for three days. Behind him, Ellen Gandy drew taut, sisterly compassion defeated by dread.

The jury filed in fast and the foreman handed the written verdict to the bailiff, Fritz Remgen, who brought it to Judge Fiehrer. The judge read aloud the verdict of murder. Straight murder, the old second degree. Schnell smiled. Bressler looked at the floor and shook his head. Holbrock smote his forehead, sighing. Ned Wortees stared straight in front of him, not a blink, no flutter of eyelid, no flicker, no wince, no twitch in the downward curve of his mouth or wrinkle in his nose. In her seat, Ellen Gandy cringed, weeping. It had come at last to what they both always knew it would.

The mandatory sentence for murder was fifteen years to life.

After the jury was dismissed, Hugh Holbrock needed to catch his breath before he could speak. As an habitual winner, he was far more visibly upset than his client, an habitual loser. Holbrock not only hated to lose, he was genuinely pained at seeing a man put away, possibly forever, in the wake of a spasm of violence Holbrock believed he was taunted into. Voluntary manslaughter could have drawn as few as four years. In his response to the verdict, Holbrock showed he had at least one more layer than the two that were visible. Beneath his professional veneer was the obvious showman, a performer who studied body language and at times appeared blatant in his insincerity and imitation. But beneath both the lawyer and the actor was a depth in which Holbrock was evangelically sincere, caring utterly, believing every word he spoke. He really did have the desire to come into his last, highest court with the certainty he had done all he could. It was a performance, and it was also his essence.

The course of the trial, like that of the Miami River wandering through town, inadvertently touched points in Hamilton that were washed and revealed by its passage. The contrast between classes, so well disguised in the itinerary of popular culture, from clothing to fast foods to television shows, became as stark as that between a lump of coal and the Kohinoor diamond. Similar elements, combined variously, led to radically disparate compounds. The Krugs and the Worteeses, like the girls from Garfield High who came to the trial, felt limited in chance and choice to their fantasies. They all knew people who made it up and out—Ken Claflin and Maria Amberson might become two of them—but these were exceptions that certified the treadmill between groveling jobs and food stamps.

They were, the Garfield girls and the two families in court, essentially in their life capsules by the age of seventeen. "I'd love to be a physical therapist," said one of the girls not so unrealistically, "but I'll be lucky if I end up behind the checkout counter in Elder-Beerman's." Television would keep these kids tranquilized until they themselves had kids. The kids would keep them busy, as they had kept their parents busy, and they would know their kids should do better than they had. When their kids began to fail at school, they would get punished, even hit, a few times and that would be the end of it.

The Hamilton middle class knew the pits when it saw them and would move school zones and neighborhoods and homes and housing policies to quarantine itself from failure, poverty, bleakness, and blackness. The middle-class kids learned fast, too. They would avoid the tranquilizers of the poor for the tranquility of the middle class. (Their own tranquilizers would be just as necessary but would cost more.) The middle class might be equally bewildered about values, but it was an easier, far more comfortable confusion.

Both classes, in their various subspecies of lower, middle, and upper, would work to serve and protect the only people with real choices, the owners. Owners were not by any means necessarily upper class, but they were always owners and they could sell. It was not, as in some Marxist morality play, that they had deliberately set up life to suit themselves. Owners were, in fact, always threatened by nonowners. They were also, alone among Hamiltonians, more threatened by taxes than death. But the institutions of property had become so fixed, the pathways to and from ownership so well trod, the protections of capital so closely identified with the social order itself, that movement or deviation involved Herculean effort. It was far simpler to go the way of the last generation, so each new litter of youngsters wore down the path a little deeper. One month after he died, Billy Krug's estranged wife, whom he had married after she was pregnant and had left before she gave birth, presented the world with his fatherless child. Six months after that, at a few minutes before ten one night in the middle of winter, Ned Wortees became a convicted murderer.

"I'm extremely disappointed," Hugh Holbrock said outside the courtroom, hardly pushing his voice above a whisper. "I'm going home to wallow."

"What I feel is lousy, just plain lousy," said Joe Bressler, dressed in the lizard and sharkskin of a race-track tout but betraying his apparel with every gloomy word and drooping gesture.

Coming down the stairs, a younger associate of Holbrock's and Bressler's shook his head. "It was a temper-of-the-times verdict," he said. "People are scared of each other, and they want to throw scary people into bins."

"I'm very pleased at the verdict," Jim Schnell said at the bottom of the stairwell opening into the cavernous ground floor of the courthouse. "It validates the jury system."

"Someone on the jury knew his rap," Judge Fiehrer said at the courthouse exit where all the principals were clustered before dashing through the February night to their cars. "Wortees' record must have been familiar to someone in that jury room because what went on at the trial itself did not justify a verdict of murder."

No one, including his lawyers, knew what to say to the convict, so the cluster simply parted, wordless, as Ned Wortees was led out by Deputy Gus De Natale to the city jail to await transportation to the state penitentiary. Ellen caught up to him in the doorway. Her tears flowed easily now, though she was biting her hand to keep from sobbing aloud. "I'll write you," she cried, then stuffed her hand back into her mouth. Her brother gave no sign he had heard.

IX

WINES 'N SUCH

"It was the right thing to do."

"Don't sweat it, pal. You done good."

"Who the hell *doesn't* have brother-in-law problems? So don't show up at Thanksgiving next year. But leave the .38 for target practice on burglars."

Wines 'n Such, a bar on North Second Street with aspirations to elegance, had more than enough room for two conversations on a snowy night in the middle of the week. Three men at a table interrupted their talk about football to welcome a fourth, one of the Krug-Wortees jurors, who had come in to announce the result of the trial. A tall young woman, brunette and earnest, tended bar while she talked about work and love to her friend, blonde and weary and much shorter, who was visiting from her own bar, the Mad Anthony Wayne on High Street. The tall woman wore a gold chain necklace that spelled "Jeanie" in tiny links against her pale throat. At the table the juror wanted only a single beer with his friends, who had begun drinking earlier and planned to finish much later. When they had reassured him that a verdict of murder was exactly what Ned Wortees deserved, the juror left and the three got back to football.

One of the men was a high school assistant coach of several sports. Another had a great muscle for a head, crowding out on the sides to leathery ears, and a mouth that seemed always either to be pouring out words or pouring down drink. He was a powerful, gray ram of a man who had once played in the Rose Bowl and now was an insurance broker. The third was smooth and dark-haired, with a thin mustache, a spectator whose knowledge of sports apparently helped him while he sold aluminum siding. As they drank, the three recalled the football teams of Paul Brown and Woody Hayes, who inspired stories throughout the Midwest but especially in Ohio where they were world-class heroes.

"God, but that boy could run all day and night," the assistant coach said.

"You think Woody didn't know that?" the Rose Bowl alumnus said. "Why do you think he tried out the single wing in spring practice that year? Everybody said he was crazy, but Woody was just trying to find out if Damion could run *and* throw *and* call signals." When he drank or ate his pretzels, the Rose Bowler gave the impression of stoking himself.

The salesman put his drink down and said gravely, "A noble experiment. Doomed, but noble."

"The above-average passer was never born that Paul Brown couldn't take and turn into All-Pro QB," the assistant coach said. "Honorable mention for sure."

"It's your large tables with your oldies, that's who you get at the Mad Anthony," the blonde woman who worked there told Jeanie, who was drying glasses behind the Wines 'n Such bar. "They want a lot of service, and they don't want to give you anything for it. When the mayor and them comes in after a council meeting they'll tip you decent, but the old ones will sit there all night while you run your fanny off and they'll say, 'thank you my dear,' and hobble out without dropping a quarter."

"I've always said large tables should have an automatic gratuity charge," Jeanie said. "I've said that here when they told me they couldn't give me a raise."

"Yet you try it out and the gimpy ones will scream H-E double toothpicks about Social Security in their golden years, which I want to tell them I need some security right now or I'm not going to have any golden years."

The three men had passed into a wet spell in which they dealt each other the anecdotal phrases of sportswriters for afternoon dailies.

"Woody took the ribbing as long as he could, but at length it got his always rather excitable goat," the aluminum siding salesman said.

In the tradition of tribes who alternately flog their idols and grovel at their feet, the old Rose Bowler cranked out his own wisdom. "You know his trouble, don't you? The trouble with Woody was Woody got so he couldn't win the big one anymore."

"That's just probably because there was no one in the state," the salesman said, "be he governor, college president, or even former All-American, that Woody had to listen to. The man was a law unto himself."

"As long as Paul Brown breathes, there's a man in Ohio Woody Hayes ought to listen to," the assistant coach said.

"So did you hear from your friend?" the short woman at the bar asked.

"Frankly, Martita, do me a favor and don't ask," Jeanie said.

"But it's almost March," Martita said.

The men were fading into press agents' blurbs, each giving portions of stories the others had known for a long time.

"To which the intrepid Brown replied," the assistant coach said.

"So when the fullback arrived drunk at the banquet," the Rose Bowler said.

"Woody could stand it no longer," the salesman said.

"Will you gents have another round?" Jeanie asked, without leaving her position at the bar.

"Only if it'll fit in my hollow leg, honey," the salesman said.

"Back during the Big Event I had this sergeant that got drunk every night," the Rose Bowler said. "He'd make me tell about catching the pass in the end zone in that last five seconds on New Year's Day."

"The fullback had taxed even the unflappable Brown to the utmost," the salesman said.

"Okay, so you'll all have one more," Jeanie said, mixing a martini for the salesman and double old-fashioneds for the others. She turned to Martita. "I don't know where he is and personally, I don't care."

"Well, was he in South Africa or North Africa or middle Africa when you last heard from him?" Martita asked.

"I guess he's near Kinshasa, someplace with a river and a lot of ants. At least that's where he went for Christmas."

"So what does he say?"

"Woody finally exploded," the assistant coach said.

"Even after I told the sarj I never caught the damn pass he still made me tell the story like I had," the Rose Bowler said. "And then he'd go into this old cheer of his own from someplace out in East Christ. 'Give 'em the axe, the axe, the axe. Give 'em the axe, the axe, the axe. Give 'em the axe, give 'em the axe, give 'em the axe WHERE?' "

"Can you imagine," Jeanie said, "he has to teach them how to read before he can sell them anything."

" 'Right in the neck, the neck, the neck. Right in the neck, the neck, the neck. Right in the neck, right in the neck, right in the neck THERE!' Every goddamn night," the Rose Bowler said.

" 'I don't mind your fighting in the dormitory,' Woody thundered," the salesman said.

" 'And I can't fault you for a couple of fumbles now and again,' " the assistant coach said, quoting not Woody Hayes but a blurb-stuffed figure set up to represent him.

"He got to signing his letters with the last line in French," Jeanie said.

"Which I would tell him to forget it, if I got something like that," Martita said.

" 'But when you show up drunk at an awards dinner,' " the

Rose Bowler said, almost bellowing as he shrugged off his old sergeant and rejoined the common legend his friends were absorbed in.

"Still, I thought how romantic anyway. French!" Jeanie said.

"I guess you're right," Martita said.

" 'And interrupt an alumni speech I am attempting to give to the very people who have supported you all season,' " the assistant coach said.

" 'Even my celebrated patience begins to wear thin, boy, especially when your remarks include unkind and inaccurate references to my own origin,' " the Rose Bowler said.

"So I finally sent him a telegram. I must have written ten letters, but I didn't send them. I sent this cable instead."

"How did it go?" Martita asked.

"Old Woody really told the fullback what stop to get off at," the assistant coach said.

"In no uncertain terms, like he could have cared less," the salesman said.

"It went like this," Jeanie said. " 'Please come home. Stop. I'd write, but I'm crazy without you. Stop. I love you. Stop. And I'll never stop. Stop. Love, Jeanie.' "

"That's sweet," Martita said. "Did it work?"

"So the fullback went on out of there meek as a shorn lamb, graduated only a year late, and made All-Pro five straight times," the Rose Bowler said.

"End of story," the salesman said.

"I never heard from him since," Jeanie said.

X

STRIKE

"I'm a liberal from Brooklyn. My family has always been working people on both sides. I never thought I'd hear myself use the term 'outside agitators,' but it's outside agitators that are causing the strike at Fred Harding's Hamilton Tool"—Pat Landi, Hamilton's Director of Community Development, at a Rotary meeting.

"Hamilton was much slower to unionize than the big cities of the Northeast and Midwest. This used to be as anti-union a town as you could find. Old Boss Rentschler—his real name was Adam but nobody ever called him anything but Boss, including his wife I'm sure—he started the foundry that became the basis of the Rentschler fortune here. Well, in the early 1900s, Boss Rentschler threatened to move his whole foundry out of Hamilton rather than give his workers an increase of ten cents a *day*."
—George Cummins, retired lawyer, local historian.

Even the sprouting labor movement of the 1930s left Hamilton with very few, and very weak, union shops. It was not until the 1950s and 1960s that the big national unions got around to the smaller communities that had held them off for so long. When the ferment of the late sixties finally swept most of Hamilton's factory jobs into the organized labor camp, a number of companies moved to Sunbelt boom towns where no unions yet existed. Others merged into conglomerates which then closed their Hamilton facilities. The cause was not unionism alone but also automation and the shifting of industrial empires from blue-collar to service occupations. The result was that Hamilton lost over six thousand factory jobs, amounting to one-third of its labor force. The companies that stayed fought the unions both fairly and unfairly, and when the old industrialists lost, it was as though an earthquake had transfigured forever the design of a beloved landscape.

Early one June, a strike was called at the Hamilton Tool Company, where approximately four hundred workers built heavy machinery. While picketers marched at the plant gates, city officials met downtown, disagreeing on what, if anything, they might do. Mayor Witt said he hoped the strike would be short and urged labor and management to accept federal arbitration. They did, but the mediator found both sides had their legs stuck solidly in tar. Businessmen at Rotary shook their heads and remembered the time before unions.

At the Rotary luncheons, the story was told affectionately and nostalgically of what happened to Hamilton's *eminence grise*, William Beckett, when the paperworkers' union at last arrived at his company near the end of the 1960s. The Beckett Paper Company, Hamilton's oldest business, had been founded in 1848 by William Beckett I. His son, Thomas Beckett, had carried on and left the business to his own son, William Beckett II. In an Italian village, each of these male Becketts would have been the acknowledged *padrone*. He would have decided what nourished the community, what degraded it and must be shunned. In Hamilton, in soil where aristocracy, with economic roots as firmly implanted as in Europe, was vulnerable to shifting gusts of popular opinion and so grew less confidently, the Becketts could never be certain for long of their position as moral magistrates. There was always, even in the nineteenth century, resistance, bitterness, and challenge.

But at least Hamilton's other first families were with the Becketts. Until, as everyone in Hamilton said, the coming of Fisher.
Fisher was the beginning of the end of the old order. The industrialists of Hamilton could chart their troubles from Fisher's
advent the way a doctor charts the course of a disease. When
domestic automobile production began again after World War
II, a subsidiary of General Motors, the Fisher Body Company,
wanted to establish itself in Hamilton. The leading merchants
in town saw Fisher as a blessing to their enterprises. New jobs
would bring prosperity and more customers. But for the industrialists, who generally did not deal with local consumers, there
was a dark side to the blessing. The men who owned factories,
led by William Beckett, had a vision of Fisher as a demon that
would blight their community.

Fisher meant unions. Unions meant that local manufacturers
would have to pay more for their own help. At the very least,
Fisher would compete for Hamilton's available labor, giving
workers the option to switch jobs for more money. Fisher, structured into the General Motors wage scale, paid much more than
any factory in Hamilton and had been unionized since the
1930s. Worst of all, the union was the United Auto Workers,
whose leader, Walter Reuther, was regarded frankly by most
Hamilton industrialists as a Communist. "I'm anti-union, I'll
state that freely," William Beckett said. "Unions are far worse
than the evils they are supposed to correct."

The manufacturers, more powerful than the merchants and
senior in the town's hierarchy, stopped Fisher Body at the city
limits. They controlled enough of local government to insure
that Fisher was not offered the services, tax breaks, or cheap
land that communities use to attract new business. It was an
expensive victory. The Fisher fight split the two branches of
Hamilton's royalty, commerce and industry, destroying an alliance that had ruled for more than a century. Industry seemed
to have won against both commerce and Fisher, but the issue
had broken the town's traditional establishment into factions
whose interests diverged.

Fisher came anyway. The company wanted to draw on Hamilton's well-trained labor force, so it planted itself, like a creature
from space, just over the town line in a sleepy little junction
called Fairfield. Hamilton had its wages raised, got unions, and
provided Fisher with workers. Fairfield got all Fisher's taxes, a
building boom, and prosperity that enabled it to put up signs
billing itself as "Opportunity City." It never became more than
a fast-food franchise of a town, having no center, only "devel-
opments" and "projects," but it had more money than it could
count. Hamilton, which could have revived its own center and
rebuilt its schools with Fisher's taxes, got nothing at all.

Still, Bill Beckett held out against unions at his own plant. He
had over four hundred workers, and he knew all their first
names and many of their family histories. He knew which ones,
like his own family, had been with Beckett Paper for three generations; which ones had drinking problems; who could be
counted on when there was discontent; whose son had a prison
record but would turn out all right if the Beckett Paper Company could only find a place for him in the sorting room. The
best and most ambitous workers, potential union sympathizers,
were often promoted to positions of at least minor management
responsibility. Chronic malcontents were fired. Nothing was
more natural. It was also natural for Bill Beckett's wife, Fritzie,
to take hundreds of turkeys to the workers each Thanksgiving.
Bill Beckett was first stunned, then amazed, then hurt, and finally angry when enough of his workers became pro-union to
force a vote. He had his managers point out that he raised
wages faster, provided more benefits, and paid better pensions
than were called for in the union contract. That was true
enough, said the pro-union workers, but as long as they had no
bargaining unit, those raises and benefits and pensions were Bill
Beckett's gift, not a paperworker's right. Children got gifts;
adults had rights.

"The day they had the final vote on the union out at Beckett,
I went over to Fritzie and Bill's house in the afternoon," said
Dorothy Beeler, an old family friend. "We were all going down

to a big party in Cincinnati that night. Bill wasn't home yet when I got to the Becketts, so we sat around talking about the vote. Fritzie was a little tense, but she was confident, just the way Bill had been when we had last seen him. The phone rang and Fritzie jumped to answer it herself. She held on for a moment, listening. She asked one question, 'Are you sure?' Then she hung up. She turned from the phone and didn't even tell us the call had been about the union question or what the vote had been. She just said, with tears pouring down her face, 'No more Thanksgiving turkeys.' Fritzie had loved taking those turkeys around, but the workers loved getting the turkeys too. I've heard them say so. A few minutes later, Bill walked in looking like he had no flesh, no blood, only bones. He was drained of everything, as though he'd been knocked out. The union just broke his heart. When she stopped crying, Fritzie whispered to me to say something to cheer Bill up, but no one could think of anything. Of course, the party down in Cincinnati was off."

Against the background of hostility toward unions among the upper class, it was not surprising that most middle-class Hamiltonians felt the strike at Hamilton Tool was the work of outsiders. The Rotary lunch, held weekly at the YWCA, attracted an establishment that regarded union raises as a cause of inflation second only to wasteful federal projects. "These unions come in and they figure they're not earning the workers' dues and loyalty unless they show their muscle now and then," said a lunching Rotarian. One table in the YWCA held not just a selection of the middle class but several of the most influential men in Hamilton. Fred Harding, whose family owned the Hamilton Tool Company, was surrounded by a leading banker, the publisher of the newspaper, the owner of the radio station, and the local U.S. congressman, Representative Tom Kindness. The banker was Tom Rentschler, who was also Bill Beckett's nephew. Between the Becketts and Rentschlers, Hamilton's industrial history could be traced like a voyage of Drake or a campaign of Caesar. Many of the other one hundred fifty Rotarians in the room flicked glances at the table where Harding and Rentschler sat, inclined their heads toward it, found excuses to walk over and ask the opinion of one of the men there. Those who spoke to Fred Harding told him they were with him all the way.

Here at this table, close together, were the communications and financial leaders of Hamilton, sitting right next to their friend, the beleaguered president of the struck company that was now in its fiftieth year of doing local business. It was not so much conflict as concert of interest. Everybody wanted to see the strike settled amicably. More important, settled immediately. Most preferable, of course, would be for there to have been no strike at all. No strike would have meant the labor contract continued as before, which would have meant the company had the same deal with the workers. Which meant no (or minimal) raises for the help while the company was free to raise its own prices. Everything on the side of a peaceful, cheerful community was also on the side of the status quo, which meant no improvement for those not in positions of ownership. Not everyone at the table agreed on the important issues, either locally or nationally. The Hamilton establishment was almost as splintered as the rest of the community. Whereas Congressman Tom Kindness and Fred Harding were usually described as arch-conservatives, at least one of their luncheon companions held views often associated with liberal Democrats. Yet Fred Harding was their friend, their identification was with him and his family, and their sympathies were on the side of things as they were. Especially since, as everyone agreed, the strike had been foisted on the community by outside agitators.

"All I have to do is vote for a strike and go out on a picket line, and the next thing you know, I'm collecting both my strike benefits from the union *and* food stamps," Tom Kindness said to a fellow Rotarian who shyly approached this table where men looked more forceful, more able to run things, more in charge than elsewhere in the room. Congressman Kindness, in fact, had perhaps the most modest success of anyone at the table. He had been a middle-level lawyer for the Champion Paper Company, Hamilton's biggest home-grown business until it moved its headquarters to New York in the 1960s and then on to Stamford, Connecticut, in the 1970s. When he discovered he was not going much higher at Champion, Kindness made a smart right turn and headed into politics. He was good-natured, well-liked, and somewhat shorter than the other men at the table, to whom he had never been any kind of threat. "By letting strikers get food stamps," Kindness continued, "the government is in the position of taking sides in a labor dispute. In effect, you are subsidizing the union position, helping the strikers stay out on strike and therefore penalizing the company." Congressman Kindness winked at his timid but grateful listener as he reached out to shake the hand of the next supplicant. "Goddamn right," Fred Harding muttered to his friend Tom Rentschler. "We've got ourselves an All-American strike out there, and from the looks of things it'll be going on for quite a while."

An American strike, as opposed to a French or a Polish strike where the ends are as political as they are economic, tends not to be an occasion for romantic ferment or ideological self-discovery. As much drudgery is often associated with the strike itself as with the work that goes undone. Ever since most of the American labor movement decided it would prefer a larger slice of the capital pie to a change in the pie's ingredients and in the movement's relationship to them, strikes have been more tedious than revolutionary. Getting onto a picket line may at first provide some variation from the usual factory routine, at least some fresh air. But as a novelty, picketing lasts about half an hour. After that, with the exception of a police incident or clash with strikebreakers—each of which is unpleasant and fearful—there is only walking and waiting. Hour after hour, week after week, while everyone's savings, food stamps or not, dwindle.

"They're plain not paying enough," said a picketer outside the big tool factory where he had worked for eleven years. Hamilton Tool was a one-storyed off-white sprawl of concrete, occupying about a third of a large city block—always called a square in Hamilton—in a rundown, residential, integrated neighborhood. The other two-thirds of the block were taken up by the plant's parking lot, which was, during the strike, empty except for a few trucks and the cars of supervisory personnel.

A dozen or so picketers walked slowly back and forth in front of each of the three, widely separated gates into the huge parking lot. Their union was the same UAW that represented the workers at Fisher Body, whose presence had once scared and infuriated Hamilton's industrial leaders. In a sense, the industrialists had been proven right, since after thirty years Fisher still led the way in the area's hourly wages. Though Walter Reuther and the old CIO were long dead, the UAW was still regarded downtown as the toughest union in Hamilton. The strikers knew this, but instead of feeling powerful they felt encircled, besieged, embattled.

"The paper only tells about disturbances, like a cherry bomb that got thrown at the boss's window," said a young blond toolmaker who had worked at Hamilton Tool for a year. "Not a word about what we're striking for. It isn't only Fisher that pays more to their UAW members. So do the local G.E. and Ford plants. We need more money, a contract tied to cost-of-living increases, a better medical plan, shift preference for those that have been here five years or more, and additional vacation time."

The blond man, Rick Price, was, at twenty-four, the youngest union representative at the company. He carried a sign that said Hamilton Tool was unfair to its workers. Next to him was an older man wearing a sandwich board proclaiming that UAW Local 1688 was on strike. Originally from Latvia, he was in his middle fifties and had been a fitter at Hamilton Tool for twenty years. He felt loyalty both to the company and his fellow workers. "I getting near retirement," he said in a heavy accent, "so this strike matters not much for me, but the young ones should have the benefits like the other UAW factories. We make wonderful machines at Hamilton Tool, and I put my kid through college from here, but Mr. Harding must pay you enough to live."

Early in the strike, many of the wives were even more determined than their husbands to wring concessions from the company. A woman marching with her husband was confident, obdurate. "They can meet with the mediators as much as they want," she said. "Until we get what we want it's all hot air. The workers' message is to our leadership, not just the company. We're hungry and we need rent money and we need to pay bills, and we sure can't do it on the sidewalk with the men not working. But we have to make them see how much we mean it. With all this inflation we ought to have a cost-of-living along with our hourly raises, but so far the company refuses even to talk about that. We'll stay out all summer if we have to."

The woman's husband, tall and skinny and very suspicious, moved away, refusing to talk. When I pursued him, naively assuming that the harder someone is to talk to the more valuable he must be, his shyness quickly became accusatory. Why should he talk to a reporter when the newspaper was so unfair to the union? What proof did I have that I was not a spy for the company? In fact, though he did not say this, I was dressed far more like an office worker than a union member. I may also have looked and talked like one, and surely my hands were those of the desk-bound. Now I spoke carefully and slowly to him, condescendingly slowly I later realized, not wanting to lose the chance to hear what he might say. Whatever I seemed to be selling, he wasn't buying. He stalked off in the middle of a self-conscious statement about how I did not work for the company or the newspaper either, though it was true some of my questions relating to the strike might sound like a reporter's, but basically I was interested much more in how . . .

By then he was twenty yards away, brandishing his fists, and ordering me to get away from the picket line. As I retreated across the street, I was followed by the eleven-year veteran who had initially announced that the strike was over the plain issue of pay. Introducing himself as Al Bowling, he spoke with a mixture of pride and bitterness about Hamilton Tool. "We make the best collators anywhere in the world and printing presses that can do things no one else's can. But the company is very conservative in its dealings with its help and far behind the other factories in this area. I grant you it's not the company's fault the cost of living is going out of this world, but it's not ours either. You've got to earn enough to eat on, and right now we're not doing that. With a wife and three kids, fifty dollars a week in strike benefits doesn't stretch too far. But if it's a choice between the benefits or signing a contract for three years like the one management wants, that fifty dollars is going to have to last. Plus food stamps, if and when you can get them. The company has offered us eighty cents an hour spread over three years, and that is nowhere near good enough. Of course, the union is starting out higher than we expect to get, but that's bargaining, isn't it?"

Al Bowling looked more worried than defiant. He liked where he worked and wanted to stay there. He was proud that he saw each piece of machinery through the whole manufacturing process and was not a mere assembler. Yet those who worked on assembly lines at other plants were paid better. It also disturbed Al Bowling that the company was continuing to do business during the strike.

"Right now the foreman and some of the office personnel are probably doing my job. Strangers are going in and out all day, maybe scabs," he said. "We see trucks loaded up driving in and out all the time, and I doubt the office help are drawing salary for playing cards."

Just then a gigantic semi rented from Avis turned in toward the main gate. Rick Price, the spirited toolmaker who had been with the company only a year, stood in front of the semi—bravely, foolishly, or both—for a few agonizing seconds blocking its way into the plant parking lot. The Latvian urged him to stand aside, and the semi rolled onto the Hamilton Tool domain.

Al Bowling crossed the street to rejoin the picketers pacing in front of the cyclone fence that separated company property from the dilapidated neighborhood that had become the strikers' territory. The union members all lived in considerably better neighborhoods than the slum surrounding Hamilton Tool, and they were unsympathetic to the company's charge of vandalism. "They claim we threw that cherry bomb into their front office," a weatherbeaten man of about thirty said in a Kentucky twang. "They have no proof we did it, and I don't know who would. Anybody living in this area has the chance more than we do, plus twice the reason, since Hamilton Tool feeds off this neighborhood and don't give nothing back. Still, they's four hundred of us and maybe someone did throw that cherry bomb, but the only harm was a broken window."

"The company did something much worse," said the Latvian fitter. "They bring in strikebreakers, they call it protection force, but the knuckles is all scabs."

"One of them hit one of us with his car," Rick Price said. "The knuckles guys are a bunch of goons and scabs that wish they could be cops but can't pass the tests."

"What does that mean, the knuckles guys? They go around slugging you?" I asked.

"Sometimes they do, that's for sure," said Al Bowling as a couple of his fellow picketers chuckled. "No, their security guard company is called knuckles, N-U-C-K-O-L-S." The protection agency possessed another of the local names too aptly allegorical for any story since *Pilgrim's Progress*.

The UAW members said the police were on the scene within minutes of the cherry bomb explosion, but still had not responded after four days to the union's call for the arrest of the Nuckols guard who had hit the striker with his car. The worker was not badly hurt, but the incident still constituted an assault. Was the worker obstructing the car's path, even momentarily, the way the toolmaker had stood in front of the Avis truck? They claimed he was only marching in front of the cyclone fence, not the actual plant entrance, when he was sideswiped.

"We hold nothing against the foremen or the office people either," Al Bowling said. "They have to stay in there and work or they'll be fired. Some of them used to be us—union guys— and we don't begrudge their promotions. But Hamilton Tool has hired goons and scabs, the Nuckols people, to do our jobs during a labor dispute, and that they should not have done."

More than a week after the striking UAW member was knocked down by the car, the police did arrive to investigate. They questioned union men and Nuckols employees alike, and after an hour they arrested the driver whose car had hit the striker. But the men walking picket could not see why the three-minute drive from police headquarters had taken a week. They complained that the whole community was too conservative to see their point of view, and that the police, in particular, were extremely one-sided in their approach to maintaining order during the strike. They were angry also at the Hamilton *Journal-News*. They seemed to have special, different resentments toward the police and the newspaper. They were mad at the police because as diligent union members, well above the bottom of the economic scale, the UAW men were very much in favor of law and order. Many of them came from the same neighborhoods as the police and had known them all their lives. They were on the same side as the police in almost every dispute, and now they felt betrayed by a segment of official Hamilton they regarded as a natural ally. They were bitter at the *Journal-News* (the media as they called it) for being, they charged, an organ of the establishment, the town crier for Hamilton Tool management and its friends in what they referred to as the power structure downtown.

"They tell people outsiders are stirring us up," Rick Price, the young toolmaker, said. "Do they think we're so stupid we don't know when we're being paid two dollars an hour less than guys at other plants who don't have half our skills? What we're really afraid of is that the national union may want peace so much they'll make a sweetheart deal with management and encourage us to settle before we get what's coming to us. But those guys at Rotary, they all think one way. This town is run by five or six of them. The Rentschlers, Becketts, Fittons, Slonekers. If they wanted their buddy, Fred Harding, to settle this strike, it would be over tomorrow." Then he repeated the refrain that had so much currency in Hamilton it took on the force of incantation, "It's not what you know, but who you know."

The battle lines in the strike were drawn as much along lines of faith as along those of position. The union members believed firmly that no one was on their side except their own membership. Everyone else was their enemy, and the enemy was united. They had no sense of an establishment in too much disarray to agree on a dam, a bridge, or even a school for their community. They did not realize that the Rotarians' friendship for their fellow member, Fred Harding, and their sympathy for his struck plant, would lead to nothing more conspiratorial than headshaking and nostalgia for the pre-union days. For their part, the business community believed that loyal Hamilton workers would never go out on strike unless someone from the outside were laying down an oil slick of discontent and putting a torch to it. "If a big national union doesn't call a strike every few years," one of them said, "what's it in business for?" He emphasized the complete lack of understanding between two sides who were ready to do everything to each other but listen.

Inside the embattled tool company offices, the siege atmosphere was genuine, even though orchestrated by Musak. The offices were bright with the fluorescence that makes the young look old and the old look dead. Though "In" and "Out" boxes were mostly empty, the attempt at brave good cheer was hardly less insistent than that at Dunkirk. "About a hundred of us hardy souls are carrying on," said Marcie June, a receptionist, while I waited to see Fred Harding. "We're doing the best we can with what we've got." The staff was taking orders for equipment they would not be able to deliver on time, writing letters asking to be forgiven for their shipping delays due to "labor problems."

"Get out of that candy," Marcie June said to a friend who had dropped by as though business were usual. "Take your cotton-pickin' fingers out of there or I'll have you kicked out of Weight Watchers. I love those shoes you're wearing. Spiffy. Your department has just about died, hasn't it? You might as well have funeral services for it. Don't try to go through that door over there. That's from the day they wouldn't let us in." She was referring to the cherry bomb that blew in a window and damaged a door.

Tall, husky, florid, hawk-nosed, visibly muscled even through his monogrammed striped shirt, Fred Harding was every inch a proof of Emerson's assertion, "A business is but the lengthened shadow of a man." In his midforties, exuding strength, he did not look like someone it would be easy or wise to cross.

His parents had run a printing shop in Dayton, though one of his grandfathers had come from Hamilton. He had not founded Hamilton Tool, or grappled his way to the top, but instead followed a company tradition of marrying the boss's daughter. Still, no one familiar with Hamilton Tool would say he had not mastered his business. Harding's manner was commanding, and he surveyed his own position, along with the rest of industrial Hamilton, the way he might assess a battlefield during a lull.

"I met my father-in-law, old Mr. Franzman, before I met my wife, actually. He had been everything but a salesman here— engineer, accountant, treasurer, senior executive, finally president. Oscar Slichter, from an old Hamilton German family, founded the company in 1927. He had three daughters and three sons. Only one son came into the business, and he died. Bill Franzman was Slichter's son-in-law, and now I am Franzman's son-in-law. But I came here to work, not to inherit.

"What I have always liked here was the smallness of the place. No corporate hassle. The company is accused of being a provincial cul-de-sac, but that's what recommends it to me. A family-owned enterprise with its roots right here in Hamilton. Like many other communities we are increasingly afflicted with absentee ownership. Old Hamilton companies have now merged, and the decisions that govern thousands of lives here are made elsewhere. These companies are now just divisions in a conglomerate. That means the civic leadership is not bolstered any more by locally directed groups that can make up their own minds on everything from plant expansion to charitable contributions. The transient managers look on their stints here as stepping stones to somewhere else—Seattle, Chicago, Los Angeles, Buenos Aires.

"The town now has an Appalachian flavor. I'm not saying that's bad, but it's different. In the strike here that means there's some violence we never would have had before. It started with the cherry bomb, but there have been a couple of our trucks shot at, too. The Appalachians have brought a coal field psychology that says labor and management have always been at war and always will be. There's an unwritten Geneva Convention on strikes—it's all right to throw eggs at the boss's window, which they have done, but you can't bomb the plant. With people getting so mad, though, you can't tell what they're going to do. Frankly, if I was out on a picket line myself, I could think up a lot more devilment than they've done so far. But if things keep up this way, anything could happen. Yesterday we had thirty-five or forty wives demonstrating out there, and they were pretty steamed up." Harding did not mention that he immediately went to court and got an injunction barring the women, or any other non-union members, from the picket line in the future.

"The old-line workers who have been with us fifteen, twenty years are not the problem in this strike," Harding said. "It's the young fellows out of the vocational schools who are doing the kicking, and that's who the union leadership work on most. What they're asking is nice stuff, all those benefits and holidays, but I just can't give it. If I yielded I'd be making a going-out-of-town settlement, which I don't want to do. Some companies have done that, given in on everything their union asks, signed a ludicrous contract, and then left town. I don't want to leave Hamilton.

"There's a strong and understandable feeling among the workers that they don't want us to subcontract the work out during the strike. But really we have no choice. We have orders, and we have to fill them or see the business go to our competitors. If our own people are not going to do our manufacturing for us, we've got to get someone else who will. We may keep some of those subcontractors after the strike, which will make the workers bitter, but if they do a better job for us, and a cheaper one, we'd be fools not to stick with them, wouldn't we? Meanwhile, we just have to be patient. All over town, everywhere I go, people say to me, 'Hang in there, Fred. Hang tough.'

"Sometimes trying to communicate with the workers is like getting in a kicking contest with a mule. The point is, the mule is not going to get hurt. There's only about twenty-five of them doing all the griping anyway. If we become a pistol-whipped, horse-whipped town like Dayton, we're not going to grow. The schools here ought to be teaching the economics of business. It's the investment of capital that allows labor to be employed. Labor is only worth what it produces. If they taught school that way, you'd have kids growing up realizing the limits of unionization. Unionism in corporate affairs is like vandalism in the streets.

"The press doesn't understand either. They play down the strike because they don't want to advertise the fact that one more employer is catching hell from the red-neck element that's leading the workers. They just figure the town doesn't need another black eye, so they don't tell what's really going on. They don't report on the trucks we've had shot up. Incidents like that open wounds that will never heal. We've had to take our own measures in response to what's been done to us. We've hired goons, I'll admit that, to outgoon the goons who have committed violence against us. The strike leaders are drunk with power, getting everyone all stirred up with promises they'll never be able to deliver. It's just like what JFK did with the colored people of this country. You have people doing a job, contented with their lot, and then someone comes along and says everything should be better, a great deal better. After that, no one is satisfied with less than a million dollars."

Fred Harding believed not only in the rightness but the righteousness of his cause, which was traditional entrepreneurial capitalism. It was another way of believing that survival of the fittest produces the strongest society. While not hiding the fact that he came to prominence through marriage, Harding would not laze away a day, and he did not expect anyone else to, either. If he did not take into consideration the advantages his upbringing, education, and even his physical size had given him, that meant he did not have to apologize for those attributes. He felt he had reached his perch on his own merits, and some of his merits enabled him to marry the boss's daughter. He was not ashamed of this, he was almost exuberant about it. Fred Harding was bosslike because he was the boss. It was nothing to be humble about. It was the simple, controlling fact of his life.

The existence, the presence, of Fred Harding at the center of the strike was a reminder that American businessmen, perhaps alone among all of us, know what they want. Their bottom line *is* the bottom line. Profits may not be all they want—a safe society, varied culture, free choice, baseball, music could be among their other wishes—but profits are basic, prior to everything else. Lincoln told us labor was prior to capital, but we do not believe him. In America, capital and profits are still sacramental. As Fred Harding's august townsman William Beckett frequently put it, profits were not only an economic necessity but a social responsibility. They fuel every other engine in the society.

Fred Harding knew what he had and what he wanted. He also knew how to hang onto it. He was not running a penny arcade or an empire, but he was not convening a seminar in group expression either. The union could strike, but it could not take Hamilton Tool. The moat of ownership was too wide and too deep for the strikers to ford, even if they wanted to. And most of them did not want to.

Al Bowling's loyalty was intense and divided. Since he had been at Hamilton Tool eleven years, he had an attachment to his job that predated the UAW, which had organized the toolworkers only four years prior to the strike. Still, like the other strikers, he had no desire to go back to work until he was making what he regarded as a livable wage. He was a man who wanted to have a good time every day of his life. "I hope I'll enjoy myself until one morning I'm walking down the street," he said, "and then a quick 'pop' and I'm gone." He could in no sense of the word, however, be called carefree.

Not quite forty, Al Bowling had the high, lined forehead of a worrier. Although his hair was still dark brown with a suggestion at the edges, not of gray, but of deep red, care had worn into his face the way wind weathers a sailor's. He had blue eyes that drooped just a bit, not sad, but not filled with hope. They gave him an aspect of thoughtfulness since they seemed at once to be looking both outward and inward.

"I pay $183.00 a month on this house," he said. "That means I'll be paying until the end of the century. The fifty a week in strike benefits doesn't travel too far when you have house and car payments, does it?" Although he did not live in a fashionable neighborhood, Al Bowling was proud of having moved his wife and daughter out of the poorer, older East Side to the cleaner, newer West Side. He had two children by a former marriage, but they did not live with him. The Bowlings' house was small but commodious, and they were most at home in their downstairs recreation room, whose centerpiece was a couch upholstered in a fabric of furry gold.

Diane Bowling, who was at Taft High School, had had black friends when they lived on the East Side, where she went to Junior High; on the West Side she had none. "The kids over here are much less down to earth, and they're snobbish about the Garfield kids over there," she said. "On this side of the river you have your Becketts and your Slonekers, and we don't mix with them. No one I know at school goes out with the rich boys. I don't mean we're poor, we're not below average, but we're surer than hell not above. Professional people sort of make me ill at ease. In our parking lot at Taft you'll see a new Dodge van, a sports car, a foreign convertible. Meanwhile, my Dad drives a ten-year-old Plymouth to work—when he gets to go to work."

Her mother, Mona Bowling, was riding out the strike by

stretching food stamps over the twenty-one meals a week she had to prepare. The Bowlings would eat noodle soup and cheeseburgers for dinner during the strike, but it was not as though they were giving up a normal fare of oysters Rockefeller followed by chateaubriand. A contented housewife, Mona Bowling was cheerful about her family's position while her husband was on the picket line, saving her sympathy for others. "We're not really hurting yet," she said in the fourth week of the strike. "We need the stamps and benefits, yet Al is a master mechanic and he is picking up stray car jobs almost every day. The ones I feel sorry for are the real young ones, just married. They're losing their homes and cars because they can't keep up the payments. My side of our family is very close-knit, and we would all help each other if we ever needed it. I have eight brothers and sisters, all living in Hamilton, and we are each other's best friends. Al's father was from Kentucky and his mother was from Hamilton, but they're both dead so most of the family is on my side."

"Amen," said Al. "When her and her sisters and brothers get going you'd think you was in New York City. We went there once and stayed at the Holiday Inn. The whole place was too crowded. They had a sign up warning us about taking walks. When we did go out, we'd see just gobs and gobs of destitute, and that means trouble anywhere. I saw coloreds playing cards on the street at two o'clock in the morning. We got right out of there and came home.

"I've never felt the snobbery Diane talked about here in Hamilton. These older families are more well-to-do than we are. Their sons get better jobs than we do. But I have to say they're also better qualified, by the time they've finished their education, than we workers are. I guess it's true, though, that if Diane went out with a well-off boy, it might bother me because I wouldn't feel on their equal.

"The only place I'd feel right up with any of them is in church. Not that I'm all that religious, but then I'm no atheist. I was raised a Catholic, but Mona's a Presbyterian and that's where we go when we go. When you're forty years old you can figure you're about halfway around the track, so you better start making your peace with somebody. But every time I give the Church five dollars, it doesn't do me any good though it does make them five dollars richer, and I'm not sure I want to make them richer. The way I feel now, while I'm here I want to keep busy, and after that the hell with it.

"Long before the strike happened, we planned to go to Las Vegas on a three-week car trip this summer, and we're still going to do it. We'll go up to a friend's cottage in Michigan, then to the Truman Library, then out through Yellowstone and down to the Grand Canyon and Las Vegas. I'm going to have a good trip if I have to spend the rest of the year paying for it. Going gambling when you're on strike seems like a good idea to me, even though I have to give up the benefits and the food stamps while we're on the trip. After all, the strike itself is a gamble, isn't it?

"Prices are so high and the working man is getting squeezed from every direction. I can't see how our system can condone that. Since the death of JFK I think the country's been going downhill. A religious person would say we're headed for destruction. Politicians are a pack of thieves, and when there's a war, big business gets the politicians to make us do the fighting for them. When you think about what they've done, you go nuttier than a fruitcake. If Nixon did all we know he did, he did worse too, and if that's true, other presidents must have done stuff too.

"About the least my country can do for me is let me draw these food stamps during the strike. I worked and paid my taxes to buy those stamps, so I earned them. Not like some bum who just sits around all his life as a freeloader, or a woman who keeps having babies and charging them to the government. I can partially agree with Congressman Kindness that the government subsidizes strikers by letting them get stamps. But that's nothing compared to the subsidies the companies get. The government subsidizes the companies with every tax break you can name, with tariffs that keep out foreign competition, and by giving the companies the upper hand in the wage-price ladder. If you ask me, the big companies in America are on welfare themselves in their relationship with the government.

"There's welfare for the rich and poor. The rich get it in tax breaks; the poor get it in direct payments. The working guy in the middle gets stuck with paying the taxes and every other rotten deal there is. Everybody in this country is riding on the working man's back. The government, the manufacturers, the people on welfare, everybody. They'll put a freeze on wages, and they might even put one on prices, but I never yet saw them successfully put a freeze on profits. No wonder we go out on strike now and then just to keep our sanity. What do I want from this strike? Oh, the whole damn world I guess. We won't get it, but we'll sure try like hell to make them pay us what we're worth."

XI

SETTLEMENT

It would be hard to find a single element in the community that contributed more during the strike to the misunderstanding between the two sides or among the general public than the Hamilton *Journal-News*. The strike was in its sixth week before the paper saw fit to print the issues dividing labor from management. When it finally did so, the context was a story about striker rowdiness.

PICKETS BLOCK PLANT; UNION REPORTS DEMANDS

"Non-union employees of the strike-ridden Hamilton Tool Co. were sent home this morning by management officials after picket carriers barred them from entering the plant." When it had quoted the police, Hamilton Tool's vice-president of labor and industrial relations, and detailed the company's plans for getting an injunction against the strikers, the story got around to the strike issues in its final paragraph. These were listed as "cost of living adjustments, shift preference, a dental plan, a better hospitalization plan, two additional paid holidays, pension benefit money, 'substantial' [the newspaper's quotation marks] hourly raises, vacation improvements and other items." The paper had concentrated, as in its earlier and subsequent reporting during the strike, on the plight of the "strike-ridden" company, giving only the back of its hand to what the UAW and management were arguing about. Yet it seemed to be imputing too much purpose to the paper's coverage to call it pro-management; it was simply pro-peace. The paper boosted Hamilton. A strike tarnished the image of a community that needed new business.

A pattern emerged, however, in the longer haul of the paper's industrial coverage.

In the last seven stories the *Journal-News* ran about Hamilton Tool prior to the strike, four dealt with executive promotions at the company, two with plant expansion, one with Hamilton Tool's victory in a fire safety contest. When the strike began, the first story, headlined "STRIKERS PICKET," emphasized that the office and engineering staffs were still at work. The next story, entitled "NO PROGRESS SEEN IN TOOL PLANT STRIKE," said that the newspaper's attempts to reach the president of the union or the chairman of the bargaining committee "have been unsuccessful." (Various union members reacted to this story in a similar manner: "Bullshit. We're all in the phone book, and we're out there on the picket line every day. They can reach us anytime they want to, which they don't.") The paper carried on with stories of alleged striker vandalism and lack of progress toward settlement before, in the sixth week, at last getting around to a meager description of the union position.

The *Journal-News*' main local columnist, a jolly town booster not usually given to contentiousness, printed an item, intended as light humor, in which he equated labor disputes with terrorism: "You look at the news—strikes, bombings, muggings—and it makes a fella wonder, maybe the Indians should have had stricter immigration laws."

When Hamilton Tool obtained its desired injunction against strikers blocking the gates to the plant, the paper printed the judge's instruction that "management or other personnel entering the plant are to exercise reasonable care in driving through the plant, to avoid injury to the pickets." This was a reference to a story the paper itself never reported, the running down of the picketing union member by the strikebreaking driver for the Nuckols company. Unruly pickets were news; unruly strikebreakers—or even the presence of the strikebreaking firm —were not.

In view of the coverage of the strike by his paper, an imagination would not have to leap too boldly to conjure up a *Journal-News* editor who would be a union-baiting right-winger impatient for any chance to exalt bosses over workers. This, indeed, was the image UAW members themselves cherished of Managing Editor Jim Blount. Nothing could be further from the impression he conveyed in person. Jim Blount was a pleasant, studious editor who, far more than his fictional colleague, Clark Kent, deserved the alliterative epithet, "mild-mannered." He was concerned about his paper's strike coverage, but hardly apologetic. If there was one motive that colored the portrait of his town Blount endeavored to paint each afternoon, it was that Hamilton should look good to outsiders.

"Perhaps we ought to be out there more with the UAW, but frankly, we don't want to spread the idea that Hamilton is a troubled town with a big labor problem," Blount said, leaning back from his desk where a small sign was good-naturedly reminiscent of Harry Truman: "The buck stops here." Blount was not hard-bitten about any of the local issues his paper reported, and toward his employees he was genial and devoted. Outside his family, his passions were reserved for Hamilton as a community and the Civil War as the solemn and eternal benchmark in our national history. A provincial editor who loved his town and had chosen to stay in it rather than become a refugee on a big-city daily, Blount wished he could do a more thorough penetration of Hamilton's difficulties. "But we get caught between wanting to report all the news and feeling the need to promote the town."

I had to ask if he was promoting Hamilton when he reported violence by the strikers but not by the company and its hired strikebreakers.

"What it comes down to is the company representative calls us almost every day. The union keeps shifting its demands, and the composition of the strike committee keeps changing. They don't contact us, and they're not easy to reach. Several times they haven't called us back when we were on deadline. We have a shortage of manpower, and we can't just be sending people out to chase them."

"Yet you have enough manpower to cover antique car rallies and city softball tournaments."

"Well, look, there is this delicate balance we have to maintain between our readers who are isolated but faithful Hamiltonians and the transients whose lives are essentially outside, who come here to make some money and then move on. The first only want to hear what they want to hear about the community, and the second are interested in the rest of the world and are sublimely unconcerned with goings-on in Hamilton."

Questions arose for the amiable managing editor, as they would arise for him later in a far more treacherously divisive crisis: What can a good man do in a bad situation? How far can he go in offending his friends before they are no longer his friends? How much truth can he tell before he is no longer permitted to tell any? Can he do more good by boosting his environment or by describing it accurately? Jim Blount was hardly insensitive to these questions. He simply had not found answers that satisfied him.

The sign on Jim Blount's desk might, after all, be wishful thinking. Demonstrably, the buck did not stop there. Given that he was not the publisher and that the *Journal-News* was part of a moderately large chain, perhaps only about twenty-five cents of the decision-making dollar actually came to rest in Jim Blount's own hands.

The fact remained that the *Journal-News* treated the Hamilton Tool strike like a stinking onion. Don't look at it or it will make you cry; don't smell it or it will make you sick. Carry it, if you must, very daintily. Eventually, it will go away. Jim Blount did not dispatch a reporter to talk to rank and file unionists, nor to local UAW headquarters, nor to seek out the chairman of the bargaining committee, a prominent, accessible Hamiltonian who later was elected to city council.

As a result, the community remained suspicious and uninformed. The press left its readership somewhat antiunion but solidly ignorant. There was no investigation into company accusations of worker violence; no detailed airing of strike issues; no test of the union's assertion that UAW workers at other local plants were paid more than at Hamilton Tool. The newspaper, a daily communicator, was serving actually to aggravate rather than heal the community's fragmentation. With small regard for the etymological connection between community and communicate, the *Journal-News* both led and exemplified the lack of communication among the sum of Hamilton's parts.

The atmosphere at strike central, the UAW headquarters half a block from Hamilton Tool, combined elements of a command post with those of a submarine. Pulsing through the large yellow upstairs room with its folding chairs and blackboards was an alternating current that the rest of the world was hostile and that it had also ceased to exist. Union members not on picket duty milled around the headquarters. Bound by little except their solidarity against the company, the strikers could have been picked out from one section of a crowd at a ballgame—fat and thin, skeptical and trusting, mean and generous, hopeful and desperate. They were grown men of all ages between eighteen and sixty-three, with accents from Ireland to Czechoslovakia to Kentucky. Most of them were white, but the blacks were vocal and articulate.

Successive waves of immigration into Hamilton had prevented, as they had in the country at large, the establishment of a working-class ethic. No sooner had the English and Scottish Protestants from Massachusetts and Virginia settled the town than they found themselves, beginning in the 1840s, in a religious and ethnic confrontation with Irish Catholics. By the 1870s the Germans, both Protestant and Catholic, had further divided the workers. The Eastern Europeans and Jews, arriving at the end of the century, found, ironically, a better life while sealing off the possibility of working-class unity. A Polish worker in Hamilton tended to identify not with his fellow foundrymen who were Italian and Russian, but with another Pole who had succeeded and become a doctor. The employers were not ignorant of this blessing. Starting before 1920, Hamilton's factory owners sent their managers into the hills of Kentucky and Tennessee to hire farmers and miners and mountaineers to come north where they would work for less than laborers who were threatening to organize. Later, the black northern migration helped weaken unions, break strikes, and keep the working class even more divided against itself. A publication from the Hamilton Chamber of Commerce in the 1940s, trying to make the town as alluring as possible to potential entrepreneurs, boasted about the fragmentation of the workers. "The varied labor classes are a benefit to the community," the chamber proclaimed, "for it is a recognized fact that the presence of only a few classes of labor in large numbers in any community tends to produce a strong labor group that, too often, attracts radical leaders."

Yet there they finally were, at strike central, the workers of Hamilton Tool, diverse and bickering and motley, harmoniously linked for the moment against their employer. Most of the strikers were simply gathered in case there was news, using the union hall as information source and social club. Some manned tables with alphabetical designations (A through D, E through H, and so on) for the distribution of strike benefit checks. Others made lists of who had walked picket at what times and when they would next be needed. Someone had hung on the wall, apparently as a joke, a child's plastic carbine. All the furniture

—several wooden chairs, moveable blackboards, dozens of folding metal chairs, card tables pushed together—looked temporary, which it was not.

Rick Price, low man in the union hierarchy but still a union representative, held a walkie-talkie for communicating with the picket lines both at the main plant nearby and at Hamilton Tool's other factory two miles away. He was regarded, at twenty-four, as a real comer by both union and management and was aware he might soon have to make a choice. "I'm still not sure what I'd do if the company wants to promote me to a position like foreman, where I wouldn't be in the union anymore," he said. "I'd be going up against all these guys who are my buddies. It's happened to others. Some of us think the company promotes whoever looks like he'll make an effective union leader. Of course, the company *would* want to promote someone who is effective, so it's hard to tell what their reasons are."

Rumors flew around the union hall as though it were an army barracks. The eight-week-old strike was causing jitters.

"I hear Fred Harding's been looking at plant sites in the South," said an older man with distinguished gray sideburns.

"They've been giving a lot of work to a shop down in Fairfield during the strike," said a thoughtful man who wore trifocals.

"Buddy of mine works for Frigidaire up in Dayton, tells me Hamilton's a dying town for labor," a large black man said. "My brother already left to work in Cincinnati. It's better for a black man there anyway."

"Wait a minute, Bill, no matter what color you are you're not going to make big money in Hamilton," said an unshaven white striker looking the same age, about thirty, as the black man.

"That's the truth. But a smart black man, like my brother, he's going to get himself on out of this town. Nobody here is pulling down thirty-five thousand, are they? That's what my brother's doing. We're lucky if we get twelve, maybe fifteen."

Near the entrance, strikers not on picket duty made sandwiches and Kool-Aid for men outside on the line. A commotion in the doorway spilled the food and drink all over the floor.

Two men came in together, laughing, jostling each other. A burly, hulking white man, huge and scarred, was paired with an equally burly black man. The white man, Robert Adkins, managed to scowl even while he laughed. The black man, Babe Shirley, had a broad, expansive face given more to grinning. Rick Price was sitting at one of the strike benefit tables, having traded his walkie-talkie for a nude-girl magazine, as Adkins approached. Along with the UAW list, the table held a Bible, which bounced off onto the floor as Adkins banged his fist down.

"Hey, I'm happy you boys have a Bible in here because if you don't want to walk picket you better get right with your Lord," Robert Adkins said, "on account of I'll kill the sombitch who don't get out there on the line when his turn comes up." Adkins found a can of Lite Beer somewhere and took it down in one open-throated swig.

Rick Price shoved his magazine beneath the papers on his table so that a single bared nipple was all that showed under the T through Z list of UAW men. "We don't have a problem with anyone who's supposed to picket," Rick Price said. "Everybody's volunteering for extra time. The Nuckols bunch, that's the bad ones."

Price handled Adkins as though trying to steer a bull away from an innocent target toward a guilty one. At the mention of Nuckols, Adkins did indeed snort.

"Nuckols! Between me and Babe, we could take *fifteen* fuckin' Nuckols guys. Black power is stronger than Nuckols power, ain't it, Babe?"

"Right, right," said Babe Shirley, smiling. "We could take all them mothers."

Adkins, who looked a ton, put away another Lite Beer in less than a gulp. For a moment he weaved angrily and heavily around the room. Coming to a stop again in front of the table where Rick Price sat, Adkins pulled a pistol out of his pants pocket, waved it around the room, and slapped it on the table. "All right, sombitch," he bellowed to no one in particular, "we mean business!"

What kind of business he meant was not immediately apparent, but Rick Price picked the pistol off the table and checked to see that it was unloaded. Adkins was scarred over his left eye and on his upper cheek. He looked tough, pugnacious, and not overly contemplative—a fairly lethal combination. From his battle marks he was clearly not afraid of a fight. He said he had been following a truck driven by a Nuckols man until he lost it somewhere on the road to Cincinnati. "Okay, listen to this," Adkins said to me, as he prepared to indulge himself in his own personal form of media manipulation, "I'd like you to write down that Robert D. Adkins says, of Hamilton Tool, fuck 'em. That means all them sombitches on up to Fred Harding, the president. Fuck him too. Fuck all of 'em."

"Not a clock or a window in the whole damn town," Al Bowling said when he returned from Las Vegas in the thirteenth week of the strike. "It was fun, though. I won the first day, half inebriated, I got up two hundred ten, two hundred twenty dollars. But they slowly dwindle it away from you, and when we left after three days I guess I was out eighty dollars. Pretty lucky, in a way, though the wife wasn't going to let me go any deeper in the hole. They have it figured so you'll stay at those tables and never ask what time it's getting to be. Before and after Vegas we were driving and camping in state parks. It was great for us. We had saved up and I would have gone even if I had to borrow because I worked forty-nine weeks to earn that trip."

"The Folies bergère was fantastic," Mona Bowling said, "and we had a complete ball there, but one time in Las Vegas is enough for me. Of course, Al didn't get his stamps while we were there, but he's getting them now and he's still managing to pick up mechanic work that gets him about half what he makes when he's working at the plant.

"I don't know what the company's going to do, though. At the meeting the other night everything seemed very angry, ready to explode. It's getting deep now, going on four months. A lot of the fellows really seem bitter, and the wives who were so firm before now just want the men to go back. The younger people are starting to lose their homes. They're looking for other full-time jobs to save themselves, and I doubt they'll ever go back to Hamilton Tool."

Inside Hamilton Tool, during the fifteenth week, there was still work to be done, but it was not going well. "A file clerk can't turn around and become a machinist overnight," said a man who had tried it. Factory supervisors were running equipment they had not looked at in the years since their elevation to management. They felt uneasy around office personnel. Contempt seemed to flow in both directions.

The strike had been a challenge at first. People had been put back into contact with the fundament of the business, its actual product. The first weeks had seen a regeneration of the company spirit as middle managers rose to the occasion and found out what they could do if they had to. "But people who didn't mind filling in on the line as a stop-gap measure," said a department head, "get pretty tired of doing it month after month. After all, if they wanted to be factory workers, that's what they'd be. Also, everybody is pretty fed up with having so many of these Nuckols types around."

From secretaries to vice presidents, the office personnel were taking jury duty, accrued vacation time, remembering aged relatives who had not been visited in years. "The damn thing is just being kept going by a few hardheads," Fred Harding told them. "The rest of the strikers want to come back to work." Yet everyone looked bored and grim now. The Muzak even broke down, Percy Faith or possibly Mantovani fading to an ominous hush one afternoon. Days stretched out like little Saharas. An executive was known to be interviewing for a position at a rival firm in Cincinnati. The staff and the situation were becoming equally skeletal.

Russell Posey had gone to work for Nuckols Associates when the Marine Corps decided he was not one of the few good men it was looking for. After moving to Hamilton from Kentucky, he had responded to a recruiting sign that said, "Nobody likes to fight, but somebody has to know how . . ." The next week he had taken the Marine tests, but he had not finished high school and his teeth were green. He never knew whether it was poor teeth or his lack of education that cooked him with the Corps. He had done a little body building and he did not mind mixing it up when he had to—"look at it this way," his big brother told him, "you ain't never gonna lose no pearly whites in a fight, why not learn how to use them dukes"—so it seemed natural to become a security guard. Nuckols sent him to help out at Hamilton Tool.

The old protection guards for the tool company had been the Pinkerton Agency. After the strike began, the UAW's major complaint against Hamilton Tool was the hiring of the Nuckols people. Union members spoke of the Pinkertons wistfully. These were the same Pinkertons who from the 1870s in Pennsylvania with the miners, to 1914 in Colorado with the railroad workers, through the 1930s and the Little Steel strike in Chicago, had been the scourge of the labor movement, beating and gassing and shooting strikers. Now, in Hamilton, Pinkertons were just a benign group of watchmen whose contract was up and who were being replaced by a certifiable gang of goons. Pinkertons had become like hall monitors in a junior high school, while Nuckols had become Pinkertons.

When Russell Posey left his Hamilton Tool shift one midnight in the sixteenth week of the strike, his car was surrounded by shouting, angry picketers. He rolled up his windows and locked all the doors of his car as the picketers blocked his path. Later, he was not sure whether or not he gave the finger to them. He thought of running one or two down just to make his escape, but someone put a boulder in front of the car and he could not move without wrecking his chassis. In a moment his car was being rocked so heavily he started getting dizzy. He rolled down one window just a crack and pleaded to be allowed to return home. He said he was a hard-working man just like the strikers themselves.

"You choose a damn funny line of hard work, scabbing away our pay," one of the strikers told him. Then a rock tore through his windshield. Someone had a tire tool and started breaking his other windows. "Okay, enough," someone else said, "he's learned his lesson. Let him go."

"I won't come back to work here again during the strike," Russell Posey said.

The picketers were turning him loose, he later told investigating officers, when two giants on motorcycles pulled up. He could not identify them, but one was black and one was white. They dragged him out of his car and beat him with their fists and a chain until he was blue. When they let him go, the white one said, "That should hold the bastard."

Russell Posey told the police that even if they made an arrest, he did not want to press charges.

Cecil Hampton, a UAW official down from Dayton, met at the Holiday Inn with John Stewart, chairman of the union bargaining committee at Hamilton Tool. They both knew the wives were impatient, and they also knew the men were desperate but determined. Stewart told Hampton the membership had turned down the last company proposal overwhelmingly. Hamilton Tool's representative had described this as the company's "final offer." Hampton told Stewart he did not know how much better they could do. Stewart told Hampton not everybody was showing up at the meetings anymore, and they were losing men to other jobs.

At strike central, UAW men lined up to receive their strike benefits, listless in the seventeenth week. The night before, a Nuckols guard had been arrested for larceny in downtown Hamilton. "It was some kid breaking into the pizza parlor," a middle-aged man said. "He ran off and another Nuckols guy hid him for a while but got so scared when the cops came he turned him right over. The thief was that kid with hair down to his fucking shoulders." Next to the middle-aged man were two of his fellow strikers, both very young, each with long hair. They turned away and went to the back of the line.

In a corner, several union members played a card game called "pitch" as single-mindedly as any group of retirees in St. Petersburg. One of them was Rick Price, the young toolmaker who had been part of the union leadership at the beginning of the summer. He had been effective as an irritable picketer, unpredictable and slightly renegade. Now his spirit seemed dulled. "Jesus, that was ancient history, me holding a union position. You couldn't *give* me anything like that now. I don't ever want to go back onto the leadership committee." A gray, stooped man snickered that nobody wanted Rick anyway. A dog who had wandered into the union hall to get out of the driving autumn rain jumped up onto a table and ate several sandwiches intended for the picket line.

At ten A.M. one Tuesday in late October, nineteen and one half weeks after the strike had begun so hopefully in early June, UAW members were called to the large union hall in Fairfield. They were convened to consider the results of the latest mediation session between their leaders and company representatives. Both Cecil Hampton and John Stewart told them, wearily, they did not think they could do any better.

Too late for a news story, but just in time for a page one headline and a single sentence in the early afternoon edition of the *Journal-News,* the members decided.

TOOL ACCEPTS NEW CONTRACT
Bulletin

Hamilton Tool Co. workers today voted 205 to 164 to accept a four-year contract calling for hourly wage increases totaling $1.80 cents over the life of the contract.

"Screw me once," Fred Harding said, ruing the strike one day shortly after the plant was back in operation, "and it's your

fault. Screw me twice and it's mine. They felt we had no backbone, that they had us over a barrel because we had a new
building, a hell of a mortgage, and couldn't afford to fall behind
on deliveries. So while we were negotiating a new contract in
good faith, the union came in and asked for the rights of management. They wanted approval over our ability to place work
on the outside and over the identity of the vendors and subcontractors themselves. No way. They even wanted a one-year contract so we would have to do this all over again next year. Yet
we did have to give more than was healthy, a lot more than we
ever expected. Right now we have a mighty low tolerance for
people screwing off. They misread our friendliness for weakness. Never again. Now we'll fire anyone who's dogging it. We
fired a guy sixty-one years old who has been here thirty-four
years—over half his life—but is no longer doing enough. The
man's daughter called the chairman of the board and cried.
Nothing doing. Not now. He couldn't do the work anymore."

Inside the plant the manufacturing and assembly of printing
presses, collators, and the rest of Hamilton Tool's products went
on smoothly again. As befit the high-precision work both labor
and management were proud of, the large factory was clean,
bright, orderly, and even relatively free of the pandemonium of
noise that was the by-product at most of Hamilton's plants.
Compared with the heat and clatter of Hamilton Foundry or
the battle din thrown off by the clash of automobile armor at
Fisher Body, Hamilton Tool was a library.

The punched paper tapes called out the feed, the speed and
the tool to mill, ream, or tap the hole in a piece of metal to its
desired size. But each of the automated processes, though it cut
down on human error, needed an operator with special skills.
Al Bowling worked a numerically controlled boring mill turning
out a printing press brakeshoe. He knew how to run approximately one-quarter of Hamilton Tool's manufacturing processes, which was considered the machinist's equivalent of being
a grand master at chess.

Everyone on both sides said things would never be the same,

that labor and management had exhausted each other's patience, good will, and bank accounts. Yet everyone in the plant would still call the boss by his first name when he walked by. "Hey Fred," the operator of a blanchard grinder would call out, "don't give me no more raises. I can't afford it!"

"See, taxes and inflation are the problem," Harding said to a supervisor. "It's the government that's everybody's natural enemy."

"You got a nice tan, Fred," was the extent of Al Bowling's greeting.

Fred Harding remained bitter for months. Publicly, he accused unions in general of "horse-whipping and pistol-whipping this town." Privately, he was no less angry. "Unless we come to grips with this problem that is thrust upon us by 'organized labor,'" he wrote one of his banking friends, "Hamilton might as well put up a sign at the city limits, 'WILL THE LAST COMPANY TO LEAVE TOWN PLEASE TURN OUT THE LIGHTS.'"

Not that the workers were jubilant. Even with his vacation in Las Vegas and his food stamps, Al Bowling remained shaken by the strike. Chaos had entered everyone's life, he thought, and the result was no one came out satisfied. "This settlement is not the worst," he said. "It's not the best. It's liveable. It would have taken too long to get the cost-of-living provision we needed, and by then everyone would have been at each other's throats. And it isn't just us against Fred Harding. We're both caught by the politicians. You can't tax Fred too much because then he can't move the dollar around to make the economy go. Plus you got to stop taxing the working man to death. He's carrying the whole load on his back. People that work are supporting people that don't work while politicians tell one lie after another. I wouldn't trust one of them in a rest room with a muzzle on. Maybe we need a leader who will get us all to like being cheated. That's what a good leader is for, isn't it? To bring us together, make us happy while we're getting cheated. If you sit and think too much about this whole thing, it'll drive you batty."

XII

MALLIE'S

Testimonial:

"I started going to Mallie's when this beautician down in Fairfield frosted my hair awful, and the whole front part of it about fell out. Right before this wedding rehearsal I was in. I knew how bad it must be when I started crying so hard I couldn't see. She had stretched my skin terrible and burned me while she was doing the frosting. I went over to Mallie's with all my hair in front broken and falling out, practically bald above my forehead. I got a headache just combing it.

"When I sat down in Mallie's I thought no one was paying attention to me they were talking so fast about so much other stuff. You could get an education there. But Mallie took and rinsed me out and started me on a natural conditioner. She moved everything around until it covered the bad spots. She fluffed me up a little and made me all right for the rehearsal, and I've been at Mallie's every Friday since, except when we go to Michigan in August."

—Waitress in Eaton Manor
Hamilton's highest
priced restaurant

Mallie's was a social marketplace posing as a beauty salon for Hamiltoniennes of all classes, mostly upper middle. Its owner was a doughty hairdresser in her late forties, as deeply idealistic in her religious devotions as she was utterly pragmatic in doing business. "Fool me once and you did wrong," Mallie liked to say, echoing Fred Harding at Hamilton Tool. "Fool me twice and I'll stuff your ears down your throat."

Outside, Mallie's was a plain white clapboard house on a modest West Side residential street a few blocks from where Ned Wortees killed his brother-in-law, Billy Krug. Inside on a busy day, to a male visitor unfamiliar with the panorama of transparent plastic domes, electric curlers, rainbow-hued rinses, and strategically angled mirrors that multiplied the throng, Mallie's might have been a surgical amphitheater or a space-age armory. A person could find salvation there or get lost forever. Signs implored: UNIPERM WANTS YOU! (a woman in an Uncle Sam hat pointing out at the viewer) and BEAUTY TALKS—BETTER LISTEN! and VITA FLUFF REVITALIZES, MAKES HAIR LOOK & FEEL REBORN—born again, like the Pentecostal experience of the proprietor herself. People came to Mallie's—mostly women but a few men as well —like pilgrims to Lourdes, seeking ministration for the one completely vestigial portion of their exteriors, the unwieldy overgrowth at the tops of their heads. Yet the life of the parlor centered several inches below the scalp, where the conversation arranged itself in patterns that varied from sidewalk gossip to psychoanalysis. The star was Mallie. Her fans said she would do their hair better, dead or alive, than anyone else in Hamilton. Her critics called Mallie's the rumor bowl.

"I couldn't have made it without my mother helping me bring up the kids, but my aunt did her share too," Mallie would say cheerfully. "The twenty-three-year-old just got her license as an X-ray technician, the twenty-two-year-old's finishing up his education, and my little girl at home's just twelve. My first husband brought me into hairdressing, but also to the bridge. I stayed with him as long as I could, and I prayed for him, and I did everything anyone told me to, but the alcohol won. It was finally get out or go under. There was no helping him, so I got out."

Girl under drier: "I get brown, that's all I ever do."

Woman under drier: "You're lucky. Some get brown, some pink in the sun. All I ever do is burn, sugar."

Girl under drier: "Remember last time when I told you I was going to be in a wedding. This guy that ushered's brother started dating me."

Mallie: "Real nice, honey. Here, look at your bangs."

Girl emerging from drier: "I trust you. It started on my birthday. His family has this place at the lake. Huge. This man at school worked on my bangs, he's supposed to be the hairstylist there, but look how he screwed them up."

Mallie: "If you blow your part, that takes away your set look and makes it feathered and softer. I don't want to go shorter in front because it looks too trimmed."

Girl: "So he's coming over tonight to meet my folks. My father says it's too soon but my mom wants to get a look at him. For once I agree with my dad. Ooh, I like what you did, can I get some of that shampoo?"

Mallie: "That's eleven-fifty altogether. Your ends won't need trimming every time, just your bangs. Good luck tonight, whichever. Tell Betty at the register to give you the shampoo and not to charge you a full set since we just did from the crown down."

When one of her assistants left to start her own shop, Mallie gave her advertising posters, lent her money, and sent over the tint formulas and special sets for each of the regular customers she knew the employee would be taking with her. "I wanted her to have a chance, and competition is good for you, keeps you on your toes," Mallie said. She went on, repeating what so many in Hamilton, particularly those to the south of twenty-five thousand dollars a year, regarded as the golden rule. "What matters here is not what you know, but who you know. So I'm glad to help her. Besides, I'm galloping, she's just going at a steady gait. We get a whole cross-section in here—the elite, the Jewish trade, the working people. The place caters to the average, yet I also have the cream of the town. I don't have the colored yet, my regular clientele wouldn't like it, but I've done them sometimes on a private basis. The colored's indignation is understandable; I consider myself as close to without prejudice as I can get, but I did start out in the Kentucky hills, just a briarhopper, or an O'Tuck as they say here. This legal secretary that's Japanese comes in with the most gorgeous hair I've ever seen. A legal secretary gets paid very well for a woman. She has this beautiful skin."

Mallie herself had beautiful skin with a translucent complexion that seemed neither to need the cosmetic aspect of her trade nor to have been disturbed by the fast-food franchises that ring Hamilton. Approaching fifty, she still had no lines on her forehead, only tiny laugh creases by her large brown eyes, which widened, as did her expressive nostrils, when she was insistent. Underneath the soft planes of her cheeks, her angular muscles animated her face and italicized her speech whenever she was excited, which was much of the time. She poured every corpuscle of her energy into her talk.

"Not one customer in forty knows my full name is Mallie Willis Pendergrass, so I just use 'Mallie' everywhere, " she said. "I guess I'd have to be reckoned a success now, but I had my spills. When my first husband, the alcoholic, was going downhill, he stopped being able to fix hair, and I didn't know what I was doing yet. Our business was no good. I wanted him to overcome his sickness, but nothing I tried helped. He was depressed, I was depressed, he was drunk, and I had two newborns and no money. One night I took my two little babies up on the bridge over the Miami. I just stood there, babes in my arms, looking down at the water. I don't even like to *mention* suicide, but I guess that was what was in my mind. Right out loud I asked the Lord, 'Should I live? If you're real, God, let me know. Give me the desire to go on.' Suddenly, I don't know why or how, standing there with my babies on the bridge, peace descended on me. Just this flat-out peace. Up to that moment I had believed in God only because I'd been taught to. But this feeling of goodness came over me then, and I knew He was real, and He was with me. I got faith right there. I knew if I could hold onto Him, a door would open and I'd be all right and my babies would be all right. That's how it happened. He gave us His peace and goodness. His word is Life, and that night on the bridge I received the infilling of His Love.

"Since then, I've built my business and raised my family with my second husband, who's in furniture. Not pushing my own faith on anybody, I help others mostly by just listening."

She was a creative listener, able to draw conclusions without condemning. She was also a creative repeater, disguising her stories so they could not be traced to a source. When a customer confided in Mallie, she did so knowing Mallie might incorporate the tale into a parable much the way a psychiatrist uses case histories to illustrate the thesis of a paper. Psychiatrists, however, were only the very last resort in Mallie's world.

"Men tell their bartenders," Mallie would say. "Women tell their hairdressers. Ladies who have lost husbands or found a lump on their breast or their kids take dope or they know their husbands are running around on them—they're all here. A lady has no communication with her husband, but she wants to save her marriage anyhow, son and daughter already grown up and moved away. This town is full of cheating. Men get to an age, possibly midforties, they're looking for a young gal. Sometimes these are men who were helped through college and graduate school by their wives supporting them, then the wives have a few children and get to look their age, first thing you know the men are off.

"A banker I know started hanging out at Waldo's Supper Club by himself. Bad sign. Pretty soon he's marrying a woman with two kids of her own, and not long after that he died of a heart attack. Okay, I see the Lord's hand in that, but it's not always so simple. There's this very, very prominent citizen whose first wife thought he was king. She worshiped the chair he sat on. She tried to ignore his chasing, and she used liquor to help her. He met his second wife in a bar and left his first. The first wife was so in love with him and looked up to him so much, she just couldn't face life without him. She died of alcoholism. Both the first and second wives had me do their hair for years.

He's left the second one now and is married a third time, not fifty yet.

"There's this lawyer constantly leaving his wife for other women. She herself is young to start with, so good, and still pretty. To me she's got everything, yet the lawyer's out chasing. One of my customers who has cancer tells me the wife should have known that about him in the first place. He just has to fool around. He has never been much as a husband, but he's a terrific boyfriend.

"A lady who's still young made an early marriage that didn't work. She and her husband played 'switch' with the couple across the street. She married the switch, this was a man she idolized. She had two kids by him, but then she started coming in and asking me questions about myself, like 'Are you a jealous wife?' That was a sign. It turned out he cheated on her, of course, and it hurt her so bad that after a long time she did the same thing. They got a divorce, with the father getting the children, and he remarried within a week. Now she shacks up, and would love to have her kids, but she can't. Her mom is an invalid and she has to take care of her. If the second husband had treated her right, I think everything would have worked out for her. She worshipped that man so much she would heat up his shaving cream in the morning and put his socks on him before he'd even get out of bed. Now she's a medical technician.

"I know at least three hundred customers real well. By the time they've been married ten years, fifty percent have real problems with their marriages. By the time they've been married twenty years, I'd have to say all of them have had problems or heartache, either with their kids or husbands. At least one customer a month will come in and say, 'My husband wants out.' I get real down sometimes, I know so much dirt. I pray for all of them, though."

Mallie's mind seemed not unlike her eyes, which continually darted around the parlor seeking out the new, reacquainting themselves with the familiar. The salon was usually filled with enough customers that Mallie would have only to turn her eyes in a given direction to see a half dozen women whose private lives were part of her scholarship. If they were young women, Mallie, the social historian, probably knew the lives of their mothers as well. Few of her customers minded, and those who did stopped being customers. When one of her admirers described Mallie as an eager, well-meaning busybody, her neighbor under the next drier simply nodded affectionately.

Mallie's own family was not exempt from her scrutiny. Her husband's first wife would occasionally telephone at home and ask to speak to him. "Now, she was real mean to Howard when they were married," Mallie would say, as though she were describing the results of a computer print-out that plainly confirmed her unified field theory of civilization, "yet here she is calling him up after he was already married to me. If I answered she'd just say, 'Hello, let me talk to Howard.' She begged Howard to see her again—*begged* him. This caused a great deal of conflict. Familiarity can breed an itch too, you know. I took the phone this one time and I said, 'Never bother me again. I don't want you calling here anymore. You been sniffing around Howard, but he's my husband now, he's not yours!' Bam, down with the receiver. It was stormy there for a while, and what with Howard's diabetes he'd get a bit jumpy himself at times where he's usually so calm you couldn't get him to move if burglars came in and tore the woodwork off the wall." But the triangle, for once, ended happily, proving that Mallie, the defender of the hearth, could also be Mallie the forgiver, particularly if business was involved. "Now I set her hair. She came in one day just before her and Howard's son Carl's wedding, and she apologized and asked me to straighten her hair out, which was a mess. She trusted me professionally. So I combed it forward, which got the tangles out, and the rest was easy. She has accepted Christ now, and just the other day she gave an Oriental girl a Bible half in English and half in Japanese."

While Mallie skipped around the thrones of her domain—an empress, a servant, a dervish—her assistants tended their own customers, their hands flying gently over the trusting heads of young girls and old ladies, the prominent and the anonymous, the rich and the almost poor. If it was a Saturday morning, most of Mallie's employees would have their own hair up in curlers, readying themselves for a dance, a drive-in, a rock concert, or just bar-hopping. On a busy day, which any Saturday was, the sibilance of hair spray being propelled through the shop was so constant as to become almost white noise. Mallie let others do the shampoos, straightening, conditioning, tints, curling, setting, rolls, permanents, and coloring, but she did most of the comb-outs and haircuts. "Anyone can set it, if the haircut is right," she said. "That's the foundation. Gloria is the only younger beautician I trust with the cutting."

With her hair dyed almost white, showing up brown only in the roots of her part, Gloria was in her twelfth year of dressing hair. Her arched, carefully plucked eyebrows were just a little darker than her whitened hair. Otherwise, her trim small features gave her a conventional, if not quite glamorous, prettiness. But then, no one was truly glamorous inside the shop because the elements of everyone's looks—teased hair, tweezed brows, painted nails, rouged cheeks—were all so commonly debated and meticulously tended that it was almost impossible not to be aware of feminine artifice at all times.

"My own customers," Gloria said, "aren't like Mallie's, mine tend not to be the classy ones and they're freer about what they do. When they do something, they don't usually have the hang-ups the older ones do." She spoke up for herself easily, yet Gloria was eager for Mallie's approval and generally had a look of faint worry. This never stopped her from declaring herself. She was not so much a liberated woman as an uninhibited, grown-up girl not looking forward to her next birthday, which would be her thirtieth. Whenever it was clean, she wore her low-cut white cotton dress that showed her pretty skin and was held up only by two thin shoulder straps. After being married twice, both times as a teenager, Gloria was living with a welder who worked in Cincinnati.

"Me and Jeff spend our Friday nights at separate bars," Glo-

ria said. "It doesn't mean much, it's just something we like to
do. It gives us a sense of freedom, like we're not so tied down.
Last night I saw a guy at a bar who's married to this girl I work
with in a restaurant since I can't make enough here. She has to
work fourteen hours to get by, so she's hardly ever home, and I
know her husband messes off on her. She herself has told me
she only has sex once every six months, and there's no woman
alive with a faithful husband who only makes love to her twice
a year. He'd be backed up to his ears! No way that could be.
And she'd be overflowing after they did make it.

"This customer, who's married with three kids, she's in love
with a married guy whose wife also comes here. She messes with
him, see, over at the Capri late in the afternoon, and then she
pays the motel bill. She's kind of fat, and she knows she's not
the only one he's running with because once she called the Capri
and asked for him and sure enough this other woman answers
the phone from his room. She still puts by a little of her market
money from her husband, who does not play around himself,
until she's saved enough to pay for two hours at the Capri. She
borrowed some stag movies and she's taken a projector over
there to use in the motel to turn her and her boyfriend on.
Myself, I don't need films, they make me laugh.

"People don't criticize me and Jeff for living together. Jeff's
sister lives with a guy in his forties. She's got a little boy as good
as gold, which the guy is very nice to. But he doesn't like her to
go out by herself, even just one night a week like I do. He gets
nervous, and she gets mad. We can see him losing her, day by
day, but there's nothing anyone can do. She still goes with her
ex-husband when he comes around. I couldn't hack that.

"No one I know was a virgin when they got married. I got
married first when I was fourteen because I didn't know about
the pill. I dropped out of Garfield after one year. My twins were
born dead. My husband was fifteen and we stayed together two
years though he was running around. My second husband I met
when I was seventeen. He was six years older and I got pregnant
right after I met him, though I was using the pill by then, but I

thought that's okay because he's twenty-three and he has money. His grandfather was a doctor, his parents had this big white house. But Craig was in construction, a black sheep, and pretty soon he was messing. We had two beautiful kids, adorable babies, the youngest is now eleven. I left him because I caught him—lots of times. After a while we had fourteen subpoenas going back and forth between us, we were each charging the other with so much of this and that. He's a part-time cop so we both had pretty good lawyers. The rest of the time he works at Fisher Body, where my father also worked. Once my father quit drinking he took extremely good care of my mother after her stroke, so that was good. I finally gave up my children. He's real good to them and he has a new wife who's nice, she made the dress I have on so I have no complaints there. The only trouble is, he's running on her, too.

"When Jeff first suggested we live together, I said no way, I'm never getting married again and I'm never starting another family. Yet it works out. We like our freedom, but we prefer each other. I guess we maybe have sex four times a week though it could be more often. When Jeff is welding nearby instead of Cincinnati, I'll trot home over lunch for a nooner. I could easily do it three times a day, not every single day, but on a day when there's an opportunity. It's the best form of recreation. Do you know why men can lie on their sides better than women? Because they've got a kickstand. Mallie would die if she heard that one."

Mallie did not like swearing or dirty (as opposed to ethnic) jokes. She also did not like gossip, which violated her religious scruples. She no more encouraged the flow of rumor in her shop than a sponge encourages water to spill. But there she was, in the direct path of most of the idle words in Hamilton. So she heard them, and she remembered. What pleased her far more were the spontaneous celebrations that could erupt in the salon. They might happen right in the middle of the regular chorus.

Young woman in Gloria's chair: "How many did she say will

be in the wedding? Her roommates are coming down from college, aren't they?"

Gloria: "I won't scalp you, but I'll cut some of this out to give you some style, just thinning. Four roommates."

Mallie: "Now bring these down, Ernestine, yeah, these forward ones. Like bangs. Not bangs but sort of like bangs. These top pieces, be sure to hold them up and fold them back."

Ruby the manicurist: "Everyone had it wrong about Billy Krug. I live right next door, and he never had a chance. Poor Irma Krug has lost all three of her boys one way or another."

Ernestine: "You can please everybody but your children. Your own kids are hardest to set hair for."

Woman in Mallie's chair: "Did you hear Marge say she saw the mayor and Anita come out of a dance hall in Dayton last weekend? Didn't look like they were feeling much pain either."

Gloria: "All right, honey. Do you want to do it yourself, or will you wait until someone here has time to set it?"

Mallie: "It wasn't Marge, and it wasn't last weekend. Frankly, I don't put any store in that mayor-and-Anita talk anyhow."

Woman in Mallie's chair: "I'm just telling you what Marge said. Have you seen my sunglasses? Silver frames. I can't move without them, and I'm in a hurry."

Mallie: "Go straight home and you'll find them on the kitchen counter by the phone where you dropped them when you heard the mayor-and-Anita story."

Several customers laughed as the woman from Mallie's chair leered at her and started out of the shop. In the doorway she passed a large, sixtyish woman whose smile was as broad as her face. The two appeared to be well acquainted, but not to have known they would be entering and leaving Mallie's at the same time. Each started to look away, saw no escape, and cast a frozen greeting at the other. There was the sense that, through no fault of either, they had become former friends, perhaps because their husbands had had a business or political disagreement on which was staked the entire pile of loyalty in each family. "I hear congratulations are in order, Dorothy," the woman from Mallie's chair said as she quickly finished her exit.

Mallie was working on a customer in the back when she suddenly saw the woman who had just passed her ex-friend in the doorway. "Well, here she is, everyone. Let's give her a hand. Who does she look like, Phyllis or Jack?"

The large lady, whose name was Dorothy, bowed to the applause as she took her place in Mallie's chair. She was almost weeping with delight. "Who she looks like is me, that's who."

All the electric curlers and *Vogue*s were set down temporarily while everyone in the shop paused to hear the new grandmother exult as she had her hair tinted from brownish gray to grayish brown.

Dorothy: "The baby was already born when I got there, 9:30 A.M. I couldn't believe it. The plane to Chicago was late."

Mallie: "Helen, as soon as you fix Dorothy's color, will you get on over here. What's she like?"

Dorothy: "A little baby, no hair."

Mallie: "Come on, you're too modest."

Dorothy: "I'm so flaked out I don't know what anybody looks like."

Chorus: "I told you it would be a girl. I knew it."

"I was only in labor the first time for an hour and a half. The second time only twenty-five minutes. The doctors said it was from being so active."

"Gloria went right from the shop to have hers. So did I."

"Phone, Marlene. Maybe it's your boyfriend."

"She doesn't have one."

"Will she go back to work?"

"I'll bet never."

"I'd like to go back as soon as the youngest hits twelve. Dan says no way."

Dorothy: "Well, she'd like to."

"What did she do before?"

Dorothy: "Hold onto your hats. She worked for Planned Parenthood."

"Hah—didn't do her much good."

Dorothy: "No, they wanted it. She only gained nine pounds the whole time. Will somebody please make Marlene mad? I want her to give me a rough shampoo."

Young woman in Gloria's chair: "Did you hear about the briarhopper who wanted a baby but he couldn't get it up so he went to his doctor and said, 'Doc, I'm feeling so sluggish, nothing my wife does helps.' The doctor said, 'Well, when you wake up every morning, run five miles. Try that for a week and then call me.' "

Mallie: "I don't think I like this one."

Young woman in Gloria's chair: "Because it's about briars or because it's dirty?"

Mallie: "Because it's dirty. Being from Kentucky I can stand a hillbilly story."

Dorothy: "I couldn't believe how proud Jack was. He doesn't even smoke and he was strutting around the hospital trying to buy cigars so he could offer them to everyone on the floor."

Young woman in Gloria's chair: "The dirty part's already over. So the briarhopper did what the doctor told him every day for a week and then he called back. The doctor asked him how he was. 'I don't know, Doc,' the briar says. The doctor says, 'Then how's your sex life?' The briar says, 'I don't know that either.' 'Why?' the doctor asks. 'Well,' says the briar, 'It's seven days later and I'm thirty-five miles from home.' "

Mallie: "You think we're so dumb try poking your nose up one of our creeks sometime when you're not supposed to."

Lady reading *Vogue* under drier: "Oh Mallie, you know you don't mind. There was this briarhopper who drove up from Kentucky to see the Cincinnati Reds play. He got up on the highway just south of the city and he saw a big road sign that said 'CINCINNATI LEFT.' He turned around and went right back home."

Dorothy: "Jerry couldn't even go up to Chicago with me because he can't get away during the summer since that's when all the boys in the store take their vacations. I want him to take me to Europe again to go to the one place I haven't been, Copenhagen, but I only want to go there when the Tivoli is open and it closes in September and we can't go till then."

Lady with *Vogue:* "My husband gave me a choice between California and a Datsun. I took the Datsun."

Young woman in Gloria's chair: "What's Tivoli?"

Gloria: "That salesman in here the other day told me this story about why the briars came to Hamilton."

Mallie: "I don't like him. I don't want to hear it."

Gloria: "He's queer."

Mallie: "No, he's not."

Gloria: "Gay as a goose."

Mallie: "He's odd, I'll give you that. I know we have some schoolteachers here that live together, maybe they're homos, maybe they're not. I guess if you look around, we've got some of everything."

Lady with *Vogue:* "Show us how he walks, Gloria."

Gloria (mincing over to a sink as everyone but Mallie laughs): "He's showing me this new line of rinses and telling me he was living up in Dayton with two other guys, but he made them move out because they wasn't paying their share of the rent."

Young woman in Gloria's chair: "How *did* the briars get to Hamilton?"

Gloria (mincing back to her customer): "Well, he said, do you know why there are so many briars in Hamilton and so many blacks in Cincinnati?"

Lady with *Vogue:* "I'll bite."

Gloria: "Cincinnati got first pick."

Mallie: "That one hates everybody."

Which said it all, really, since the joke depended on its hearers already taking for granted the low ranking of blacks. The joke would be meaningless if turned around. It was essential to the humor of the text that you assumed blacks were undesirable, the most undesirable people around, in fact, until you were confronted with the O'Tucks—Kentuckians living in Ohio. Only then were you permitted the conclusion that someone who is white can be so unwelcome even a black is preferable. The air in Mallie's was heavy after the joke. A few titters quickly faded to silence. It was not that any one of the women was ready to ascend the ramparts of egalitarianism, only that the joke was mean enough to remind them all of problems and hostility beyond the reach of the kind of humor it meant to convey. The judgment against O'Tucks and blacks was so strong as to overwhelm the lighthearted municipal aspect of the joke—that its source was a Daytonian, gay or straight, who was knocking off both Hamilton and Cincinnati with one sick stone. Mallie seemed to look for a way out of the moment. She found it when she began to apply the tint to the new grandmother's hair. "Only her hairdresser knows for sure, and she's telling everyone."

Dorothy: "You wouldn't dare. Jerry took me to the airport, see, and then he went to the club to play golf. Mark called with the news, but I'm in the plane and Jerry's on the golf course, so the steward puts a sign on his locker that says, 'IT'S A GIRL!' Naturally, when Jerry comes in and sees the news, he's so happy he has to go downstairs and tell my whole canasta group. So everyone in the world knows the story but me on the plane to Chicago. I rush to the hospital and say, 'I'm Phyllis Kaufman's mother, how is she?' They say she's had her baby, they're both fine. I say, 'What do you mean fine, will somebody please tell me what it is, boy, girl, or monkey?' They say girl, and I start to cry. Can I have a cigarette, Mallie? They show me through the glass and I cry more. Seven pounds. I'm hysterical. This perfect little angel with fingernails and dreams, how can anybody not believe in God?"

Mallie: "That's what I say. Will that hold you, Dorothy, or do you want another appointment next week?"

After everyone had left—customers, beauticians, assistants—Mallie would tidy her shop before going home. The shop, of course, *was* her home in a way that nowhere else could be, if only because the coordinates of her identity were so fixed there. Relaxing as she put each curler and tray in its place, her life and her work fused as they do only in those who have found a calling more congenial to them than any other they could universally imagine.

If the phone rang, she was ready with last-minute advice.

"Which is it now, honey, your hair came out, or did the color come off? Your hair—at the roots? You used what? Clairol Colorbath? No, you need more than cholesterol. They've overlapped the bleach. Get PPT. You need to use it religiously. If the strength's gone and the stuff lapped over into the virgin hair that had no bleach, the rest of the hair will go. Come Monday at ten. We'll figure something."

Back to her tidying, Mallie turned from one pole of her expertise to the other. The pivot was as natural as to a second baseman wheeling away from his shortstop to relay the throw to first on a double play.

"That lady on the phone got involved at a distance with a married man in Toledo whose wife knew about her and threatened to divorce him," Mallie recollected. "She was married herself, but she had known the married man earlier. The woman in Toledo warned her husband not to come down here to see her, but he did it anyway. So this lady came in one day, before she had that awful bleach put on by someone else, and she said, 'I know you know what I'm doing, Mallie. You don't condone it, but you don't sit in judgment on me. Thank you.' I told her for her kids' sake she shouldn't do this unless she's going to go off and make a new home with the man from Toledo. She got some sense then, and both her and the man went to their spouses with full confessions and apologies. This lady's husband forgave her, though her hair's falling out from the bleach, but I don't know what's going on in Toledo, I hear it's not too good.

"I don't allow talk about explicit sex in here. I kicked one woman out of the shop for profanity eight years ago, and just last month she came back. I wouldn't hold a grudge that long. I try to help them if they need it and I can, which I can't always. I had a troubled customer who was very flashy and swore a lot. She was very demanding in here and didn't like it if I set anyone else's hair. I said she'd have to quit acting like that or leave, and she got more polite, but a little cold. I told her not to hang out in bars like she did after her husband went off with his secretary. In a few months she did change and become less troubled. We all thought she was better, calmer. But I was wrong. She put a hose in her car and the next thing we knew I had to go over to Klaus-Weigel to do her hair for the funeral.

"I do the heads of the dead for the Klaus-Weigel Funeral Home, plus all the hair for my own customers when they die. This used to be terrible when I first started. It was like putting a hairpin in a rock. I couldn't eat for three days and I was still vomiting. I must have washed my hands fifty times after the first corpse. One of my first was this twelve-year-old girl who had hepatitis. While I was setting it, her head moved, probably just some nerve that still worked from when she was alive, but I about fainted. I had a funny feeling on another corpse while I was doing her, something was wrong, and later I found out she had lived a wicked life. When I did this young girl who had killed herself, I felt so weird I talked to her. 'Where are you?' I asked her. 'Do you know this body is just your temporary home, just the place you stayed for a while? When you depart, your soul goes to God if you've been good. If you haven't, well I happen to believe in both heaven and hell.'

"Little elderly ladies is who you get mostly. The first time I did one alone, after the funeral director and all the morticians had gone home, I was giving her a nice set but feeling funny all by myself. She was lying in there just as easy, though. Suddenly, I hear this high squeaky voice that says, 'Ow, you got water in my ear.' I like to have jumped four feet in the air. My husband Howard had sneaked in and was using a falsetto voice. I almost killed him.

"Going in to do my own mother was hard. It was like a dream while I was getting ready to set her. I had these terrible visions, and I couldn't sleep the night before. But as soon as I saw her in there with peace on her, it was real and I remembered how beautiful she had died.

"She had cancer, she was really smothering to death from a lung tumor that metastasized, but she never lost her faith at the end. She called us each in to her around her bed, and she told us our shortcomings. She was so sweet about it. Then we told her to stop talking and get some rest and we waited outside her room. But she wouldn't be quiet. 'How are you going to get me across that water?' we heard her say. 'They said I couldn't talk to them, but they didn't say I couldn't talk to you. Are you going to use a boat, or what? You're lighting the way, I know that, but when are you going to let me see your face. If this is dying, it's not bad at all. No, No! Yes, yes!' My sister doesn't know what's going on so she goes back in and asks, 'Who are you talking to?' My mother says, 'I'm talking to God, leave me be.' And then she goes right on. 'I'll never leave you nor forsake you. No, no. I'll be with you all the way, even unto the end. Yes, yes.' There she is, talking to God and answering in His voice at the same time. That was Him saying He wouldn't forsake her to the end, she never talked like that.

'She called us to her again. 'I'm a citizen of both worlds,' she said. 'Part of me has crossed over already, part of me is still with you. Maybe this will be the night He comes for me. Poppie, get close to that gate, I'll be up there soon. I want to hug you around the neck and thank you for teaching me about God.' She was talking to her own father, who had already died. My brother says, 'She makes it sound so beautiful you want to crawl into bed and go right along with her.' She was having trouble breathing because the smothering was getting her, but when she talked to God she was normal.

"That night about three A.M. I was dozing on the couch. She choked, and I heard her ask me to sing to her. At this time I had some nodes on my vocal chords that made me so hoarse I'd had to drop out of the choir. I went to my mother and I tried to sing for her, but I couldn't get a peep out of my voice. I cried and told Mom I hated to fail her, but I was too hoarse to sing. She touched my throat then and she said her next to last words, 'Oh God, let Mallie sing! Please, God let her sing for me.'

"Well, I took a deep breath and I lifted up my voice and I sang. 'Sweet Jesus, sweet Jesus, what a wonder you are, brighter than a morning star.' The tumor in her chest got calm and she became at peace. She hadn't been able to get divine healing because the Bible says we have to keep our appointments and this was hers. But she wasn't suffering anymore. Her eyes started to weaken. My father came near the bed and he stood right by her head so she could see his crushed finger from the accident when he worked at Champion, and she could know it was him by the finger because she could hardly see anything at that point. 'Oh Nanny, don't go,' Pa cried. 'But Scott,' she says, 'it's so pleasing in the hills and valleys over here, it won't be long till you'll get to come too.' That was all.

"She got perfectly all right, and in a few minutes everything in her just stopped. It will be five years in December. I've never been hoarse since."

Finished now with her fussing about the shop, Mallie was ready to go home to wash her own hair and set it. Not that it needed this attention, just that for Mallie her work was also her leisure. She put some shampoo in her purse and switched off the lights. "Stay green and keep growing," she said. "Don't get ripe or you'll rot."

XIII

RUMOR

The figures in a rumour can be subjected to the same
principle of dream interpretation.
                    —C. J. Jung, *Civilization in Transition*

Deep in the ghetto, bounded by railroad tracks on one side
and an incongruously stately funeral home on another, is a
playground containing a basketball court with weeds growing
through its cracks, old tire swings, seesaws, several street lamps
with smashed bulbs, and an expanse of grass normally as much
in need of care as the neighborhood surrounding it. A strange
memorial dominates the center of the small park. Defended by
a fence of wrought-iron pickets, a trapezoidal concrete block
serves as pedestal for a pocked sandstone globe that is almost a
replica of the earth. Almost except for a curious difference. The
sandstone globe is hollow in both its polar regions and tilted on
its axis so that visitors can look straight through its center and
see the stately funeral home across from the North Pole. Dedicated to an early Hamiltonian, the globe is a monument to his
dream. The dream was first spread abroad in the town, after-

ward to the country at large, and finally to Europe's learned societies for acceptance as a scientific postulate that could change history. It began as a rumor.

The Theory of Polar Voids swept through Hamilton in 1824. Captain John Cleves Symmes, nephew and namesake of the old Judge Symmes who had founded Hamilton in the imperial expectation it would become "the great metropolis of the entire West," had fantasies of his own concerning frontiers beyond the surface of the known world. Disappointed in both his military and business careers, Captain Symmes conceived the idea that the earth was open at either end, or, as his few Hamilton critics had it, that there were "holes in the Poles." Symmes was an imaginative man whose vanity was forever getting in the way of his ambition. While in the Army he had fought a duel with a fellow officer who had simply observed, Symmes said, "that I was not generally considered as a gentleman." Both men received wounds from which they never fully recovered and immediately became friends for life. When he left the Army after being commended for gallantry against the British in the War of 1812, Symmes set up at St. Louis as an Indian trader and troop supplier. Neither the Indians nor the federal garrison could keep Symmes from going bankrupt.

While he was failing as a merchant, Symmes was raising four children of his own to add to the six he inherited when he married the widow of another army captain. With a huge family and small bank account, Symmes escaped into his theories. In a later generation he might have tried to become a test pilot—his bravery was as well documented as his hunger for adventure— or a science fiction writer. In the 1820s, Symmes remained a dreamer. When he came home a failure to Hamilton, Symmes brought with him his "Theory of Concentric Spheres, Polar Voids, and Open Poles."

What was as striking as Symmes's theory was the reception it was accorded in his hometown, particularly in view of the way it was greeted elsewhere. He had no trouble gaining converts in Hamilton. Even the town's first historian, a highly literate merchant named James McBride, believed Symmes's story. Symmes put it about that he had evidence there were fertile lands *inside* both the North and South Poles. The area was bountiful, with a rich variety of fruit and vegetables feeding the numerous well-nourished animal species that enjoyed themselves there. Symmes claimed to have studied the migratory habits of reindeer—he was serious, he was not talking Santa and Rudolph—and to have concluded that when they disappeared in the far north they were merely hieing themselves to the abundance inside the North Pole. If reindeer, why not men?

"I declare the earth is hollow and habitable within," Symmes said in a circular issued "To all the World." He proposed a polar expedition of the faithful to test his theory. Just as his uncle had been able to persuade the skeptical Little Turtle to withdraw his Miami Indians from the territory where Hamilton was founded, the younger Symmes convinced his far more gullible fellow citizens that there might really be a green and pleasant expanse inside each Pole. With a soupçon of charm and reams of rhetoric, and with the certainty of Chicken Little describing the falling sky, Captain Symmes propounded his theories at every tavern and street corner. Hamilton listened. The whole town was interested, and dozens of Hamiltonians actually wanted to accompany Symmes. He asked for "one hundred brave companions" to venture to the interior of the North Pole with him.

The point was, there was not a shred of evidence. It was no arguable theory at all, only a story. Captain Symmes did not even pose as a scientist. Yet one night, in May 1824, he filled the old Hamilton courthouse with everyone who could squeeze in. When he finished his lecture, he not only picked up more volunteers who must have figured that life inside the North Pole could not be tougher than the frontier winter they had just endured, but also received an endorsement from the entire audience. "We esteem Symmes's Theory of the Earth," the assembly resolved, "deserving of serious examination and worthy of the attention of the American people."

Armed with this resolution and the enthusiasm of the community, Symmes went beyond the protective pale of Hamilton. He needed financial support as well as the expert advice of those who might conceivably know something about polar exploration. If he had only been content to keep his idea at home, Symmes might have ripened into an eccentric local character advancing into old age with honor, admiration and just a few chuckles. But Symmes had to take his story abroad, and the story did not travel well.

He asked the Ohio State Assembly for a motion favoring his cause and a recommendation to Congress that it appropriate funds for the expedition. The assembly tabled the motion. Symmes was able to persuade Senator Richard Johnson of Kentucky, a junior colleague of Henry Clay and later vice-president under Van Buren, to petition the Senate for funds to fit out two ships and equip the rest of the polar expedition. In order to gain support, Symmes said he was now willing to test his theory at either of the two Poles, whichever the Senate thought most appropriate for exploration. The Senate, however, was still out to lunch with the Monroe Doctrine it had received the year before. A similar petition from Symmes was ignored by the House of Representatives. Symmes took his cause to the public and was booked on a lecture tour, but he was hooted and egged from rostrums in Philadelphia, New York, and Boston.

Though he could not afford a voyage himself, Symmes dispatched his obsession to Europe. "I calculate on the good offices of Great Britain and France," he said, "for they nurse and patronize the sciences with ardor." In London, where he had sent numerous copies of the Polar Voids circular, Symmes' theory "was overwhelmed with ridicule as the production of a distempered imagination." At the Academy of Science in Paris, where Symmes had managed to have it presented by a French count, the theory was regarded as an insupportable hoax. In 1825 Symmes applied to the Court of St. Petersburg for permission to accompany a Russian Polar expedition. His hopes soared temporarily when he was accepted by the Czar, but Symmes was unable to outfit himself and get to Russia "for want of means." The expedition left without him.

Captain Symmes' heart was broken, his health destroyed. The successive humiliations were more than he could bear. He confessed he was "considered by many as a madman for my pains." Returning in decline to Hamilton, the Captain died while still in his forties. But his town remembered him and erected the hollow globe monument to Symmes that still stands in the ghetto whose dreams are as blighted as his own.

The hold Symmes's Polar Voids had on the community was matched one hundred fifty years later by an entirely different kind of story. True or false, it gripped the upper classes of Hamilton the way rumors only can when they embrace the fantasies of a community. In this case the fantasy had human form. The gossip everywhere was that the mayor was having an affair with one of the most attractive and prominent women in town. It was not only the best rumor around, it was heated up by the obvious sex appeal of both parties, by the fact they were each married to someone else, and by a featured cross-cultural ingredient that made it a perfect American (illicit) love story.

In a quiet way the presumed affair was highly publicized, in high school cafeterias, in Mallie's Beauty Salon, at the country club. Even people who never listened to gossip could not help hearing about the supposed relationship between the driven, energetic Mayor Frank Witt and the beauteous Anita Weisman, a vivacious brunette, part-time teacher of disturbed children, decidedly upper-middle-class housewife, and the only Jew in the Junior League of Hamilton. The self-made Protestant businessman-politician and the rich, graceful Jewish princess. Each of them was acknowledged a good Hamiltonian, but the talk was that each had too much dash, drive, voltage for Hamilton. From the New London Hills tennis courts to the City Club downtown, it was said they were too big—detractors had it that they *thought* they were too big—for a small town. They could have been contenders in a much larger arena. Frank Witt, for

Christ's sake, could be running Louisville or Cincinnati, or he could be senator. Anita Weisman would be a star anywhere, socially or professionally, but here she was stuck in Hamilton as a housewife.

The talk circled Frank Witt and Anita Weisman like a bird of prey, now scrutinizing their every move, now scenting the air for whatever might be tucked in the breeze, now poised, now swooping to envelop the victims and their families. The Weismans had two sons, the Witts two daughters. Al Weisman owned several restaurants around the county and a popular catering service. Joan Witt came from a large but not prosperous Hamilton family, some of whom thought she had high-hatted them since her husband became mayor. The thing was, the parties of the third and fourth part were themselves very appealing—Al Weisman a good-natured, well-liked St. Bernard of a restaurateur, Joan Witt a pert and pretty blonde with perhaps a few strands of white just beginning to sneak in among the gold.

The couples, as it happened, were good friends. That was how the rumor began: they went away for a brief vacation together. Within weeks it was hard to find anyone in Hamilton making more than $40,000 a year who had not heard that Frank Witt and Anita Weisman were having an affair. There was no scandal because there was no proof; no one seemed upset and no one acted hurt. The story stayed confined to the middle and upper classes of Hamilton although a few of the mayor's political enemies moralized that he was not fit for town leadership if he could not keep his own house in order. But for most people who caught the rumor and passed it along, the mayor's relationship with such a beautiful woman simply enhanced his own appeal. He had been hospitalized with a weak heart during the previous campaign, and the rumor of an affair seemed only to reassure Hamiltonians that their dynamic mayor was restored to full health.

Over a pitcher of beer one night after a council meeting, a fellow city official asked if the rumor were true. The handsome mayor snorted, he chuckled, he turned away and changed the subject. Some gossip is so complimentary you would have to be a fool to deny it or a braggart to confirm it. Frank Witt was neither.

Anita Weisman, however, did not mind talking about the rumor. Olive skinned, with flashing eyes that radiated both confidence and confidentiality, she deserved her reputation as a brunette knockout. She was sensual without being either soft or hard, vibrant without the affectation of surprised innocence that sometimes accompanies her kind of alertness. Depending on her mood, Anita Weisman denied the affair with candor, casualness, earnestness, annoyance, or humor.

"Did somebody tell you the gossip about Frank Witt and me?" she asked.

"Not just somebody," I said, unsure as to where the conversation could go from there.

"Oh my God. You mean everybody?"

"No, but a number of people mention it enough so there's the sense that it's part of the currency, at least on your social level."

"I guess the gossip was irresistible, and once it got started people had to repeat it. A couple of summers ago Frank and Joan Witt took a cottage with us up in Michigan. A good deal of the time Joan and I were alone with our kids because our husbands had to stay here working. When Al and Frank were able to join us, we all had a lovely time together. There were picnics, hikes, cocktail parties with other families from Hamilton. We may have gone through a case of vodka a little too quickly while we were there, but at no time was there even a suggestion of my getting physically involved with Frank. My goodness, our children were all right there in the house. Maybe the story was started by someone who saw the four of us at a cocktail party.

"But by the time we got back to town the rumor was in full flight. My own mother even asked me about it. I laughed it off, I couldn't believe it. But then we all started to hear about it everywhere. A friend of Al's warned him to keep an eye on his wife. People were whispering about it downtown behind the mayor's back. A cousin of Joan's spread it wherever she went.

"Finally, we had a two-family meeting to discuss what to do. We seriously considered not seeing each other socially anymore, at least for a while. Then we decided we would be giving in to the rumor, and why let a malicious piece of gossip ruin our lives? So the next summer we all went right back and rented the cottage again up in Michigan. A few times I've gone places with Frank when Al didn't feel like coming along and Joan couldn't. Once I helped him put on his bow tie when it fell off at a Christmas party. You should have heard them after that."

Didn't all the gossip ever make her long for the anonymity of a big city?

"I guess I was upset for about one afternoon. Then I thought well, it's my life. I probably fed the rumor a bit at parties and dances by being openly friendly, maybe even affectionate, toward Frank. This is a town where just having lunch in Cincinnati with someone else's spouse can lead to embarrassing talk. In fact, it can lead to a big fight. But I've never wanted to be in a big city. People I hardly know say 'hi' to me here every day. I live happily and well. Anywhere you go you feel the warmth— in backyards or stores or gatherings. You should have seen my son's Bar Mitzvah, it was the best time anybody ever had. Of course, the Witts were there and Frank's a wonderful dancer. He danced with me, and I guess that pushed the rumor along, too. But I can't help that. I like it here.

"If I yearn for anything, it's for the sixties. They were my decade, but I wasn't in them. Al and I got married so young I didn't really have a chance to move around and live the kind of life that kids in the sixties had. I miss that. Maybe that was the way to live. I never even got to park and neck. I don't know, maybe if I had it to do all over again I'd do the same thing. Certainly, I wouldn't let gossip determine who my friends were."

The rumor about Anita Weisman and Frank Witt had a corollary. When Hamilton grew tired of it, a twist was added. Frank and Anita were through with each other, people said, but now

Joan Witt and Al Weisman had fallen madly in love. The supposed switch enlivened many a dull evening.

The Witts and the Weismans went on seeing each other, perhaps a little less frequently. The rumor was sometimes amusing, sometimes annoying, but it could not help making all four of them self-conscious. To that degree it damaged their friendship, diminished their closeness. Though the gossip faded eventually, it had worked its way into the fantasy life of a large segment of the community.

In the end the real vigor of the story, indeed its sexiness, had nothing to do with its truth or falsity but with its use as fuel for the imaginations of others. The rumor literally fed on itself until it was as big and important as any other communal obsession, from the fear that integration would rot the schools to the conviction that getting ahead had less to do with talent than connection. The point was not that any of these notions was true or false, merely that they burrowed into the collective town mind with a mythic intensity far out of proportion to their practical application in anyone's life.

On the gossip level, stories about Anita Weisman and Frank Witt flourished with less viciousness than sheer vicarious pleasure. The rumor was not only a defense against boredom, it was an attempt to give meaning and morality to the surrounding dailiness, to order life—even humdrum life—against chaos. Anita Weisman was surpassingly glamorous in Hamilton, Frank Witt was powerful; they made a famous couple. The objects of both envy and contempt, they filled a void—not as huge as Captain Symmes's Polar Voids, but all the same a vacancy in people's lives. Unlike Symmes, they were not, of course, spreading the story themselves, but like him, they engaged the town's fantasies. As to whether they themselves actually did make the match rumor decreed for them, no one else would ever know, really.

XIV

FIRST FAMILY

Before he went back into the air force during the Korean War, Bill Beckett was driving his twelve-year-old daughter Emily to a friend's house one Saturday morning. Emily was retailing her school gossip about who was most popular, which girl had only one ratty dress, which boys were cute. Usually her father could be counted on to interrupt that it was not nice to make fun of unfortunate girls with soiled dresses. This morning he said nothing. Was he worried about business? The town? At the time, her father was not only Hamilton's leading industrialist but also its mayor. He looked grim, stricken, not the irritated way he got when something was wrong at the paper company or city hall. He could be moody, Emily already knew well, but he seldom was when they were out driving together on a Satur-day.

Without warning, Bill Beckett pulled off onto a shoulder. Emily looked at him to ask if anything had happened to the car, but her father was resting his head on the steering wheel, sob-bing. Emily had never seen him like this before, and she did not know what to do. Whatever was going on, she thought she should not be there. Because of the kind of man her father was

—controlled, strong, unbending—she was at once shocked, ashamed, elated. A car went by them, then another, like years in Emily's life. Yet it could not have been more than thirty or forty seconds before Bill Beckett raised his head and said simply, "He did it himself." Then he drove on, delivering his daughter to her friend's house on time. Emily felt afterward she could almost hear herself growing up during the moment by the side of the road. She knew enough not to ask what or who her father had meant because she could figure that out for herself.

Unlike most people in town the Becketts had ancestors that counted. As all light can be measured by its diminished power in relation to the sun, the social classes of Hamilton could be seen from one perspective as existing only to magnify the illumination of the first families. These several families, clans really, traced their lineage either to the founding of the town, the growth of its industry, or both. Beyond that, they counted back to Pennsylvania and Massachusetts, and from there to England, Scotland, and Germany. When Bill Beckett's grandfather, the first William Beckett, had founded the Beckett Paper Company in 1848, he had help from his father-in-law, John Woods. As the town's first entrepreneur, Woods made fortunes in everything he touched, from land to railroads to manufactured goods. With a timely loan and shrewd advice from Woods, Beckett built his paper mill into an enterprise that barely survived the Civil War to thrive in the late nineteenth-century publishing boom. But according to Hamilton legend, there was an unseen cost in William Beckett's alliance with John Woods.

Woods had several daughters who married into what became Hamilton's best families, all multiplying and prospering by the 1870s. Woods himself, however, was subject to fits of melancholy, terrifying bouts of wrath and despair which, it was said, were bequeathed to his descendants. The Becketts, for generations the most prosperous of all, were also hardest hit by the so-called "Woods strain." They contended over the years with alcoholism, depression, even suicide. What Emily Beckett had

discovered that Saturday morning over thirty years ago was that
her favorite uncle, Daniel Beckett, had not in fact died from an
early heart attack, as the family put out and the loyal newspaper
repeated, but had asphyxiated himself in his garage while his
wife was asleep upstairs.

Bill Beckett, or William Beckett II as he was occasionally
called, reigned in Hamilton from the 1920s into the 1980s. As
in England, reigning did not necessarily mean ruling. In the
1920s, Bill Beckett was a young man, perhaps only Prince of
Wales, and by the 1980s he had relinquished most of his power
to emerge as elder statesman and unofficial chairman of the
board of the Hamilton establishment. Still, during most of that
long period, excepting when he was away at war, very few issues
were decided in Hamilton without Bill Beckett's strong leadership. Twice he was mayor, many times he was a city councilman.
Three decades later he was still remembered, though he denied
a key role, for having blocked the entry of the Fisher Body
Company into Hamilton's labor market, and he was widely
given credit, or blame, for the fact that unions were so slow to
gain even a toehold in the community. Yet he was also a patron
who led the reform of city government, as his grandfather had
a century earlier, and supported the arts unstintingly. His critics
said he ran the town through his business, his wealth, and his
various political posts, and that he manipulated every municipal
dealing to his own advantage. Admirers said he participated
actively and generously in the life of the community, contribut-
ing not only his talents but also his money to many civic and
cultural organizations that substantially benefited Hamilton.

Even after his retirement from the Beckett Paper Company
in the mid-1970s, no one was neutral toward Bill Beckett.

"They don't come like Uncle Bill anymore," said his nephew,
the banker Tom Rentschler. "He's done more for this town than
anyone since his grandfather, William the Conqueror."

"He has lorded it over the town for too long, and he's gotten
away with some things he doesn't talk about," said a daughter
of one of the other first families.

A former employee revered him. "He's a good man to work for, very fair, and he helped me put my kids through college," she said.

"He's an arrogant old S.B. if you'll pardon the expression," said another former employee. "A rich man's son who kept decent industry out of Hamilton, yet, by God, he's a psychologist and a good judge of men. For years he knew just how to keep the union out by hiring a whole family, including the one black sheep who drank too much. Then he'd give everyone that stuffed dead bird at Thanksgiving and they'd all vote against the union when the time came."

"It's too bad Bill Beckett is anti-Semitic because he's so well educated and cultured. He deprives himself of our company and we're deprived of his," said a prominent member of Hamilton's Jewish community.

"Nonsense," said another, "he's no anti-Semite. We've served together on several of the same committees, and he's never been anything but friendly."

"Old Bill's a fine boy and not too bad a tennis player," said the nonagenarian doyenne, twenty years Bill Beckett's senior, of another old family.

"Who wants to touch the hand Bill Beckett's hand touched?" asked a clerk at Elder-Beerman's department store one day after waiting on him.

Whether patron or scourge, his environment, like his past, circled the man. Bill Beckett's garden, designed by him and nourished by his wife to express the more exotic yearnings of her husband, was spectacular, like that of an ancient and immaculately kept English estate. Yew trees mingled with weeping spruce, ferns, flowering crab apple, a grape arbor; beside a serpentine brick wall built by Bill Beckett himself were coralbells, dusty miller, geraniums, Queen Anne's lace, succulent white pine with long-stalked green cones and tassels. The garden was structured by hedges and brief plots of deep green lawn, dotted with Hosta lilies and American Beauty roses, presided over by a stately ash tree and a great oak whose pedigree rivaled that of its owner. From the ash hung a swing that fifty years of Becketts had grown up on.

The elegance of the Beckett house was quieter. It was stated simply in deep couches, plush carpets, old tables, silver trays, portraits of the ancestors. Bill Beckett, it was agreed by those who knew the family's past, was like his grandfather. William Beckett I had a stern, straight mouth turned slightly down at the corners, with eyes of such probity and determination that, it was said, a dishonest man could not even look at his photograph without turning away. When Bill Beckett himself entered a room, whether it was one of his own or in the home of a friend or downtown in the City Club, Hamiltonians would visibly strive to look casual. Men tried to be inconspicuous as they felt their tie knots to check for straightness, their middle suit button to see if it was fastened. Bolder ones would talk louder to make it less obvious they were inclining their heads to hear what Mr. Beckett had to say. Women smiled wanly as they worried about their hair and turned their good sides toward the slightly stooping, exquisitely groomed, aristocratic sparrow who had just graced their presence with his own. The right glance from him could illuminate an evening; he had another glance that could reduce anyone to feeling like a termite.

"Bill Beckett is A-One," a policeman had said while describing Hamilton's hierarchy. "The Becketts are the seeds of this town." It seemed relevant that he chose "seeds" over "roots." Seeds, of course, precede roots and bear even less resemblance to the branches, leaves, and efflorescences of the fully grown plant. Whether or not he intended it to, the policeman's words implied a primal relationship between the Becketts and what the rest of Hamilton had become. If the Becketts were seeds, Hamilton was bush and tree, flower and thorn.

Though he loomed grandly over the town, Bill Beckett's physique was tidy, and seven decades had bent him a little. The movement of no muscle, however, was wasted as he pursued his forward course. His gaze, whether it included a spry smile or the hereditary grimace reflected in the family portraits on his walls, influenced a room the way a sunset's pigments are spread over everything it touches. If he were at Trinity Episcopal Church, sweeping in wearing his majestic blue choir robe, parishioners suppressed the impulse to turn from their hymnals, but no one sat ignorant of his entrance. Elsewhere, he favored dark suits with a dotted bowtie on a striped button-down shirt.

At home, the master was no less presentable than his house or his garden. His straight, thinning gray hair was combed back close and tight on his scalp. His large azure eyes stared evenly as they had at obedient associates and dissident unionists alike for half a century. Below a nose that was a prominent pink, Bill Beckett's set lips turned down, not dourly, but with the assured punctiliousness of a schoolmaster up in his lessons. He sat perfectly still when he talked, his life emerging less as story than history, a history both bright and bleak.

"My great-grandfather came here from Pennsylvania before 1800. Before that members of my family presume to trace themselves back to the martyred Archbishop of Canterbury, Thomas à Becket. But Becket was a Catholic priest not allowed to marry, so if he had sons what does that make me?" Bill Beckett gave a pleased little laugh that contained the rustle of dry leaves, not quite a cackle. His daughters thought he communed with the past, particularly with his own ancestors, not because he was getting old himself, but because he had no sons. Two baby boys had been stillborn to his wife, Fritzie Beckett; only her daughters had survived. Bill Beckett spent enough time in the past so that when he spoke of his dead relatives he even included what would have been their present ages.

"My grandfather was born in Hamilton and would be one hundred fifty-nine now. The Beckett Paper Company he founded is one hundred thirty-two. My father would be one hundred twenty. Since I have no sons I am the last of the Becketts, and I can't grieve. I wouldn't want to inflict that on anyone. I am satisfied there will be no future Becketts."

Bill Beckett's daughters, Emily and Lucy, felt he indeed had wished for sons long ago, but they agreed it was not easy to be

a Beckett. There had been so much accomplishment that everyone in the family was expected to produce. Excellence was only
the norm. There had been enough tragedy for each generation
to carry, along with the compulsion to achieve, a dread of the
consequences of failure. His brother Dan was not the only victim of despair in Bill Beckett's family. Altogether, he had lost
two brothers, a sister, an uncle, and a niece to suicide. In other
societies or centuries, an invading army or the plague might
have cut such a swath. Among European Jewry a single family
could lose more to the crematoria. But in one family in a quiet
Middle Western town, a rash of suicides was almost unthink-
able.

The tendency to succeed among the Becketts was at least
equally strong. Bill Beckett's great-grandfather, John Woods,
may have suffered from melancholy, but it did not stop him
from bringing a canal and railroads through Hamilton, nor
from clearing swampland to build factories, hydraulics, a law
firm, and a financial empire. Bill Beckett himself, in addition to
his paper company, became chairman of the board of trustees
of Miami University at Oxford and held board memberships at
a life insurance company, Cincinnati Gas and Electric, a bank,
and a radio station. A lover and promoter of music, he not only
sang in his church choir but was also chairman of the board of
the Cincinnati Symphony Orchestra. His grandfather and both
his parents had preceded him as the ornaments of Hamiltonian
professional and social life. Bill Beckett's mother, Mary, who
presided over the town's society for decades, set standards of
behavior and performance that seemed to recede upward
whenever a member of her family approached them. In an
alternating current of affection and pressure, she doted on her
brood and found them desperately short of her mark, sending
signals that both nurtured and confused. She insisted on obe-
dience to her wishes and respected no one until he or she had
broken away. An aristocrat who believed in democracy, she used
her influence to keep the Junior League out of Hamilton, not
because it would have admitted the likes of Anita Weisman, but

because, in the nineteen thirties and forties, it would not have. The Junior League eventually came anyway, and a couple of decades later it accepted Anita Weisman. But Mary Beckett, hating snobbery, had virtually no friends who did not share the essential aspects of her own background, and she issued the most exclusive invitations in Hamilton. Each fair-weather Sunday after church, she gave decorous little tennis gatherings at which, it was often maintained, the town's business and social destiny were decided.

It could be tormenting to try to follow such acts. One of the sons of the first William Beckett could not bear the burdens of being a Beckett in Hamilton and drifted west to Omaha in the 1870s. In the 1970s Bill Beckett's eldest daughter Lucy felt if she stayed in town she could neither live down the past nor up to it, so she moved to Cleveland.

But fear of failure did not seem to account for so many suicides in one family. Meditations on suicide often call it internalized aggression, homicidal rage finding no object acceptable other than the self. An ego is undone either because it is insufficiently developed or cannot place its alienated self within a caring environment. It boils and panics and looks for an exit. Suicides within a family, sometimes repeating themselves on the same date years later, as occurred with two pairs of Beckett relatives, mark the annals of self-annihilation, but the urge to imitate or even join is not enough to destroy an individual. Various Becketts were afflicted with depression, alcoholism, sterility, feelings of inferiority, but so are members of most large families in which suicide is never experienced. Freud said, "no one finds the mental energy to kill himself unless, in the first place, he is . . . at the same time killing an object with whom he has identified himself, and in the second place, is turning against someone else." The Church calls suicide a sin not only against God but against the continuity of mankind. In his own periodic despondency, Bill Beckett's recourse was neither to psychology nor theology but to that most quintessentially American attribute, self-control.

"It is not easy to be a Beckett," Bill Beckett would say, "but keeping a grip on yourself does wonders. Suspicions and accusations are always directed at the prominent, especially if they have shown assertiveness and a demonstration of enterprise. There is some inspiration, I believe, in my ancestors and their attainments. I have failed to live up to them in some ways and excelled them in others. Being a Beckett seems a cushy thing to someone down the road, but we are as liable to be overwhelmed by despair, obviously, as anyone. I don't know why certain of my relatives did away with themselves. 'The Woods strain?' I've had infinite occasions to ponder, and I've never thought of a more satisfactory explanation.

"My mother met each adversity with stoicism and determination. She held on to what was hers—in life and death. Mother always cited King Lear. Had he not disposed of his kingdom and his authority, she felt, his story would not have been so tragic. For herself, she retained all property until the end and provided in her will for her shares in the Beckett Paper Company to continue to be held in trust after her death. She knew she could only control up to a point and then had to hope for the best. Not everyone could survive with those hopes." Bill Beckett paused an instant, then added a filial doxology. " 'As it was in the beginning, is now and ever shall be, world without end.' "

But he would pick right up again in his controlled sparrow's way, Hamilton's restrained *eminence grise,* to continue his version of the world. Bill Beckett often appeared to have something on his mind other than what he was permitting himself to express, but perhaps it was only that he was looking at the reflection of what he said inside himself, listening for its echo. Sometimes what he seemed to hear would then bound up from his recesses to be verbalized, revealing him more naturally than his exactitude and candor.

"We had a huge old three-storied house across from the Beckett Paper Company. That's where I grew up, and my mother stayed there her whole life, even when the neighborhood declined. Nowadays, executives would shudder at the thought of living next door to their factories, but that's what we did. After my mother died I couldn't bear to see it become a rooming-house, so I had it torn down for a parking lot that we needed. After that, my sisters never mentioned it again, wouldn't even let it come up in conversation, wouldn't go along the street where it had been, wouldn't visit the paper company itself. They never forgave me, but my God, I think of the old house too. I dream of it every night. Sometimes I'm outside, sometimes inside, but every night I see that house." Bill Beckett's dreaming probably contained neither more nor less of his wishes and dread than anyone else's, but his musings on the house he grew up in, however factual, were enriched by a component of fantasy. It was as though his memory, if properly applied to a target, could lead him through a locked door into another existence, back into the old house itself.

"The house withstood the flood that came in 1913 and destroyed so much of Hamilton. My father had horses drowned, almost everyone did. The water rose thirteen feet where the paper mill was and destroyed it. But the house stood. Although we were marooned upstairs, we stayed dry just inches away from the high-water mark. Hundreds of people in homes smaller than ours were simply carried off by the flood. I happened to have measles at the time, but we had food and extra supplies of coal. The Red Cross went from home to home in rowboats throwing bread and apples to people trapped inside. Dirt came out of cracks in the floors all the rest of my childhood, flood mud."

The 1913 flood, ravaging Hamilton a few days after Easter, divided the town's history from its memory. Before the flood was a kind of legendary time when whatever happened was unreclaimable. The flood swept much of the town away and killed one hundred eighty-three Hamiltonians. Ministers compared the flood to the Flood. The rising waters were seen as a combination of God's wrath against general sin, and vengeance for the particular vice of tampering with nature, because the growing town had earlier diverted the Miami River from its own natural, looping course into a curve more favorable to Hamilton industry. It was not hard to convince the ten thousand people whose homes were destroyed by the flood that they had been struck from on high. Flood mud was the remnant of their chastisement. Elders gained veneration for having lived through it, as though they had been at Waterloo or Chickamauga, while younger generations respected the blind force of nature and fate. When the terror had been retold often enough, it became only a story for grandchildren to marvel at. The flood marked off ancient from modern times in Hamilton, the history of the community from the memory of an individual. Like a dream whose details vanish while its mood remains, much of Hamilton's past was consumed in the flood, but the town's heritage endured. Remembering when water came so close to destroying all he knew, Bill Beckett's imagination was briefly engaged as if a gear had been shifted within him.

"I dream I'm in the swing, too, the old swing hanging from the ash," he said, momentarily leaping past the distinction between his childhood house that stood against the flood and his present home with the elegant garden. "I sit in that swing and I swing high over the whole town. I have an image of people gazing up at me and dancing in the streets. Cheering for me. My people loving me. What a vision!

"And what a joke," he added, bringing himself down from the swing to the firm soil of his garden. "The laugh was on me. I was once in the state senate, having decided that it was a civic duty to serve in public life and winning a seat during the Eisenhower landslide of 1956. I ran for reelection confidently, sure I could finish what I'd started. I couldn't imagine they wouldn't vote me back in. But it was a big Democratic year and they didn't love me after all, and I lost, so the hell with them.

"Since I couldn't run the Beckett Paper Company by phone from Columbus anyway, the voters did me a favor. But I think the principle of citizen political participation is sound. Business leaders should take their turn in politics, or high offices will all go to the demagogues. That's why I served as mayor and that's why I went to the state senate. It grieves me to see the absence of authentic community leaders. Mayor Witt's good here, we could use a dozen more of him, but he gets no support. The idea is abroad that if a leader proposes something, it must be for selfish reasons. So the outstanding citizens, discouraged before they start, don't go into politics. Important public offices are filled by pedestrian hacks. Hamilton reflects the nation. There are plenty of great men in the United States today, but they are leading private lives. I guess I'm just a common scold."

Pausing, Bill Beckett stared at his Taxus hedge by the serpentine wall he had put there with his own hands, and adjusted his bowtie. He walked to a bench in the middle of his garden and sat perfectly still, neither clasping his hands nor threading his fingers together as he gathered his reflections. When he was young Bill Beckett had studied engineering at MIT; he had never lost the precision. His blue eyes, catching the sun and adding their own gleam, included the contradictions his daughters felt in their father—tense and wanting fun, proud and critical, powerful and fearing his demons.

At his most serious, Bill Beckett thought of business. Rather than continue in engineering, he had come home to run the paper company. He had no regrets. Business for him was more than a livelihood, more even than a way of life. It was a philosophy of life, it was the way creation organized itself most productively.

"You never suffer from another man's success," he said. "Whatever my competitor can do, I can do better. Therefore, I am better off if he is successful since I have only to improve upon what he has already proved possible. Another man's gain does not diminish me but enhances my opportunities. His success can only be bad if he achieves it in a degenerate or ignorant manner, such as by cutting market prices in an attempt to control demand. Price wars destroy profits and ultimately hurt us all, the public too. Cutting prices is a business sin. Profits are not only an economic necessity but a social responsibility. They have manifestly been the best way to build our civilization, support our culture, maintain our continuity with the best in the American past.

"I deplore the decline of paternalism. The Beckett Paper Company was a family in the days before unionization. It is much harder to make a profit, please your customer and to turn out a good product now than it was in pre-union days. There is slackness, poor productivity, indifferent workmanship, constant wrangling. We feel a pistol is being pointed at our heads all the time, at the public's head as well. Forcing wages up has been the greatest single source of inflation, it's nearly destroyed the economy. I used to raise wages faster and further before the union came, and I did it voluntarily. In the old days it wasn't just my father and my grandfather and I who loved being at work; all the people there loved it. Almost all. It was a joy to be at the Beckett Paper Company before the union came, a joy to be there every day! Every single day carried its own pleasure. Then the agitators came and sowed their poison, and it's never been the same since."

Bill Beckett will one day be accorded substantial obituary space, not only in Hamilton, but surely in Cincinnati and Dayton, and possibly more distant cities as well. His virtually textbook Calvinist conservatism may be noted as much as his board memberships and community contributions. The obituarist could suggest gently that Mr. Beckett might have been more at home in an age when pay raises were not regarded as a worker's right but an employer's gift. But the factual account will miss the life, sailing right by it like a ship passing an island where someone is marooned, as the young Bill Beckett was once marooned during the 1913 flood. To him, the tragedies of two brothers and one sister were a warning. The specter of suicide could destroy him or it could goad him, like a classical hero being tested by the gods, toward a destiny more exalted than he would otherwise have achieved. Dr. Johnson might ascribe to Bill Beckett, as he did to Richard Savage, the general fault of harshness, the general excellence of dignity. Bill Beckett became the rare American aristocrat whose sufferings transformed him, like those of Franklin Roosevelt (whom he both admired and despised), from a rich man's son into a leader.

The symbols in such a life tended to merge, after seven decades, with fragments of reality. Memory and metaphor were not always easy to distinguish. In Bill Beckett's dreams, his mother's house, the home he had destroyed after her death, held him again. In other dreams, when he was in his old garden swing, a swinger over his whole town, he received the adulation of multitudes. Was Thomas à Becket concealed in that house, waiting once more for Henry II's assassins? Was there a regal fantasy—being born again, this time a king—riding on the swing that hung from a genuine family tree, the great ash that was older than the town of Hamilton? Would it be revealing to call his mother's house a womb that he had finally—though not without guilt—outgrown, the swinging emblematic of both sex and power? Or would this simply obscure the man within the dreams more certainly than a glacial recitation of his vital statistics? Bill Beckett, given to speculation in ideas, if not money, had thought about these things. He did not know.

Near the close of our last visit together, he made a wandering promenade to a far corner of his garden. When he bent to consider his Hosta lilies, his daughter Emily remarked quietly that her father was no doubt adoring them as well as becoming irritated because they were not growing faster. Bill Beckett looked up.

"Whatever it means, I have an active dream life. Communion with my forebears is part of it, yet there's more. Composed as I am, I still have a very energetic group of dreams. Adventurous. I would say 'unspeakably' adventurous. As always. I asked an old friend the other day if things were really as different from the past as they seemed to be. 'Totally different,' he told me. 'There are no old fuddy-duddies anymore.' That stopped me. I realized that meant we had become them," said the last of the Becketts.

XV

HIS HONOR—
Hamilton United

When Mayor Frank Witt decided to hold the regular council meeting on the evening of Washington's birthday, as scheduled, the grumbles were muted. It was the middle of the week, and most people had taken the holiday as part of a long weekend combined, in the new fashion, with Lincoln's birthday. Some council members thought the father of the country was still due his own day as he had been in their childhoods, which would have allowed them the night off. But their own children had gone to school that morning, and they themselves had worked, so they sat amiably with Mayor Witt in his office until it was time for the meeting to begin.

Muzak was spreading its toneless cheer through the office, and after "Pennies from Heaven" gave way to "Vaya con Dios," Mayor Witt rose unsteadily to shut it off. "Extra beer at dinner, Frank?" asked the portly councilman, Stanton Newkirk. He was joking, they were good friends.

"Not hardly, Stan." The mayor could allow himself a country phrase now that it was almost fashionable for a prominent Hamiltonian to have some Kentucky in him. Frank Witt had been born in Hamilton, but part of his family was up from the Kentucky hills and one great-grandmother had been a full-blooded Cherokee. The great-grandmother was preserved in Mayor Witt's appealing combination of large bones and delicate features, giving the impression of both power and sensitivity. The features were pulled together now into a tight wince. "Doctor said this afternoon I have a urinary infection. It's got me in some real pain."

"Tonight shouldn't be tough, Frank," Ann Antenen, the vice-mayor, said. "We'll be out of here by eight-thirty." It was almost seven-thirty, the official time for the beginning of council sessions.

"I hope so. I want to say something about energy, though." Frank Witt was concerned that Hamiltonians, in the coldest winter on record, were leaving their furnaces on while they were away from home all day. He had bailed out the neighboring town of Fairfield twice in the last six months, in the summer by letting it have some of Hamilton's water, and now with propane gas to heat the Fairfield schools.

The winter was especially fierce. A few weeks earlier, Frank and Joan Witt had been on their way to Washington for a mayors' conference with the President when a blizzard had snowed them in at the Cincinnati airport. They managed to get to a Cincinnati hotel, but the roads back to Hamilton were impassable. The following day there was no highway open to the airport, which was still closed anyway. The hotel kitchen shut down, then the heat went. "Yeah, romantic, stranded in a hotel like that," Frank Witt told a friend when he finally got home two days later, "but the night we were supposed to eat at the White House we sat in our freezing room sharing a bag of potato chips. I'll take the White House. When we got back to Hamilton, though, it never looked so good."

Infection or not, the forty-two-year-old Frank Witt walked from his office with the bearing of a professional athlete—a heavy build over a flat stomach and a nimble step—perhaps a just-retired athlete about to go on to his next career. Since becoming mayor he had been selected as one of the five outstanding young men in Ohio and voted Hamilton's Man of the Year, a sort of municipal most-valuable-player award. Many friends and a few political enemies already assumed he had too much energy to be satisfied forever in Hamilton, energy that simply could not be contained by the town. They predicted he would look for a statewide office, possibly go national before long. Noticing that tonight, as usual, there were only a half-dozen visitors scattered around the ample benches of the imposing council chamber on the top floor of the City Building, Frank Witt shook his head. He may even have scowled. "So many things affect John Q., but he won't, in all deference to him, show up and get informed," the mayor often said. "That's the challenge in this job, getting John Q. interested in what's going on around him. This is such a deeply fragmented community that the fragments don't even speak to one another, and they paper it all over with politeness. If we weren't polite, I guess we'd be in a fight every month."

Flanked by the other six council members, the mayor took his seat at the council table in front of a huge mural purporting to represent early days in Hamilton. A trapper in a coonskin cap was accompanied by several frontiersmen and militiamen in the tricornered hats of the Revolution. They carried muskets. In the background was the benign, natural countryside of nostalgia; great trees shaded gentle meadows while peaceful Indians toiled innocently at the land. The mural's title was "Founding of the Fortress—Fort Hamilton, October 1791." The caption read, "And so was born a city."

There was a brief prayer and the pledge of allegiance. Council members put lavalier microphones around their necks so the meeting could be recorded. The roll was called and the minutes of the previous meeting were read by a woman with the voice of a computer. This being so much rote, Hamilton's director of community development, Pat Landi, barely paid attention. He was thinking of a phone call he took that afternoon from a businessman in Florida who had given him a lead on a Canadian company wanting to build a plant somewhere in Ohio. Why not here? After the meeting he would tell the mayor and they would figure out how to lure the Canadians. If Hamilton got the new plant, Frank Witt would not be shy about taking the credit, but that was politics. Pat Landi was a civil servant; he was used to elected officials.

The municipal budget was under discussion as the council session began. City employees were due for a salary increase. After that would come a resolution to renew the license of the foster home for mentally retarded children. A member of the mental health board would be heard briefly. A zoning ordinance was to be passed switching some lots on the East Side from single-unit to multiple-family homes; that meant another neighborhood was sliding down a notch. Next, the council would consider a resolution for a street in the Second Ward ghetto to change its name in honor of a black soldier who had died in Vietnam. After they passed an ordinance to help a local businessman by allowing him to use a city alley as his own property, the council would adjourn. Ann Antenen was right; the agenda was easy.

The council got no further, however, than the city budget. A three-part question was asked of the city manager, Jack Kirsch, concerning expenditures. He paused a little before beginning to pick his way carefully through the answer. This was the kind of moment that always made Frank Witt nervous. He had other things to do, the council meetings could not begin to service his drive or his quickness. If only he could vault over the tedium. Sometimes he would interrupt to try to focus the point better, or he would tell a joke, or simply wink at a friend in the tiny audience. When a meeting seemed terminally boring, he liked to end it by saying, "If you want to soar with the eagles in the morning you can't hoot with the owls at night. Let's get out of here." On this night, Frank Witt said nothing at all as Jack Kirsch wound into the labyrinth of Hamilton's fiscal X-ray.

A sigh echoed through the council chamber from the mayor's microphone. One member thought the mayor was, though silent until now, suddenly impatient with the pace of the budget recitation and about to tell them all to speed it up. Stanton Newkirk remembered the pain Frank Witt had mentioned in his office. Ann Antenen saw an abyss opening beneath her. Pat Landi, still preoccupied with the Canadian manufacturer, thought for a moment that the mayor, disgusted with the progress of the meeting, might have let out an expletive in an undertone, a whispered, "Oh, shit." Yet this sigh seemed ominous to Landi. The sigh, amplified by the collar microphone, was longer, deeper than a sigh of impatience. It was no cursing, or grunt of agitation, or anxiety to get on to the next point or following topic. What everyone was listening to was mere air rushing to get out while it could, the hurried expulsion of Frank Witt's last breath. And then, his heart attack complete, the head of the man generally conceded to have the most vitality in Hamilton hit the council table, its bang resounding through the chamber because of the still-live microphone. For an instant the council members were as frozen as the pioneers and Indians in the mural behind the table where Mayor Witt's head lay. The next second they all rushed to him. The life squad, with its pumps and adrenaline and respirators and oxygen, was there within three minutes, but Frank Witt never breathed again.

The dead remind us. Alive, those we like best are still full of foibles. Dead, they become bearers of our values. We had better be good to them, speak no ill of them, because we are all headed in their direction. But when they have gone much earlier than we wish they had, we transform them utterly.

Think of those who die before their time. Great or anonymous—though it is the former, of course, whom we honor—their aura survives in everyone who knows them or hears of them. Alexander, Christ, Joan of Arc, Byron, Kennedy. They engender so much more faith than if they had lived out their spans. Their unmeasured promise seems the most obvious reason for this. What they would have done, if only. We never know their limits; in Christ's case, we say he had no limits at all. But another reason, more subtle, is also more important. Dying young, they never quite disappear. We always and only imagine them in their prime. What would an old gray Keats be? So we see them forever young, forever in their power, pledging more, about to do something absolutely great, even miraculous. They live on in the penumbral glow of special remorse for those who die with their promise unfulfilled. Incorporating both their hopes and their youth, their magic comes easy. One generation exaggerates; the next has a myth. After the council session on Washington's birthday—itself a form of ancestor worship—a new myth was gestating in Hamilton.

Frank Witt in life was tough, humorous, quick, ambitious, unregretful, kind, perceptive, unsatisfied. In death he was virtually all magnificence.

Bill Beckett, Hamilton's patriarch, had wished while Mayor Witt was alive that there were a dozen more of him. Not being able to hang on to the one Frank Witt it had, the town went into shock. On the sidewalks, Hamiltonians greeted each other more warmly than usual, drawing closer. Total strangers, yet not strangers at all, stood together a few moments, shaking their heads, saying, that's life, when they also meant, that's death. He was the best thing that ever happened to this town, a local booster said, and added, dying on the job was just like him. He was no saint, a level-headed friend said, but my God, how Hamilton and he needed each other. Hearing of his death, a contemporary of the mayor's sat dully at his desk and suddenly found himself incontinent for the first time in decades, his pants wet seconds before his cheeks. A former Hamiltonian wrote from Texas: "Never was a community so blessed with such a devoted, honest and outstanding leader. This devotion was only exceeded by his love of his family. That's the way things should be in America, and I'll never forget Frank for his example." The Hamilton *Journal-News* called him the most popular mayor in the city's history, "a catalyst for positive action and a beacon of enthusiasm." The paper also endorsed a proposal to rename the main bridge across the Miami River; "Let this bridge, which unites Hamilton geographically, be a memorial to Frank Witt, mayor of Hamilton, who gave so much to unite Hamilton in spirit."

Beginning to mourn what she and her husband had, were going to have, had missed altogether, Joan Witt looked resolute at the hugely crowded funeral in the First United Methodist Church. Anita and Al Weisman were a few rows back, stunned past words. City council members sat with their families scattered throughout the church. Representatives of the community fragments Frank Witt tried to bring together were all there, from the newest Kentucky arrivals who shared the mayor's heritage to the blacks whose grandparents had come to Hamilton when it was a stop on the Underground Railway to the Becketts whose people came before the town was a town.

One eulogist said Frank Witt's concern was not for Hamilton as an intangible city but for each citizen as an individual. Another said he had the rare gift of making each person in his presence comfortable, dignified, confident. Perhaps unconsciously referring to the rumor Hamilton had had so much fun with, that the mayor and Anita Weisman had been seen together as far away as Michigan, one speaker declared, "His love had no city limits." Each tribute was fully meant; there was among the throng a desire to enshrine not just Frank Witt's memory but his vitality. His family led the way. The mayor's oldest daughter Amy insisted on joining her Taft High School choirmates in singing at the service. "My father would want me to," she told a friend, "not for him, for Hamilton." Their closing hymn was "How Great Thou Art."

The City Building was closed for an hour the day of the funeral. Then the town started up again. Frank Witt's successor, Ann Antenen, quiet and reticent, partial to historic preservation in contrast to his own flamboyant passion for the future, was the first woman mayor in Hamilton's history.

XVI

HAMILTON DIVIDED

No one in Hamilton could remember when the *Messiah* at Christmas, or the Mozart *Requiem* at Easter, had ever sounded as glorious and reverential as they did under Sam Shie's direction. He was the choral director at Taft High School, handling about two hundred singers a year, and everyone—superiors, colleagues, students—rated him an excellent teacher and a superb musician. He pronounced his name "shy," and he waited patiently for people to tire of word plays on that, which generally happened by the second or third meeting. Both the boys' and girls' individual choruses, as well as the combined Taft Chorale, had won "superior" awards at state contests, though Sam Shie himself said that his real thrill came from just hearing them sing as well as they could. Shie had led the Taft Treble-Aires, including seventeen-year-old Amy Witt, in singing "How Great Thou Art" at Mayor Witt's funeral. To go with Handel and choral selections from Brahms, Shie would add Vivaldi's "Gloria" at alternate Christmases, and he was annually praised and thanked unstintingly, even by those whose musical education ended with "God Bless America." When he thought about it later, Sam Shie could not recall hearing an unkind word in Hamilton until August 1, 1978, when his nightmare began.

On that idle afternoon in the ripeness of summer, Sam Shie's world became, in both the jargon and literal senses of the word, unreal.

In the next weeks, a gentle life became an individual crisis, then a community controversy, at last a catastrophe splitting Hamilton ideologically as, long ago, the great flood had isolated the two sides of the town from one another physically. Perhaps nothing since the flood had caused so much panic. Astounding, chaotic language flowed over Hamilton as unexpectedly as the water once had. Cocksucker, motherfucker, erection, diarrhea, jerk off, get fucked. Not words and phrases heard in polite Hamiltonian company, especially at a public hearing conducted by adults. Yet there they were, big municipal toothaches, right in front of everyone in the Board of Education Building on Dayton Street. If this was a nightmare, Sam Shie was well into his third month of it when the hearings began in October, and he showed no signs of waking up.

It started when Shie went downtown on the first of August to shop at Elder-Beerman, Hamilton's largest department store. As he looked at clothing for his young son, he ran into Connie Beale, who was choral director at Wilson Junior High, a feeder school for Taft High. Sam and his wife, Mary, were friends with Connie, a radiant young blonde living alone in a new apartment. Connie, who had often visited the Shies, admired their taste and asked Sam to help her decide how to decorate her windows.

As they looked at drapes, Sam said later, he began to feel like going to the bathroom. He had recurrent colitis which caused him diarrhea, at times without much warning. Having made some drapery selections for Connie, Sam started edging toward the Elder-Beerman men's room. He ran into a music student, who delayed Sam several minutes with talk of a rock concert he had been to and questions about the chorus teacher's summer vacation. Finally shaking himself loose, Sam again started for the men's room—by this time, he said later, feeling real pressure from his bowels. Once more he ran into a friend, a former music student now working as a salesgirl in Elder-Beerman. She asked him about his plans for the choral season, and Sam patiently, though uneasily, gave a quick rundown of the Treble-Aires' schedule. Connie Beale said after the nightmare was well under way that she knew Sam was uncomfortable and anxious to get to the bathroom without wanting the embarrassment of explaining why. Sam finally got into the men's room around three P.M. while Connie continued shopping and shortly afterward left Elder-Beerman's. This is almost the last point in the story that everyone agreed on.

According to Sam Shie, when he got into the men's room he did have diarrhea. His colitis attacks kept him on the toilet longer than most people. In this instance, Sam stayed in the men's room about half an hour.

According to the police and Elder-Beerman's management, that particular men's room had become a gathering place for homosexuals. Women shoppers had complained about effeminate men rushing by them in the drapery department to get to the men's room. Other men would come out tittering and mincing in a way that some Elder-Beerman customers, especially women, were finding offensive. The store management decided to put a stop to the use of their rest room as a sexual emporium. First, they had the doors removed from the three toilet stalls. Second, they hired a security guard to patrol that part of the store and make frequent visits to the men's room.

On the afternoon of August 1, the Elder-Beerman security guard was Neal Ferdelman, an off-duty policemen dressed in civilian clothes. At twenty-two, Ferdelman was only a rookie cop but a well-regarded one whose father had also been a policeman and who himself was working toward a college degree. It was Ferdelman's first day that summer as a plain-clothes security guard for Elder-Beerman, but a year earlier he had done the same kind of off-duty work.

Shortly after three o'clock, Neal Ferdelman entered the men's room, made a quick survey, saw that only one man was inside, and left. The man was Sam Shie, who occupied the center toilet of the three stalls whose doors had been removed. Afterward, Ferdelman said he noticed that Shie was wearing red gym shorts that were pulled up around his waist so he didn't see how Shie could have been making a bowel movement. Shie said they were ordinary jockey shorts and they were down around his ankles.

Ten or fifteen minutes later, Ferdelman stopped back in the men's room, and again Shie was its only occupant. According to Ferdelman, Shie's red shorts were still pulled up around his waist. This seemed strange to Ferdelman, but he did nothing because Shie was doing nothing. According to Shie, he was having a sustained attack of diarrhea. In either case, Ferdelman left the men's room and went about his rounds in Elder-Beerman.

After another fifteen minutes, Ferdelman made his third visit to the men's room and saw that Shie was still occupying the middle stall. Ferdelman washed his hands at the sink a few feet to the right of the stall. While he was drying them, he later testified, he turned around and saw Shie masturbating. This time, Ferdelman said, Shie's red shorts were pulled down and Shie was stroking his erect penis. Shie said he was doing nothing of the sort, but was only finishing his bowel movement. Ferdelman said he saw Shie for only a few seconds out of the corner of his eye, but Shie's motions were enough to convince him he was observing masturbation. Having noticed Shie on his two previous visits to the rest room, Ferdelman concluded that the suspect was engaging in what Ohio law describes as "public indecency." Although Ferdelman did not charge Shie with homosexual solicitation, the inference on the part of Shie's detractors was that he was masturbating for the purpose of enticing Ferdelman himself, an attractive young man in street clothes, now in the rest room for the third time since Shie had sat down. Shie maintained he was simply having diarrhea.

Whether Shie was stroking his penis or not (depending on whom one listened to), there was no doubt Ferdelman now pulled out the emblem of *his* identity—his policeman's badge—and proceeded to arrest the still sedentary Shie. Both men agreed later that Shie immediately protested his innocence and asked Ferdelman to look in the toilet bowl if he wanted proof of Shie's bowel movement. Ferdelman told Shie he had no interest in looking in toilets and to pull his pants up because he was being taken into custody.

Shie was first led, handcuffed, to the security room inside Elder-Beerman. The handcuffs were removed while Ferdelman and another officer questioned Shie. He was asked if he masturbated frequently in rest rooms. Shie, a polite and trusting man of almost Billy Budd-like ingenuousness, now made what everyone, himself included, came to regard as a major mistake. He told Ferdelman and the other security guard that twenty years before, at a high school picnic while he was a student, he had once masturbated in a rest room. Never since. The two security guards, however, now had reason to believe they had caught an habitual rest room masturbator who was even willing to admit to a previous incident. They put Shie's hands behind his back, again handcuffed him, marched him out through the department store, and took him in a patrol car two blocks to the police station, where he was booked and locked in a cell.

Shie was thirty-five years old and looked perhaps twenty-eight. He and his wife, Mary, also a teacher, had been married eleven years and had an eight-year-old boy named Phil. Because Shie related to his students extremely well and had won several state contests with the chorus, he was one of the most popular teachers at Taft, occupying a position similar, if not quite as visible, to that of a victorious athletic coach. Of medium height and with a stocky build that was just a few pounds short of roly-poly, Shie generally looked—it is impossible not to say—jolly. But for his arrest in their men's room, Elder-Beerman's would undoubtedly have been delighted to consider Sam Shie for the annual position of Santa Claus. With his large, open features and a tendency to smile even when he was serious, Shie could not have looked less the part of a furtive sex offender.

But appearances, as Sam Shie found out for himself, can not only deceive, they can destroy. After an hour in his jail cell, he was permitted the customary phone call. He reached his wife at home and, by everyone's account, said to her, "You know my usual problem. Well, I was arrested in Elder-Beerman's rest

room." The police, overhearing the remark, interpreted it to
mean they had indeed apprehended a regular men's room masturbator (at least) and assumed they had a lock on the case. Sam
and Mary Shie, on the other hand, maintained that he had only
been referring to the chronic colitis that at times kept him in a
rest room longer than other people. Shie was released in his
own custody, and the police notified him he was charged with
public indecency, a euphemism that usually implies observable
nakedness such as exposing oneself in a theater or urinating on
a sidewalk.

Shie knew he was in trouble, but he did not know how much.
He hired a lawyer and called the superintendent of schools,
Robert Quisenberry. Quisenberry, who had applied for the job
after Superintendent Peter Relic went to Washington in the
wake of his local defeat on the School Bond issue, was a former
junior high school principal whose reputation was built on a
"back to basics" approach to education. Where Relic had been
an idealist with theories, Quisenberry was a pragmatist with
experience. It was a simple enough pendulum effect often seen
in changes of leadership. When Quisenberry set about restoring
school discipline and raising educational standards, it meant
school expulsions increased and that annual class failures
jumped from under 150 to over 500 because students were no
longer promoted to the next grade unless they could actually
pass tests on the material presented in class. Though he occasionally liked to play poker, Quisenberry's great extracurricular
enthusiasm was for writing, to which he gave himself with the
devotion of a boy training to become a professional ballplayer.
He had not published any fiction, but he liked to keep several
manuscripts in the mail at all times. Richard Adams, Quisenberry was fond of saying, had fifty-five rejections on *Watership
Down* before it was accepted for publication.

Quisenberry heard Shie's story on the telephone—the arrest
and Sam's denial of the charges—and drove over to his house
to see him. Shie had been granted tenure only the previous
spring and was not aware at first that his position was now in
jeopardy. Bob Quisenberry was not sure Sam would want to

discuss the situation in front of Mary, but the Shies preferred to sit in their living room while eight-year-old Phil was sent out to play. Quisenberry, a precise man of forty-two whose large glasses gave him the look of an inquisitive owl, was sympathetic but firm.

"Messy thing to have happen to your summer, isn't it, Sam?"

"I couldn't have imagined it."

"You and Mary and your little boy were probably getting ready to go somewhere." Maybe they still would; a school super-intendent could be forgiven for wanting a problem to get out of town before it can polarize the community.

"Just to the concerts in Cincinnati and Dayton. I guess we'd go as far as Columbus for the Robert Shaw Chorale."

"Sam would figure out a way to get to Chicago for the Robert Shaw Chorale," Mary said.

"I'll do anything to protect my teachers, you know that, don't you?"

"I appreciate that. This is a school system I believe in. That's why I've stayed around for ten years."

"But I've also got to protect the students. We've got a problem here—I do and you do and the whole school administration does."

"What kind of problem? How big?"

"Well, a morals charge for a schoolteacher in a town this conservative just doesn't sit too well."

"But Mr. Quisenberry," Mary said, "You've heard Sam tell you he's not guilty."

"Bob. Call me Bob. It's his word against the policeman's."

"He's making it up. I was only sitting there."

"Pretty hard to work and live in a community after something like this has happened."

"Like *what* has happened? Nothing happened, Bob."

"It's tough to call a police officer a liar and make it stick. We could help you find another position. Start fresh."

"Hamilton's my life. I love teaching at Taft."

"This could get ugly. People can be mean."

"What do I do then?"

"Go to court and win, Sam. It's the only way you can come back into a Hamilton classroom."

Shie and his lawyer, Hank Masana, prepared for trial. In the charge of public indecency, Officer Ferdelman's affidavit specified masturbation in the Elder-Beerman rest room. But by now, Neal Ferdelman was not the only witness against Shie. There were also the other security guard at Elder-Beerman's, to whom Sam had said he had once before masturbated in a men's room, as well as two more officers at the police station who had overheard Sam tell Mary about "my usual problem." This was in the secondhand category lawyers call hearsay, and some of it was at least a moral, if not legal, invasion of the privacy of husband and wife. It added up, however, to the police believing they had a relatively solid case against Sam Shie.

Before becoming a lawyer, Hank Masana had been a policeman himself and a colleague of Neal Ferdelman's father. Masana was still a friend of the Ferdelman family—a situation Shie's supporters later likened to a conspiracy—and believed the young patrolman to be a credible witness. In advising Shie about his trial prospects, Masana stressed the fact that a parade of police uniforms could be quite impressive to a jury, especially when character witnesses were all that could be summoned against them.

Sam Shie saw himself surrounded. A nonevent became a dumb little soap opera that became a detective story that would now be a courtroom drama as it hurtled to its destination as a horror movie. Sam was beginning to feel like Joseph K, trapped in the bureaucratic labyrinth of Kafka's Prague instead of being nourished by the warmth of friendly, have-a-nice-day Hamilton. The board of education had cut him adrift, now his own lawyer was suggesting the forces against him were arrayed for victory. But this was only the private side of the nightmare.

The trial would be public and would be reported in the *Journal-News* during the comparatively slow summer news season, and then all his students—plus everyone else in town—would know Sam Shie was accused of masturbating in a downtown men's room. The nicest thing he would be called when school reopened would be fag, with the language ranging downward to cocksucker and—given adolescent creativity—below. And what about Mary, what about Phil?

But there was a way to avoid scandal and public humiliation for his family and himself. Hank Masana had talked to the prosecutor, who was willing to reduce the charge of public indecency to a simple disorderly conduct if Shie would plead no contest. This would mean no jury, no public trial at all, no publicity, just a one-hundred-dollar fine for disorderly conduct. After discussions with Mary and a few friends, but not with school officials, Sam Shie pled no contest in the last week of August.

Long before Spiro Agnew used the same plea to avoid a prison sentence on the charges that removed him from the vice-presidency, the no contest plea—*nolo contendere* (I do not wish to contend) in legal Latin—was a puzzle both to lawyers and the public. It is not the same as pleading guilty, because the defendant is not admitting his own culpability in the case, but it does constitute a decision not to contest the charges as they stand. The unresolved ambiguity leaves the defendant in a kind of legal limbo and is generally interpreted by the public as an admission of guilt. Sam Shie, after his own court appearance, was recorded as having been convicted of the lesser charge, disorderly conduct.

A disorderly conduct conviction would not necessarily result in the dismissal of a teacher from the Hamilton school system. The problem for the board of education was that the no contest plea meant that Sam Shie, regardless of the lesser charge of which he was convicted, had elected *not* to dispute the facts as alleged by Officer Ferdelman. Ferdelman's affidavit stated that Shie had been masturbating in a manner to constitute, as the school board interpreted it, "an immoral act of homosexual solicitation."

Superintendent Quisenberry had sent the assistant superintendent for personnel, Donald Helms, to observe the Shie case in court. When Helms, a by-the-numbers administrator who had taught in Karachi and Athens, duly reported the conviction to Quisenberry, the two administrators felt they had no choice. They summoned Shie and asked him to resign.

"But I'm innocent. I told you that before," Shie said in the superintendent's office on Dayton Street.

"According to the court records, you've been convicted," Quisenberry told him.

"Not of the original charge, not of public indecency."

"But Ferdelman's affidavit about masturbation still stands," Helms said. "Sam, you're in a no-win situation. You walk back into that classroom, some kid's going to call you a cocksucker."

"I can take that. Sticks and stones."

"But *we* can't take it, Sam," Quisenberry said. "We have rules about students using abusive language and obscenity with teachers. Do we enforce them in other cases but not in yours? And if we enforce them in yours too, what if the student says he's only coming to the logical conclusion of your own court conviction?"

"There's profanity on half the walls at Taft," Shie said. "Last year a teacher was called a motherfucker by a student, and everyone just laughed except the teacher, who couldn't even get the principal to send the student home."

"Nobody says we're perfect," Helms said, "but we at least try. With you back in front of a class, we can't even try."

"You're just guessing about the kids," Shie said. "It might be rough for a couple of days. Why don't we just see what happens?"

"Look Sam, you and your family have suffered enough," Helms said. "We don't want to see your teaching certificate revoked. You can still go anywhere in the state—if you go now."

"Is that a threat?"

"I told you," Helms said, "it's no-win."

"We have to ask for your resignation, Sam," Quisenberry said.

"You're not getting it."

August ended as badly for Sam Shie as it had begun. At a special meeting of the board of education on the last day of the month, Shie was ordered suspended without pay. The suspension would end as soon as the board could formally terminate his contract. One month from the day of his arrest, Shie was notified he was being fired.

A tenured teacher who wants to appeal a dismissal may request a hearing presided over by a referee. At the hearing, which resembles a trial, the teacher and the school board are each represented by their own attorneys. Unlike a trial, the referee only tenders his decision to the parties in disagreement. The judgment is not binding, and if either side objects to it, the case then goes into the court of appeals. According to the wishes of the defendant, the hearing before the referee can be public or private. The *Journal-News* had published only a brief item about Shie's disorderly conduct conviction, giving no details. In that sense, the no contest plea had been successful in stopping publicity. But by the time school started, rumors about the case had leaked all over town. Shie's absence from his teaching duties, combined with his enormous popularity among the students, had led to stories ranging from his having been caught in a homosexual orgy to his having run off with a girl student half his age. Since the board itself had already gone on record as wanting to fire him, Shie decided that a public hearing was the only way to clear his name. He dropped Hank Masana, the lawyer who had represented him in the no contest plea.

A month of intense preparation followed. The Ohio Education Association voted to support Shie unequivocally and pay for his defense. They sent in their own lawyer from Dayton, Robert Dunlevey, and their local branch hired Hugh Holbrock, who had defended Ned Wortees, as well as the mass murderer, James Ruppert. Holbrock was assisted by a young colleague, Randy Rogers, who soon came to consider Shie a cause as much as a case. The school board was represented by Carl Morgenstern, the distinguished Hamilton attorney, who had resigned an elected position on the board itself in order to become its legal counsel. Morgenstern, outnumbered at the counsel table three to one, consulted specialists at Miami University's school of education regarding the effect of allowing a teacher convicted on a morals charge back into a classroom. The defense,

of course, had Shie examined by a clinical psychologist, who
also gave him a battery of tests designed to disclose as much as
possible about the subject's state of mind.

As the October date for the hearings approached, the people
of Hamilton clustered like metal filings around the two poles of
a magnet. Considering the predictability of stands on so many
local issues, as well as the general conservatism of the community, both the size and composition of Shie's support were astonishing. If a jigsaw had been turned loose in Hamilton, it could
not have arranged the sides more unpredictably. Conservatives
and liberals linked arms, or fought bitterly, with no regard for
earlier opinions they had held on any issue, local or national.
The case made enemies of friends and at least temporary allies
of former enemies.

Carl Morgenstern, often an embattled leader of liberal causes
in Hamilton and a Miami University trustee who had voted to
have the university divest itself of stock in companies doing
business in South Africa, led the fight to run Shie out of town.
As the school board's lawyer, Morgenstern argued that the
safety of the students, as well as the primacy of the superintendent in disciplinary matters, demanded that Shie be dismissed.
The usually wary teachers' union, frequently (according to its
members) fearful of crossing school boards, decided to take on
the Hamilton board with a mood approaching vengeance, possibly to atone for past docility.

William Beckett, whose admirers as well as detractors often
speculated that he would like to see the entire twentieth century
—especially the union movement—repealed, became an immediate champion of Sam Shie's cause. Beckett was enraged at
what he described as the persecution of Samuel Shie. Not often
in Bill Beckett's nearly five decades of public life had he found
himself aligned on the same side of a conflict with a labor union.
As a member of the board of the Cincinnati Symphony, Beckett
loved music and admired Sam Shie's work with the Taft chorus.
Shie had been an occasional member of the choir at Beckett's
church, Trinity Episcopal. In this instance, school board supporters claimed, Beckett found himself in a position analogous

to that of northern liberals mandating southern integration: since Beckett no longer had children in school, it was easy for him to argue that Sam Shie ought to be allowed to remain a teacher even with a morals conviction against him. Yet there was more to the steely conservative's indignation, to the fierceness with which he engaged himself as Sam Shie's partisan. William Beckett, the old *padrone,* was also sad for his town. "I don't know him well personally," Beckett said, "but Mr. Shie is being given a chance neither to defend himself before being tarred and feathered, nor to continue to practice the craft at which he is a proven master. I'm horrified to find out how much savagery there is here, particularly among the board of education. It smacks of the Salem witch-hunt. This is small-town savagery at its ugliest." It had taken almost a lifetime—Emily Beckett Reed said she couldn't imagine her father taking this stand twenty years earlier—but Bill Beckett had at last fused his nineteenth-century righteousness with the twentieth century's tolerance for diversity.

Beckett's son-in-law Terry Reed, an English professor at Miami University's Hamilton campus, was the only school board member to oppose Shie's dismissal. "He does not admit to what he's accused of," Reed said, "nor is there any indication, even if he did masturbate in that men's room, that he poses a threat to the students. If counseling or therapy is indicated, we could suggest he get some. There is certainly insufficient cause for dismissal." The rest of the board disagreed. Regarding Hamilton schoolchildren as their wards, Hamilton parents as their clients, and convinced that Sam Shie's return to the classroom would be the occasion at least for obscene jeers from the students and possibly for further transgressions by the music teacher himself, they voted literally to get him out of their system.

Some of Shie's most vocal support came from his students. When school reopened, they gathered petitions on his behalf and protested his replacement, a choral director reluctantly promoted from an elementary school. In an informal poll of thirty-one Taft teachers—the school had sixty-five altogether

—thirty said they supported Shie and wanted him to return to the classroom. One teacher, criticizing both the police and Elder-Beerman's, said that if the store management was so concerned about their rest room, they should have just locked it and had customers go to a salesperson or cashier to get a key when they wanted to use it. Removing doors from toilet stalls, she said, seemed to constitute an enticing provocation for homosexuals rather than discouragement. Adding to Elder-Beerman's obtuseness was the snooping strategy of the police; didn't the three rest room visits by the handsome young plainclothesman come pretty close to entrapment? Shie, the teacher said, was naive to tell the police he had previously masturbated in a men's room and should not have pleaded no contest in court. "He behaved stupidly, but I hope to God he wins."

Syrilla Everson was a Taft teacher who supported Shie and had known Carl Morgenstern for many years. In the present crisis, she would not speak to Morgenstern and was not sure she ever would again. But Mrs. Everson, Taft's faculty advisor to the school paper and popular tenth-grade English teacher, was not merely indignant, she was also scared. "The worst of it is that if the school board gets away with this injustice to Sam Shie," she said, "there will be no stopping them on any issue involving a teacher. And I'm afraid there will be reprisals against those of us who do speak out for Sam."

Carl Morgenstern said it was nonsense that any teachers could be reprimanded or fired for supporting Shie. "But I have to tell you this, my old friend," he said, both in acknowledgment of the fact we had now known each other several years and in a lawyer's traditional courtroom tactic of invoking an assumption of intimacy with a jury, "Shie stands convicted of masturbating in public to solicit homosexual contact. If we let him back in school, we're saying to the students we approve this type of behavior. Why should we gamble on someone like that with our kids? The fact he's a great teacher makes it even worse because he's a role model. I happen to feel we shouldn't have sex deviants in the classroom—am I old-fashioned?"

Some of Shie's more sophisticated supporters thought the

schoolchildren were in markedly less moral danger than their elders. Emily Beckett Reed laughed at the concern over who was leading whom astray. "How can today's high-school students be corrupted by *anyone?*" she asked. "I just wish I knew a *tenth* of what they know."

But Sandy Wyman, a teacher of slow learners in junior high school and a close friend of Carl Morgenstern's, said, "Why should we sanctify a guy—homosexual *or* heterosexual—who can't keep himself under control? Once he gets into public and misbehaves, he doesn't represent my concept of a teacher, and he is no one for the students to emulate, which I think a teacher should be. Shie has to go."

If opinions were not enough, there were plenty of rumors. Like a recipe that includes leftovers from several previous meals, old enmities enrich a local feud. Shie's backers claimed Assistant Superintendent Helms had been out to get Shie ever since the choral director had complained because Helms cut the music budget to give more money to the Taft football team when his son was its quarterback. Critics of the board of education charged that Joe Wolf, its president, was pursuing the case overzealously because Shie had caught Martha Wolf, Joe's daughter, writing graffiti in the music room and kicked her out of the chorus. Shie's disparagers charged that he asked for an open hearing because he knew there were students and former students who would testify about sexual advances he had made to them only if the hearings were closed and private. They said the school board had evidence that Shie had been seen going into an out-of-town men's room with a known homosexual. ("Out-of-town" in a Hamiltonian context often means the same as "beyond the pale"—a wild, hostile, immoral territory controlled by barbarians.) It was also alleged that Taft High School had once, years before, received an anonymous letter from a parent complaining that Shie had been giving expensive presents to his or her son, and couldn't this outrage please be stopped? Since the letter, if it ever existed, had been destroyed, its fumes were even more pungent as they wafted about town.

On the Sunday in October before the public hearing began,

Sam Shie was elected an elder of the First United Presbyterian Church, where he was also organist. Elders are, in effect, the church governing board. Sam had been nominated before his arrest, but the election followed several weeks of discussion among the church membership. The pastor, Tedrow Dingler, did not influence the election, although he was an enthusiastic Shie advocate. "The members wouldn't listen to me anyway," Reverend Dingler said. "The elders run the church, not the pastor. Those who were against Sam were the ones who always think you're guilty until proven innocent. Oddly enough, there wasn't much argument on the moral question. Most people know Sam, like him, think he's an awfully fine musician, and figure what he does on his own time is his own business." This hardly meant that the congregation of the First United Presbyterian Church was devoid of sexual anxiety; indeed, if the "moral question," as Reverend Dingler called it, went largely undebated, the reason may have been simple inhibition. Still, as with Bill Beckett, the potential conflict between righteousness and tolerance seemed to have been resolved on the side of the latter. It could even be claimed, again as with Bill Beckett, that First United members were fusing the two and sending a clear message of righteously tolerant defiance to the board of education.

At the center of community polarization, starring in his own nightmare, Sam Shie began to feel like a patient who had been given a local anaesthetic so he could watch part of his body being amputated. The fight itself dulled the pain temporarily, but his horror grew more vivid as he saw fresh pieces of tissue cut from him. Shie was normally an outgoing, talkative, even mercurial man who did not try, as many teachers do, to hide his feelings. "I guess the kids at school, my family, anyone who's around me doesn't have too much trouble guessing the state of my emotions," he said. "I always wanted to teach at Taft with a high school chorus. I enjoy my job, I love music, and helping kids develop their musical ability is exciting. I can't believe they don't want me to do that anymore."

When boys chewed gum during chorus, or girls put on

makeup, Sam would snap at them. "I *do* get angry, and then right away I calm down. It's over in a minute." His reputation was for good-natured, easy relationships with his students, who felt they could come to Sam with problems about music or anything else and find a sympathetic, responsive listener. No one in the school system, including those most anxious to fire him, ever rated Shie less than a superior teacher and accomplished musician. His partisans went further; he was so warm and dynamic he could even get the Taft and Garfield choruses to sing *together,* they said, thus at least symbolically bridging the East-West, rich-poor abyss that neither politicians, ministers, community leaders, nor school officials had ever been able to do.

As Shie told it, his frustration was only increased by the knowledge that most of his supporters did not care whether he had masturbated in Elder-Beerman's rest room or not. They simply wanted him restored to his job, with full back pay, and they were perfectly willing to have the school board mandate psychotherapy for the teacher. For Shie himself, no matter what happened at the hearings, he was in front of a firing squad that never should have been assembled in the first place. "The thing is," he said, "I've never been arrested for *anything,* and I'm completely innocent of the charge here. That's why these hearings have to be public—since I've got nothing to hide, the only way to stop the rumors is to put everything in the open. My record is so clean it hurts." It hurt enough so that Sam cried several times in front of friends during September and October. Remarkably, Phil was not taunted at school—third-graders, perhaps, were not yet aware enough of sex to have overt fears about it—but Mary Shie's agony was no less than her husband's. One day while she was in line at the post office, Mary was approached by an old friend whom she had not seen since the trouble began. The friend did no more than tell Mary how sorry she was and to add that she and her husband supported the Shies completely. Mary looked up at her friend, made one attempt to smile, then ran from the post office in tears.

On the eve of the hearings, compromise was rejected by both sides. The teachers' union, with Shie's implicit agreement, in-

sisted they would take nothing short of full reinstatement with
back pay for their persecuted colleague. The board of education
held to its determination to get Shie out of town. The few neu-
trals shared a feeling that if Shie did what he was accused of,
both the board and he had a complicated problem—complicated, but not unresolvable. Among all the educators of Hamilton, surely there could be devised the academic equivalent of
Shie's no contest plea, allowing him to keep his job while the
board maintained its authority. But at times armies spoiling for
battle are insulted by the mention of peace, by anything less
than victory. Given the seemingly endless anxieties about sexual
activity—endless, really, as the circumference of a circle whose
successive revolutions, like those in sex, only bring it to a point
where it can begin again—even having sex all by oneself can be
menacing. Shie was, if "guilty," not just a consenting adult but
the only one involved. Surely masturbation must be the ultimate
victimless crime. Yet the fact of his being observed, if he was,
constituted an outrage to some.

At her beauty salon, Mallie was tender and compassionate—
at first. Shie had been mercilessly abused, she felt, and his family had suffered horribly. "He's been crucified by his toes upside
down on the courthouse clock," she said. But her Pentecostal
background, similar to that of many Hamiltonians, was not con-
ducive to sexual permissiveness. "You wouldn't do what he's
accused of," she said, "if you weren't looking for somebody. A
known homosexual has no business teaching public school." She
thought a moment. "If he's guilty," she added calmly, "it's not
just a sickness, and it's not just a crime. It's a sin."

If Sam Shie did masturbate in the Elder-Beerman rest room,
a problem of some kind existed for everyone involved, from
Shie himself to the board of education and its constituency, the
parents and students of Hamilton. As in medieval Thuringia,
where possession by demons was held to be contagious, a problem existed in Hamilton if only because so many people believed
and behaved as if one did. But what if, on the other hand, Shie
did *not* do what he was accused of? The case then was no longer
a misunderstanding, but a complete miscarriage of justice, a

false accusation to the point, as William Beckett put it, of witch-hunt. A good man and his family crushed for nothing. Since there were no witnesses but the arresting officer, since the crime's only conceivable victim was Shie himself (if one can still accept self-abuse as the archaic euphemism for masturbation), it should not have been difficult to harbor a reasonable doubt as to whether anything at all happened in the Elder-Beerman rest room worthy of legal note. Yet here was the board of education with a straight face spending months of its time and more money than Sam Shie's salary (eighteen thousand dollars) just to kick him out of town; and here was the Ohio Education Association pouring outside legal advice and labor agitation into Hamilton to try to break the authority and autonomy of a local school board.

"This type of conduct renders Sam Shie unfit to continue his teaching duties at Taft High School," Carl Morgenstern said, as he opened what amounted to the prosecution case in the crowded hearing room upstairs in the Board of Education Building. During eight full days of hearings on the Shie affair, spread out over a period of four weeks to accommodate the schedules of all the lawyers, and, for Sam Shie, to prolong his view of the surgery being performed on him, the hearing room was faithfully congested with Shie loyalists. Many of them wore little hand-scissored paper badges with the words, "I Support Sam Shie." The hearings, and their extended coverage by the *Journal-News*, focused attention on moral standards and the deep divisions between various segments of the community. But although the hearings thereby became a microcosm of Hamilton's attitudes toward sex, morality, education, behavior by public officials, and police procedures, Shie's supporters were almost the only spectators. Between thirty and fifty were always present, at times spilling out into the wide stair-top hallway, which, as the hearings progressed, became the offstage center for cigarette breaks and kibitzing. "I didn't know Morgenstern could be so mean." "What are Holbrock and Dunlevey trying to pull with all their objections? No thanks, Camels make me cough." "I still don't see why Sam wanted to go public, he must have known they were going to say all this stuff which everyone is going to connect with him, even if it's not true."

Inside, sitting in the front row of spectator seats only a few feet from her husband at the defense table, Mary Shie started a piece of crewelwork on the first morning of the hearings, embroidering a deer, two starlings, and a robin redbreast all in a clump of trees, a sylvan setting to keep her nerves quiet and her fingers busy. She looked sad and wan listening to the testimony. As soon as anyone spoke to her, she was instantly smiling and eager. During recesses, she talked animatedly to supporters and greeted friends at the stair top. No one stayed in the hallway for long. Remarkably for a public event that began at nine A.M. and at times continued well into the evening, the hearings were never routine and often reached emotional peaks, blending public with private tension, becoming a theater in which, as the fate of one man was being argued, the direction of a community was being charted.

The question was, with feelings so bitter and positions so rigid, could there be any winners? If the board of education "won," the teachers would be demoralized and insecure, Shie's career wrecked, his family humiliated. How could that ultimately help the school board or the cause of learning in Hamilton? But if Shie "won," it would mean state organizations could successfully interfere in local disputes, the board of education could not effectively govern or the superintendent superintend, leading to a form of anarchy that would set an inauspicious example for the classroom. With the school board manifestly unable to conceive of any official attitude toward Sam Shie between total approval and outright dismissal, intelligent men and women on both sides, like nations girded for war, seemed to have concluded that there were only two alternatives open to them—surrender or conquer.

Morgenstern concluded his opening presentation with a promise to establish that Shie had masturbated in the Elder-Beerman rest room "with a wild, imploring look" toward Patrolman Neal Ferdelman. This, Morgenstern said, was behavior that could not be tolerated by the school superintendent, who had to uphold a standard of conduct for teachers expected by the people of the community.

Opening for the defense, the lawyer sent by the Ohio Education Association, Robert T. Dunlevey, Jr., made the assertion, perhaps unique in public tribunals, that his client committed no crime because he was only suffering from diarrhea. He characterized Shie's ten-year teaching record in Hamilton as "excellent in overall performance, his conduct exemplary and beyond reproach." Throughout the proceedings, neither Superintendent Quisenberry, nor his assistants, nor Shie's own principal at Taft, all of whom were trying to get rid of him, ever said Shie was less than a superb teacher.

Shie himself was called as the first witness for the prosecution. During this early, brief appearance, he simply denied masturbating or having an erection in the men's room, said his colitis had forced him to leave classes and public choral performances a few times, and admitted to pleading no contest in court. Carl Morgenstern asked Shie if he knew that no contest meant he was not disputing the facts as alleged by Officer Ferdelman. Shie said he understood that, but he had wanted to avoid publicity and thought he could save his job with a quick disorderly conduct conviction and a one-hundred-dollar fine.

Morgenstern and Hugh Holbrock, who was representing Shie along with Dunlevey, began early in the hearings to object to each other's questions. Their styles, appearances, and personalities clashed as much as their points of view. Holbrock was given to florid, biblical metaphor, as he had been while defending Ned Wortees for murder. He loved courtroom melodramas and had starred in many. Morgenstern framed his questions like the short sharp jabs of a hungry welterweight; it was the law itself he loved, and the contest. Holbrock's white hair and soft blue eyes were the disguise for a mind that, like the steel-belted radials in television commercials, was both versatile and adaptable to quick bumps or ruts along the way. Morgenstern had dark, resolute eyes and his hair, at fifty-seven, was still black. His mouth was firmly set, though he smiled easily, a cheerful egotist whose sense of humor was always playing tricks on his determination. Between his thin upper lip and his precise, assertive nose was a wide space that lent him the authoritative aspect of a Spanish grandee. At the Shie hearings, Morgenstern hid his twinkle behind dark glasses, resembling, for the duration, Mephistopheles on a moral mission.

When Morgenstern called Neal Ferdelman to the stand, the patrolman testified there had been eight previous arrests in the men's room for homosexual solicitation and that customers were complaining to Elder-Beerman's about harassment. It was Ferdelman's job to stop this, which was all he was trying to do in the Shie case.

Ferdelman's even, clean-cut features gave him the kind of countenance the Armed Services like to put on their posters. He was not an ordinary patrolman—nor could he have been further from the sixties stereotype of a pig with a sadistic grudge —and had only one semester to go before graduating from college, a second-generation police officer with pride in his work and the law itself. But like any good soldier in any army, Ferdelman had been trained to be wary of eccentricity and had been specifically primed by Elder-Beerman's to look for trouble in their men's room. Ferdelman passed quickly over his first two visits to the rest room, during each of which he had noticed Shie. On his third visit, the security guard was about to leave the sink when he saw that Shie "had lowered the red gym shorts and was exposing himself and masturbating."

As he continued describing what he had seen, there was little that seemed subjective or opinionated in Ferdelman's testimony. There was little, in fact, that was not as tacked down as a well-laid carpet. The patrolman made an excellent witness, because instead of becoming more vague when questioned on details, he became even more specific. Ferdelman portrayed Sam Shie's penis with structural precision that bordered on the architectonic: "The penis was at a forty-five-degree angle, erect, and he was pumping his penis."

Ferdelman's statement about the angle of erection, whether accurate or not, had at least the salutary effect of requiring the parents of Hamilton schoolchildren to get closer to geometry than they had been in decades. The vision Ferdelman evoked of the acuteness of elevation of the Shie organ left no one in the hearing room unimpressed. Careful computations would go on in bedrooms all over town for weeks, but lightning calculation in the hearing room itself produced envious gasps from the men and appreciative chuckles from the women. The referee banged his gavel for the first of many times and warned spectators that they would be evicted if they did not refrain from interrupting the witness. It was clear at least that, regardless of Shie's sexual preferences, his performance was admirably vigorous—if, indeed, there had been any performance at all, which Shie denied.

Ferdelman went on to say that when he identified himself to Shie and placed him under arrest, Shie "began to whimper and sob softly." He denied he had been masturbating then, but confessed to having masturbated previously in a public men's room. On cross-examination by Holbrock, Ferdelman admitted it was his first day on the job as a security officer charged with policing the Elder-Beerman rest room. He also said he had observed Shie's hand motions out of the corner of his eye and had waited "only a few seconds" before making the arrest. Basically, Ferdelman left the stand unscathed.

The Elder-Beerman store manager testified about the problems the store had with homosexuals in its men's room. Then two more police officers, subdued by the nature of the case perhaps, but unashamed of their role in it, attested to the police station phone call Shie had with his wife in which he referred to "my usual problem," the phrase claimed by the prosecution to refer to public masturbation and by the defense to diarrhea caused by colitis. Morgenstern was building his case carefully, its foundation being the precisely detailed police testimony.

Late in the afternoon of the first day, after she had finished her duties as a substitute teacher but before she would have to go home to fix dinner, Joan Witt quietly tip-toed into the hearing room and sat down in the back row of spectators. Eight months after Frank Witt's death, his widow looked remarkably

—or else unremarkably, a miracle only in the sense that birth
or any other occasion in nature is bewildering in its refutation
of logic and its confirmation of vitality—as she always had. She
was pretty and pert, her eyes smiled before her lips did, and it
would have been as easy to find dust on a mirror at Versailles as
to have spotted a trace of self-pity about her. In repose, listening
to the testimony, she may have looked slightly in shadow, but
perhaps she always had, and then Ferdelman's tale of hanging
around a department store men's room to catch a music teacher
masturbating, whether true or imaginary, was indeed a baleful
one. The instant she spoke, Joan Witt was both cheerful and
declarative. "Can you believe what they're trying to do to this
man? He's such a wonderful teacher. When Amy was in his
chorus she just adored him. Frank would have been outraged
by all this."

Amy was now a freshman at Miami University and the
younger Witt girl was in her last year of junior high. Besides
substitute teaching of English and home economics (still basic
training for Hamilton girls in how to be a housewife), Joan Witt
supplemented the mayor's life insurance and Social Security by
selling Avon cosmetics. She liked Avon, even the doorbell ringing, which brought her into contact with other women who
needed something, who wanted (she said) to be beautiful. She
still lived in the house they had moved into only two years before, and she had begun having a social life. The rumor mill—
one industry that would never leave Hamilton—had Joan Witt
married already to a local realtor despite the realtor's own continuing second marriage.

It was a pleasure to remember Frank, and Joan only laughed
when she thought of how, a month before he died, they had
been snowed in at a Cincinnati hotel so that they had never
gotten to Washington for a mayors' conference with the President. In the last year of his life, with his local popularity at a
crest and his diplomatic missionary work among the country's
mayors gaining recognition and support, a number of politicians had spoken to Mayor Witt about running for senator from
Ohio. He would say he didn't know yet, he just didn't know.

"But oh, the plans he had," Joan Witt said now. "No one would go around making all those speeches who wasn't hoping something would come of it. He didn't really talk about it. Sometimes I don't know if Frank actually admitted to himself how big his dreams were, but you knew he had them if you lived with him."

But even Frank Witt might have had little effect on the collision Hamilton was having with itself in the Shie case. The throng of spectators on the first days of the hearings comprised mostly Shie's friends, sympathetic teachers, and a few students who risked—and received—demerits in order to attend. Those who wanted Shie out of town stayed on their jobs, in their homes, or were seated at the prosecution table as members of the school board. Most of the community polarization around the Shie case occurred after the hearings began, when the press coverage also began.

The *Journal-News* was graphic. In a way that no Hamilton paper had done in one hundred and seventy years, the *Journal-News* put lurid testimony directly in front of its readership. It was not that Hamiltonians had never read before about sex or crime. Going back to Prohibition raids, prostitute round-ups, and Dillinger escapades in the twenties and thirties, to the gamey particulars of corruption and murder in the 1870s, to the details of carnage in the Civil War, to the robust *Intelligencer* when it was owned by William Dean Howells' father in the 1840s, to the broadsides and handbills specifying the slit throats, wife desertions, and sexual peccadillos of the early settlers, a long tradition in the Hamilton press had often left the imagination only a little space in which to stretch itself and wander. But now there was no space at all. Expletives were supplied, not deleted; instead of veiled references there were eyewitness accounts.

Yet surely the *Journal-News* was innocent of the accusations by many subscribers that it had descended to smut. Nothing was suggestive or titillating, every syllable was as declarative as a stop sign. If anything, the paper's paragraphs rang with candor in place of the insinuating evasions that had been customary in reporting local scandal. In addition to mentions of erections, diarrhea, and homosexuality, the *Journal-News* used some form of the word "masturbate" forty-six times in its first eleven stories on the hearings. But masturbation, after all, was what the case was all about. In its vividness, the *Journal-News* was possibly grafting another species of writing onto responsible journalism, adapting an alien form to new uses. But it was not pornography, only screenplay.

For Hamiltonians accustomed to generations of euphemisms in their press—euphemisms that often inflamed fantasy and speculation, such as the first-family suicides that were depicted as bizarre, almost impossible accidents—the coverage of the Shie hearings was an outrage far worse than any he was accused of. Passages such as "Morgenstern said the charges stated that Shie exposed his private parts and engaged in masturbation in a toilet stall at Elder-Beerman" brought a high tide of protest letters. Each successive story on the hearings would lead to a fresh wave of mail breaking over the *Journal-News*. Most of the letters expressed anger at the *Journal-News*, not disapproval of Sam Shie.

The passion with which these letters were filled went far beyond anything the paper—or the community—had ever known. The letters came from all over town, every neighborhood, every segment and fragment of Hamilton—high, low, and middle, white and black, northern gentry and southern migrant, east and west sides of the river, students and parents. Excerpts yield both the tone and its intensity. "I was disappointed, dismayed and disgusted that the *Journal-News* would publish such a graphic description of an incident which has yet to be proven. . . . The *Journal-News* has sunk to a new pornographic low. . . . Up to now our daily newspapers have been our last bastion of defense against the ever-increasing tide of moral decadence. . . . If this type of journalism continues your paper will be known as *The National Enquirer* of Hamilton. . . . As the mother of a young child who is just beginning to read the newspaper, I don't feel it is your job to educate him to such filth. . . . You have allowed your newspaper to become guilty of the same acts of lewdness and indecency of which he is accused and are near, if not over, the line into pornography. . . . Details of rape and murder hearings have been reported with much less color. . . . I have read stories in the *Journal-News* which, besides being almost pornographic, are so one-sided to the school board's point of view that one would feel Carl Morgenstern had written it. . . . If the *Journal-News* had given as much publicity to Sam Shie's musical activities as it is giving to his alleged misdemeanor, Hamilton might now be the music capital of the nation. . . . You have literally murdered Mr. Shie with your yellow journalism. . . . I now choose to stop taking your paper."

Sam Shie himself was astounded by the paper's coverage and the community's response to it. He had been mortified to read —and to have his students and everyone else in town read— about the supposed angle of his erection and his alleged masturbation. Mary Shie was both enraged and humiliated, while eight-year-old Phil, if he felt or even knew anything about his father's travail, bravely pretended he did not. The *Journal-News* was scrupulous about printing only what was said at the hearings (and nowhere near all the X-rated phrases), making no remarks without full attribution (if only to protect themselves), and implying nothing beyond what was actually contained in testimony. Typically, the paper would say, "Miller [Taft's principal] read the affidavit alleging Shie masturbated in a toilet stall in the Market Street level of Elder-Beerman department store," or again, "Shie said he did not have an erection as the officer said he observed and Shie testified that he was not masturbating." Most of the stories, in fact, could have been written by the *Journal-News'* lawyers; there was not a word of opinion or interpretation. Confronted with the printed details of the hearings, Sam Shie felt at first, like so many of the *Journal-News'* readers, that the paper was doing all it could to make it impossible for him ever again to teach in Hamilton. "But it looks like the articles have backfired," he said, when the paper began to print its letters-to-the-editor. "Both the letters and the support I'm getting seem to show I really could walk back into the classroom and be accepted. I wasn't so sure before, but I am now."

If Shie was the beneficiary of the backfire, managing editor

Jim Blount felt he was its victim. While the hearings were in
recess for several days, Blount took up half his editorial page
and used eighteen hundred words to defend his decision to
cover the Shie proceedings so graphically. Acknowledging the
storm that raged more around the press coverage than the case
itself, Blount's editorial attempted to justify the *Journal-News*
stories on the grounds that Shie himself had requested a public
hearing, the consequences of which would inevitably be press
coverage. Furthermore, Blount continued, "public money and
public policy" were involved, and "the conduct of teachers is of
high concern to persons in the community, particularly when it
involves sexual issues." Blount knew there was a conflict between the rights of publicity and privacy, between the community's right to know and the humiliation that had descended on
Sam Shie after—and only after—the *Journal-News* began publishing the vivid details of his alleged sexual crime. "The subject
matter and language in this case have been offensive," Blount
wrote, creating "a traumatic situation" for Shie, as well as for
the school board, yet the entire case was centrally involved with
"the community's moral standards," and the public would have
to decide whether those had been violated or not. If Shie were
guilty—and the paper took no position on whether he had actually masturbated—then the school board's action in firing him
was either defensible or an overreaction, depending on one's
view of Hamilton's moral standards.

   In private, while continuing to express no opinion as to Shie's
guilt or innocence, Blount said that the first stories in the paper
had emphasized the prosecution's contentions simply because
theirs was the first turn. The later stories would reflect the defense position when its turn came. But Blount also had personal
feelings about the case. "If Shie is innocent," he said, "he should
have contested the case in court. If he's guilty, I'd have to say,
yes, he should be fired from teaching in a public school since he
masturbated in a downtown rest room where minors have been
accosted. We have upset many readers by printing the details
brought out at the hearings. If just *reading* about it offends
them, then surely what he did—*if* he did it—*must* offend them.

This means he, in fact, did violate community moral standards and should lose his job if guilty."

Blount's reasoning did cover some of the protests, but it did not answer those who felt the paper's coverage lacerated Shie cruelly if he was guilty and convicted him falsely if innocent. In either case, readers seemed to be invoking a complex protective mechanism that often springs into action where sexual appetites are concerned. Most adult Hamiltonians would have agreed that there is a line, especially where children and public solicitation might be concerned, where sex ceases to exist solely as pure drive and becomes an occasion for that shared public concern about right and wrong that produces moral standards. But most of Hamilton would also prefer to discuss that line in the abstract. Some sense of either charity or fair play, some tender prudence, calls for a discreet public silence on the personal habits of a man with a wife and son. The newspaper's graphic, though hardly pornographic, account of the hearings did further polarize the community in the short run, but in the long run obviously brought the issue of public and private morals directly into the open where it could be debated, where, as politicians never tire of saying, a meaningful dialogue might be held.

Yet the paper's coverage itself remained the issue for many Hamiltonians. "I'm outraged at how trashy the *Journal-News* has been," Tom Rentschler said at his bank in a short burst of irritation. "Every lunch or cocktail party I go to people are mad at the paper, which the paper deserves. They made a minor error at the beginning, and now they justify and magnify it every day by using the same vicious language. Even if he did what they say, I feel like being a champion of his cause just for the way the paper is maligning him. Why don't they ever point out when the homecoming queen is seven months pregnant at the graduation ceremony?" Whatever Sam Shie had done, the paper itself seemed to have violated the community moral standards its editor, Jim Blount, was anxious to uphold. This was all the more curious since it had done nothing but bring summaries of the public hearings into the homes of its subscribers.

Dave Belew, a prominent industrialist, was sympathetic to Shie but characteristically circumspect. "If he's innocent he's already been crucified; if guilty he could still be a good teacher, but it might become difficult to operate in those circumstances," said Belew, William Beckett's nephew and handpicked successor as president of The Beckett Paper Company. "I'm a great admirer of what he's done with the choral groups. He picked our music up to the level of where it should have been. Even murders are not so graphically described in the press, but I'd hesitate to blame the paper because they feel they have a responsibility to report what goes on." Belew was taking what might be called a firm Hamilton stand, similar to that of the local minister who asserted that, yes, President Nixon had been hounded mercilessly from office—and then added that the reason was Nixon's flagrant abuse of power.

At Mallie's Salon, the hearings and the *Journal-News* coverage of them were major topics. Regardless of her own personal belief that "homosexuality is a stench in God's nostrils," Mallie fervently hoped for Sam Shie's exoneration. For weeks the Shie case was bounced between Mallie's driers and curling machines and shampoo basins. The sentiment was largely pro-Shie and anti-*Journal-News*, but there was a good deal of argument about whether the teacher had in fact been masturbating. "Frankly, honey, I don't care if he was standing on his head whistling Dixie in a snowstorm," one woman would say. "He was on his own time and he was by himself and he wasn't hurting a soul."

"You're still not listening to me, Elaine," said her friend from under the next drier, putting down her *Cosmo* and trying one more time to be reasonable. "That's not the point I'm making, which is that if he did it, he has no business in a Hamilton classroom teaching our kids."

"Why the hell not?" came from a cigarette under a third dryer. "He's in charge of music, not sex education."

The hearings themselves could have used Mallie, who, hovering over her flock like a Bo Peep resolved never to lose them, tried to accommodate everyone. "If they're having trouble in

that rest room, I can see where they might arrest someone hastily," she said as she circled from one drier to the next. "Of
course, I feel where there's that much smoke there's got to be
some fire. Yet and still, he's due his day in court."

With witnesses to the facts—more properly, allegations—
heard, the prosecution elicited testimony on community moral
standards. A parade of school officials marched to the witness
stand to say that Shie's plea of no contest in court left him unfit
to teach in Hamilton. For the defense, Hugh Holbrock asked if
masturbation itself was not a fit subject for discussion in the
schools. A school board official said it absolutely was not. "Then
why, may I ask, do you allow this film to be shown in your sex-
education classes?" Holbrock thereupon brought forward a can
of film and offered it in evidence. (Perry Mason would have had
the courtroom plunged into darkness while images flitted across
a wall opposite the jury, but Hugh Holbrock was dealing with
no real courtroom, no jury, no movie projector, and a lot of
Venetian blinds.) "This film, which your own youngsters are
currently being enlightened by, contains instructions on sex relations, including a lengthy passage on masturbation," Holbrock
said. "I commend it to the members of the school board."

From an assistant superintendent, Holbrock drew admissions
of two crimes committed by other Taft teachers, neither of
which resulted in a firing. One teacher was caught shoplifting
at the self-same Elder-Beerman's during Christmas vacation.
Pathetic as the incident was for the underpaid schoolteacher,
there was no question as to his guilt, yet he was not dismissed.
Another case was more complex and also more violent. One
teacher at Taft was living with the wife of another teacher,
leading some of their colleagues to snicker that the school
should be renamed Peyton Place High. The cuckolded teacher
attacked his tormentor one morning directly in front of the
students during a class lecture. In the brief punch-out, eyes
were blackened and names were called before students stepped
in to break up the fight between their teachers. Hamilton's legal
apparatus went right to work. An arrest, assault charges, and a
guilty plea resulted, but school officials magnanimously be-

haved as if they were in Amiens, treating the affair as a *crime passionel* requiring only indulgence, not dismissal. Holbrock asked if theft and assault were not considerably more serious— and a far greater threat if emulated by the students—than the minor misdemeanor of which Shie stood convicted. "Not to us they're not," the school official countered. "We stay away from sex deviants."

The discrepancy between Hamilton's legal and educational standards was thus displayed. The law was interested in theft and assault, but only casually concerned with sex when there was no victim. School officials, on the contrary, could look the other way on both violence and stealing, but were willing to divide the community and risk their public careers over a single alleged, altogether solitary, sex act. It was doubtful, of course, whether the school board would have been so tolerant in the assault case if the fight had been the result of homosexual, rather than heterosexual, jealousy.

When Maurice Miller, Taft's principal, came to the stand, the hearings took a more ominous turn. Known as Hank, Miller was described by a friend as "a nice likeable guy, a jock, not overly cerebral." A team man all the way, Miller's educational spirit was embodied mutely in the twelve tigers he displayed all over his office. Miller appeared approximately as sinister as an ice cream cone, but his testimony made clear that an open season on differentness could descend over Hamilton as insistently as it had in the 1690s over Salem or in the 1950s over Washington and Hollywood as sources of our national policy and popular culture. It was, of course, his geniality that made what Hank Miller said so scary. After testifying cheerily that Sam Shie was an excellent teacher who had great rapport with his students, Miller was asked by Holbrock whether the fact of masturbation in the rest room, if it was a fact, was enough by itself to make Shie unfit for teaching at Taft.

"If I know about it, it is," Miller said, not seeing yet where Holbrock was taking him.

"You mean we're faced here with that sad old American song, that golden oldie we've heard from Teapot Dome to Watergate, that a given misdeed is wrong if you get caught and right if you get away with it?"

"Objection," Morgenstern said. "He's drawing conclusions and leading the witness from here to Honolulu."

"I think I'll overrule the objection," said the referee, John Zopff, as he invariably did throughout the hearings. Zopff was an out-of-towner, a kindly looking, gray-haired lawyer whose practice was to be far more lenient with questioning than a judge would be in a court trial. "What we are trying to arrive at here is precisely what the community standards are. He may answer if he has an opinion."

"I wouldn't say it's right if you get away with it, no," Miller said, "but perhaps it's acceptable in the sense that you could still go on teaching and not be subjected to verbal abuse and taunts."

"So if it is a fact but remains unknown, you could still teach," Holbrock said. "All right then, Hank, now let's consider the opposite—let's say it's not a fact, or not a proven fact anyway. Let's say it's only a charge made by others. Does the accusation, the mere accusation itself, impair Sam Shie's ability to function in his chosen profession as a teacher in our community?"

"Yes, it does," Miller said quietly.

"Well then, let me pause one moment," Holbrock said, gesturing toward the closed door at the entrance to the hearing room, "while we all take note of two new and, to my mind, unwelcome visitors to Hamilton, Ohio. Mr. Witness, Mr. Referee, members of the school board, ladies and gentlemen, let the record reflect that the Reverend Cotton Mather and Senator Joseph McCarthy have just entered this hearing room and taken their ghostly places among us." Holbrock glared at two empty seats in the front row.

"I didn't say it was *right* for mere accusation to damage someone," Miller said.

"You didn't have to," Holbrock said. "The point is made. The point is that a man's life and career can be ruined, and his family humiliated, just because someone says something about him, just because he is publicly denounced, regardless of whether a single charge is proven against him."

"Well, there's a stigma associated with an accused man even if he's found not guilty."

"So if I throw enough stigma around, some of it's bound to stick," Holbrock said. "Do you mean if I accused you, Hank, of having an affair with a married woman, and it was *proved,* absolutely proved, to be untrue, you would still be suspect, your credibility would still have been undermined?"

"Yes, that's right. Let me add that such a charge would not only be untrue but ridiculous," Miller said as the spectators joined him in a good-natured chuckle, "but it would be damaging all the same, and it would make me less fit to be principal of a high school." Holbrock seemed to have invoked phantoms appropriate to the occasion. Under the guise of affability—a little joke—Mather and McCarthy were gaining at least a toe-hold in Hamilton.

At this point the school board was in the ironic position of trying to banish a teacher fighting an accusation he claimed was false, while giving its support to a high school principal who maintained that false accusation alone is enough to destroy a citizen. If this had been an incident studied in one of Taft's classes, a midterm examination might have asked: Which of these positions would be more destructive of our Constitutional protections, democratic rights, and the rule of law? Which man —the accused teacher or the accusing principal—was setting an example that would be more harmful to society if everyone behaved that way?

To return the hearing to what he hoped would be specifics, Carl Morgenstern asked how the Taft music program would proceed if Sam Shie were allowed back as its director. Hank Miller said he would have to curtail the program because of Shie's conduct and also because students would be lewd and unruly in his classes. This would create a discipline problem that could spread to other classes as well and might make the school virtually unmanageable.

"Why would all this happen?" Morgenstern asked.

"Because Sam Shie has violated the community moral standards and will not have the respect of the school if he is permitted to return," Miller said. "A teacher is a teacher regardless of where or when. Impressions made on young people are the same in August in the Elder-Beerman rest room as they are in the classroom in October."

"Do you know, as principal of Taft, that most of the students and almost all the teachers *desire* the return of Sam Shie?" Holbrock asked on cross-examination.

"They didn't hire me to run the school as a popularity contest," Miller said. "In order to have the best school, and the school that will in the end have the most respect for itself, we have to have standards, and in this case the whole community's standards are at stake."

Holbrock had been hearing about these standards from everyone who worked for the board of education, and he decided to probe them. "And just how do you know these standards, Hank?" he asked.

"They involve general opinion in the community about what a teacher's conduct should be. Mr. Shie has not lived up to these standards."

"I see. How have you determined these standards?"

"They are known throughout Hamilton by all the people," Miller said, and then, hearing snickers from the spectators and possibly remembering the thirteen hundred unpredictable adolescents whose waking hours were spent primarily in his jurisdiction, he added, "by all the *adults* anyway."

More snickers prompted Referee Zopff to warn the spectators against becoming a cheering or booing section for either side.

"But Hank, how do you know these standards?" Holbrock asked. "Have you taken a survey?"

"No. This is my opinion of the standards."

"Well, I'd like a list of the people who helped you form that opinion. The defense would like to call these experts in community moral standards for questioning as to how they arrived at their conclusions and why they didn't bother to put these conclusions and rules up someplace where everybody can see them."

Holbrock was developing his second line of defense. The

first, quite naturally, was that Sam Shie was not guilty of the charge, that he did not masturbate in the Elder-Beerman rest room. But the second defense took on more significance as the hearings and the community debate progressed. What were Hamilton's moral standards anyway, and who was in a position to know them? These questions were not as abstract as how many angels could dance on a pin, but they were hardly as concrete as how many Hamiltonians on a softball team, at a Rotary meeting, in a union shop. In physics, certain questions that seem almost unanswerable—the size and history of the universe, the simultaneous speed and position of a single sub-atomic particle—can, simply by being posed, enlighten the questioner as much as they perplex him. In philosophy, such questions—the limits of logic, the nature of good, the value of art—can become the central focus for a lifetime of speculation. In Hamilton, the Sam Shie case raised questions concerning community moral standards that inspired arguments whose rampant phase might last only a few weeks, but whose residual effect could go on for decades.

The heat, as always in conflicts, came first; the light, if generated at all, would appear chiefly as afterglow. In the middle of the hearings, the teachers union demanded a meeting with Managing Editor Blount of the *Journal-News*. The union's angry leaders, Mary Jo Haizman and Dennis Roberge (respectively, a teacher and an organizer), opened the confrontation with Jim Blount by threatening to boycott the newspaper if its coverage of Sam Shie did not become more sympathetic. What this would mean, if the leadership were able to enforce its will among the teachers, was the cancellation of six hundred subscriptions. Although it might be taken as a union tribute to the presumed power of the media, the fact that the teaching profession was making the threat hardly added up to a ringing affirmation of freedom of the press. How would they teach the First Amendment while they were trying to break a newspaper for printing something they did not like?

Blount explained patiently that the prosecution had its innings first and that the early coverage merely reflected that fact

by detailing the charges against Shie. When the defense presented its case, the coverage would reflect Shie's side. The
paper's policy was to print no damaging allegations about the
accused in a criminal case until they were made in open legal
proceedings, either in court or in a public hearing. The paper
had known why Shie was arrested since the beginning of August
but had, until the hearings in October, printed nothing except
that the original charge had been reduced from public indecency to disorderly conduct. Shie himself had requested that
the hearing be public, and since he was also on the public pay-
roll in a public school coming into daily contact with the children of the community, the paper thought it had a duty to
report the details of these open meetings on his dismissal.

But why, Roberge and Haizman wanted to know, was it necessary to treat Shie, a highly respected and admired teacher, as
though he were a convict when he had not been proven guilty?
Blount answered that Shie had, in fact, been convicted in court,
and that the no-contest plea, while not an admission of guilt,
was an admission of the truth of the facts as stated in Officer
Ferdelman's affidavit. The conviction for disorderly conduct
did not alter the charge of masturbation in a public rest room.
Roberge and Haizman asked why it was necessary to print allegations about masturbation, the angle of Shie's presumed erection, and other details of the police charges; these related to no
one else in the community but Shie, and the publicity served no
purpose other than to humiliate him and his family. Blount's
opinions were strongest on this point. First, the *Journal-News*
printed the hearings in detail in order to stop rumors; Shie's
detractors had gone around town saying he had been trying to
pick up boys in the rest room, and his defenders had been
claiming that he had only unzipped his fly to urinate when
Ferdelman moved in with his badge. Second, the hearings represented a strong challenge, by the union as well as Shie, to the
authority of Superintendent Quisenberry and the school board;
such proceedings were therefore of abiding public interest and
could only be covered responsibly by printing the charges and
countercharges. Finally, Quisenberry's "back-to-basics" pro-

gram—the restoration of higher levels in discipline and academic performance—was at stake, for standards were at the
heart of both the learning process and the Shie case. Though
the *Journal-News* had not been unfriendly to the progressive
reform theories of Quisenberry's predecessor, Blount himself
felt more comfortable with the current emphasis on fundamen-
tals and had supported Quisenberry enthusiastically.

Haizman and Roberge did not agree that the Shie case could
be linked to Quisenberry's whole program, or even that moral
standards had much to do with the "back-to-basics" approach to
education. Many teachers in Hamilton felt the "new" program
was simply an easier way of controlling the students and tended
to stifle spontaneity, that the return to old ways represented the
swing of a creaky pendulum at best and a reactionary, hickory-
stick repression at worst. Haizman and Roberge left the meeting
with more respect for Blount, but unsatisfied, with a frustrated
feeling that the community was splitting into two great floes of
ice doomed to drift around in arctic isolation from one another.

The positive side of the crisis was in forcing concerned townspeople, like a baseball team expected to be mediocre but suddenly finding itself up with the leaders in a tight pennant race,
to play above their normal levels, in this case, philosophically.
There were discussions of morality; the rights and duties of a
free press; the place of music in education; the rights of homosexuals; whether homosexuals should teach in schools; the age
at which children should be exposed to sex education; the line
between an individual's private and public lives. The debates
were everywhere—in bars and banks downtown, from the
Fisher Body plant on the Hamilton-Fairfield line in the southeast to Champion Paper, Mallie's Salon, and the corridors of
Taft High itself on the West Side.

When the hearings resumed after eight days' recess, school
board officials ordered Sam Shie's teacher friends back to their
classrooms. Several teachers protested that they had been sub-
poenaed as witnesses for Shie and needed to remain at the
hearings so they would be present when called. They asked
Referee Zopff to direct Superintendent Quisenberry to have

substitutes teach their classes until they had finished their testimony. Zopff said he had no power over the internal affairs of the Hamilton school system, but that he would wait for any teachers to arrive from class after they were called as witnesses. Except for Mary Shie, who continued doing crewelwork while her husband's career and toilet habits were debated, the teachers returned to their classes. Shie's cheering section was thus somewhat depleted, which was exactly what the school board wanted.

Carl Morgenstern now summoned his experts from the School of Education at Miami University. These were essentially trained-seal educationists whose function was to assert that Sam Shie had debased his profession and was no longer worthy of belonging to it. "I could not conceive how anyone could proceed in teaching with this set of circumstances behind him," one of them said grandiloquently. "There are no school districts who would hire Mr. Shie now." When Hugh Holbrock tried to shake the educationist by reminding him that Shie's colleagues and students wanted him to remain, the specialist drew himself up even tighter and said it made no difference what anyone at the school said, the charges against Shie were sufficient to destroy his effectiveness as a teacher. If the charges were proved untrue, and Shie found not guilty, the expert said Shie would still be ineffective as a teacher simply because of the publicity surrounding his case. The publicity itself, then, not the alleged masturbation, put the finishing touch on Shie's teaching career. Holbrock, to rebut the educationist, placed into evidence a petition that read: "We the undersigned wish to express our thought that Mr. Shie should be back in his position at Taft Senior High School. Immediately." It was signed by 240 Taft students.

The testimony of Superintendent Robert Quisenberry climaxed the prosecution's case. With his glasses on, the latent novelist resembled an owl; without them, a genial melon. He wore a blue pin-stripe suit with vest, and his light brown hair was combed down onto his forehead. Quisenberry, though no less determined to get rid of Shie and uphold his authority, was in a good mood. His daughter had been married over the weekend, and just that morning, NBC's "Today" show had filmed a segment in Hamilton on how Quisenberry was restoring discipline and academic ideals to his school system. "We expect a high standard of behavior from students in the school district," Quisenberry said on the witness stand, as he had earlier to the NBC film crew. "We have a similar set of standards for teachers." The NBC crew had not, of course, been told about the Shie case that was tearing apart the school system—and the community—as they filmed Quisenberry's purported triumphs.

Under questioning by Carl Morgenstern, Quisenberry said Shie had assured him after the arrest that he was innocent and that he would be found not guilty in court. "Mr. Shie and I talked about what his going back to class might mean," Quisenberry added, "and Mr. Shie said he knew that some student was bound to call him a cocksucker." At the defense table, Shie vigorously shook his head and whispered to his attorneys that he had never said "cocksucker." Defense attorney Robert Dunlevey objected to the superintendent's remark, both on grounds of hearsay and obscenity, but Referee Zopff quietly overruled. "It's in the record, let it stand."

Quisenberry said Shie had agreed that his only chance for vindication was in court. "When Shie pleaded no contest, I was shocked," Quisenberry said. "I believed his plea meant he had no confidence he would prevail. Therefore, I had to accept the statement of Officer Ferdelman that Mr. Shie had masturbated in the rest room."

"Why did you recommend Mr. Shie be fired?" Morgenstern asked.

"I recommended the termination of Mr. Shie's contract, although I believe he still has the same teaching ability, because the music program would have to be curtailed, students and parents would not want to participate, and we would have discipline problems with students who called Mr. Shie names."

As the lawyer hired by the Ohio Education Association, Robert Dunlevey pressed Quisenberry closely in cross-examination. Dunlevey was young but partly bald, with a shiny pate ringed by reddish-brown hair. With his Vanzetti-like moustache, Dunlevey could have led a student rebellion a decade earlier, and even now had the aspect of a man at the forefront of a cause, which, as each day made clearer, he was. Dunlevey began by asking the superintendent where, in all the statutory codes governing the actions of the board of education, it had been written that a teacher must be fired for a conviction on a minor misdemeanor.

"It is not written anywhere that a no-contest plea will result in the dismissal of a teacher," Quisenberry said.

"You had nothing written in this district that mandates dismissal, yet the minor misdemeanor is all you had to go on."

"When I found out the nature of the crime I went to the school board with a serious infraction of our standards and recommended termination. Now I don't say a misdemeanor necessarily results in dismissal, but what we're dealing with here is a sex offense."

"Do you consider masturbation to be an indication of homosexuality?" Dunlevey asked.

"Not in and of itself," Quisenberry said, "but what you do at home is one thing, and what you do in a public rest room is another."

"Would masturbation lessen the ability to teach?" Dunlevey asked. Was he about to move on to the old superstition that what it does do, at the very least, is grow hair on the palms of offending hands?

"It hampers him," Quisenberry said, "because his credibility is destroyed. He himself is afraid of all the names he'd be called." At the defense table, Sam Shie shook his head. In the audience, Syrilla Everson whispered to a friend that it would be hard to find a teacher at Taft, even during the heralded restoration of discipline, who had not been called a motherfucker.

"Mr. Shie said to you he'd be called a cocksucker in the classroom?" Dunlevey asked.

"Yes, he did," the superintendent said, as Shie shook his head furiously. "You see, we need a music program, not the rest of this stuff," Quisenberry continued, winding into some school board oratory. "Division, polarization, and controversy is what we'd have with Mr. Shie back in the classroom, and we have enough of that already in this town. Conviction of a sex crime is not something this community will tolerate. Masturbating publicly is repulsive, distasteful, and offensive, so I fired him."

Dunlevey's voice was suddenly hushed in contrast to Quisenberry's rhetorical flourish. "Is public masturbation a problem at Taft, Mr. Quisenberry?"

"No, it is not."

"Is pilfering and petty theft a problem?"

"Yes sir, it still is. We're doing everything we can to . . ."

"You say pilfering is a problem at school," Dunlevey cut in, "yet you let a teacher continue who had been caught shoplifting. Why is that?"

"I did not have the confidence to let Mr. Shie go on teaching. The shoplifter was not distasteful, only wrong."

"How's your mail running, Mr. Quisenberry?"

"Four to one in favor of Mr. Shie. My decision to fire him was not based on public opinion, or on how I thought people might vote, but on what I think is right."

"Is student opinion important to you?"

"It's important, but not controlling."

"All right then, Mr. Quisenberry, if you can have it both ways, so can I." Dunlevey actually rubbed his hands together in anticipation of the point he was about to score. "If student opinion is important, you should let Mr. Shie come back because they are for him." The beginnings of applause came from the spectators. "If it is not important, then it doesn't matter what they think of him or what awful names they call him, so you can let him come back because he's a meticulous, inspiring, and—in the words of all his superiors—excellent teacher." The audience erupted into cheers for Dunlevey and Shie. Referee Zopff asked for silence, and Carl Morgenstern asked that the hearing room be cleared since the spectators were disconcerting to the witnesses. Zopff told Morgenstern his point was well taken but that these proceedings were a community civics lesson everyone ought to have access to, if possible. Turning to the spectators, he said, "This may be good for the soul and I'd like you to stay, I really would. But you're going to have to be quiet."

"The problem with the young people in high school," Quisenberry said when order was restored, "is that they are of an age to experiment with life-styles, to find out which way they're going to go in life. In that context, we can't let Mr. Shie back in the classroom because the students would construe that as an acceptance and approval of a teacher who behaves this way."

"Doesn't that apply to shoplifting?"

"To a lesser degree. This is sex."

Indeed it was. Harry Everson, Syrilla's husband, bent toward another spectator and said, "Jesus Christ and all the Apostles couldn't save him now. They're just stringing him up, they might as well have the hanging right here." Yet Harry Everson himself was not ready to give up. He wore the defiant "I Support Sam Shie" badge on his lapel, as did more than half the audience.

Joan Witt wore one, too. Because of Avon work and her substitute teaching, she could come to only a few of the sessions, but she remained a firm, even indignant, Shie adherent. "The atmosphere around here is getting worse," she whispered one afternoon between witnesses. "People are becoming afraid of each other, especially teachers of administrators. It's a bad sign." Despite assurances from the superintendent's office, teachers were beginning to worry that their support of Shie would lead to cancelled contracts or at least unfavorable appraisals inserted in their records. As the next witness, Assistant Superintendent Helms, took the stand, Anita Weisman walked into the hearing room and found a seat in the row behind Joan Witt. Perhaps the old rumors really had destroyed their friendship. Did Frank Witt's death remove the only bond there was between them? Would the two speak at all, even acknowledge each other's presence? Anita did not wear a Sam Shie badge, only a small gold bumblebee on her cashmere sweater. As soon as the court stenographer began to read back some testimony, Anita Weisman leaned forward and answered a number of questions with a fond tap on Joan Witt's shoulder. "How's it going?" "Not well," Joan Witt said. "Every administrator wants Sam's scalp." When contrasted, two kinds of loveliness became lovelier still. Each woman's prettiness was haloed by her hair— Joan's prematurely white and Anita's the black of sable.

Anita looked at the table where the school board members, most of whom she knew well, sat. "He never should have entered that no-contest plea," she said.

Joan turned around. "Maybe not. He's the best music teacher you'll ever see, though. Listen, I meant to ask you, do you need any of that new bath oil?"

Still looking at the school board members, Anita answered absently. "I don't know. I guess not."

"I mean I have some on sale this week, and it's usually so expensive. You know, the Avon?"

"Let me think. The bath lotion?"

"You don't have to. It's just that it got so expensive, but it's on sale right now. This week."

"Oh. Sure then, Joan. Save me three bottles?"

Assistant Superintendent Donald Helms said school officials had not wanted to hurt Sam Shie, nor had they sought the newspaper publicity, the all-over-town gossip, that the hearings had brought about. The officials, it seemed from Helms' testimony, merely wanted Shie to slink away from Hamilton and find work in some other school district. "We wished Mr. Shie no ill-harm," the assistant superintendent of schools said. "Personally, I wouldn't want anyone convicted of a sex-related offense to teach my children. Professionally, I wouldn't think most parents would want someone convicted of a sexual crime to teach their impressionable children. I believe it would be a poor risk to place Mr. Shie back in a teaching situation. You have to take action to avoid putting your students in jeopardy."

To support the school board's contention that Sam Shie would be a disruptive influence at Taft, Helms produced three posters, known as "spirit signs," long hand-painted strips of drawing paper lettered with slogans. The first banner advised the football team to "MUTILATE MONROE," underneath which someone had penciled in, using the first word of the painted part of the sign, "Mr. Shie say's MUTILATE your meat." The second, proclaiming "JUNIOR CLASS SALE," had "Mr. Shie say's Beat em, Big Sam say's pound em" written on the sides. The third banner, again a football plea, "SHOW EM WHAT YOU CAN DO TIGERS," was accompanied by "Sam Shie say's Beat em—get fucked." It did not take Hercule Poirot to point out that the corruption of the word "says" into "say's" in all three graffiti indicated either that there was only a single miscreant at work out of thirteen hundred students or that Taft's English Department was doing a far worse job of instilling the rules of punctuation than anyone had suspected. Many other Taft teachers had also seen their names appear in graffiti and had managed to continue their duties. A number of them complained, in refutation of Superintendent Quisenberry's tight-ship claims on the "Today" show, that even when it was well known who the source of a taunt was, no disciplinary action was taken against the student.

The cross-examination of Dr. Helms was conducted by Randy Rogers, the young associate of Holbrock's. Rogers was tall and strongly built, lacking by only a couple of inches the height of a professional basketball player who weakens the opposition by fouling often and drawing fouls in return. This was close to the function Rogers performed for the defense. With Hugh Holbrock, Robert Dunlevey, and Randy Rogers all ranged against Carl Morgenstern, it was sometimes hard to tell just who the underdog was at the hearings. Sam Shie, to be sure, was a lone teacher up against a community's educational establishment which was trying to purge him. But at the hearings themselves, almost all the spectators were on Shie's side, he was being supported by the Ohio Education Association, and he had three articulate, variously styled lawyers who disputed virtually everything Carl Morgenstern or one of his witnesses said. Each came at Morgenstern from a different angle with a new tactic, trying to wear him down the way a basketball team will use a full-court press, a fast break, the setting of a pick or screen, the switching of defensive assignments to bewilder an opponent. Hugh Holbrock made long, arcing, oratorical shots from outside the key,

Robert Dunlevey dribbled spectacularly around any position Morgenstern took, and Randy Rogers would try to provoke Morgenstern into exchanges of anger and procedural wrangles. Rogers was surly to Morgenstern, who would respond by being loftily sardonic. A few times Morgenstern slipped and got mad at Rogers, who was polite to witnesses but steeled himself to a single pitch of fury when he was addressing Morgenstern. The rest of the time Rogers sat moodily at the defense table—in effect on the bench—while Holbrock and Dunlevey performed their own specialties.

"You've moved around a lot, Dr. Helms," Rogers said as he began painting a verbal picture of the peripatetic Helms as an educational careerist. "Athens, Karachi, San Bernardino County, Hamilton, and I understand you've applied for positions in the South and the West."

"Yes sir," Helms said, shifting his powerful build in the witness chair. His face itself looked well muscled. He was known as a disciplinarian and a jock, though he was cautious and restrained on the witness stand. "But I didn't get the one in the West. That was Oklahoma City."

"Now why would a man like Sam Shie stay in one place for over a decade?"

"Dedication, sir. That, and the enjoyment of working with young people." The several administrators' strategy was to say as many good things about Shie as possible, showing nothing but admiration and sympathy as they rode him out of town.

"Then how can you take that livelihood away from such a dedicated man?" Rogers asked. (A spectator said, "Damn right.")

"Objection," Morgenstern said, "he's arguing with the witness."

"I'm arguing," Rogers said, "with a parade of self-satisfied smug administrators who condemn a man and set off an explosion in a community and then move right along to the next plateau in their careers."

"And who are subjected to public humiliation," Morgenstern

said, "from the cheering section you've arranged to show up here every day like this was some basketball game." Indeed.

"We didn't ask any of the spectators to come here," Rogers snapped, "and if I were you, Mr. Morgenstern, I wouldn't talk about who is causing public humiliation around here." Several members of the audience applauded.

Referee Zopff was banging his gavel, but Morgenstern had the last word. "You're losing your cool, Randy. Haven't you been out of law school long enough to know that's unprofessional conduct?"

"I'll overrule the objection, Mr. Morgenstern," Referee Zopff said when the room was quiet. "But I'll have no more outbursts. The witness may answer the question."

"I didn't take any livelihood away from anyone," Helms said. "Mr. Shie did that to himself by his own action."

" 'By his own action,' Dr. Helms? Do you know that Mr. Shie denies that there *was* any action?"

"Richard Nixon denied that too, but the evidence proved otherwise."

"Oh, the evidence. I almost forgot. During the incident that is alleged to have taken place in the Elder-Beerman rest room, do you know if there was ejaculation?" Suddenly it seemed strange that Rogers' question had not been asked earlier.

"No sir, I do not," Helms said.

"That's because there was none, nor has there even been an accusation that ejaculation occurred. Masturbation, as all you educators surely must know, is defined by Webster as 'production of an orgasm by excitation of the genital organs.' 'Production of an orgasm,' Dr. Helms." A long, low train whistle invaded the hearing room, the engine it came from sounding as though it were struggling to catch its breath as it picked up speed passing through Hamilton. Rogers glared at Helms.

"When he pled no contest, it was an admission of the truth of the charge against him. We had no choice."

"One of the reasons for a no-contest plea," Rogers said, "is to avoid publicity. It *worked* in this case, didn't it? There *was* no publicity until this *circus* began!"

"We didn't ask for a public hearing. He did."

"Yet, if Mr. Shie had asked for a *private* hearing, you'd be sitting in that chair saying he did so because he has something to hide, wouldn't you?"

"Objection," Morgenstern said, "not only argumentative but insulting."

"I'll withdraw that," Rogers said. "He knows I'm right. No further questions."

That night, with the school board's case closed, Sam Shie surveyed the stage he was on. He could see, if not yet feel, limits to his own endurance. At a West Side dinner with friends, Mary told him he was holding up beautifully. This sounded like wishful thinking to Sam. What he had first loved about Mary was her ability to sense the direction his emotions were moving in before they got there. Sam told Mary he was—in addition to feeling besieged, harassed, persecuted—beginning to get tired. "If I'm feeling sorry for myself, maybe I'm entitled." One of the Shies' dinner companions, the music teacher Connie Beale, who had been with Sam in Elder-Beerman the day he was arrested, said this was the worst time, it had to get better. Sam saw it two ways. Sometimes he thought it would get much worse, but he would win. Other times he saw even his community support as an omen that he would eventually be cast out by Hamilton when people wearied of him and his cause. Though this was hardly the kind of attention Sam liked to bask in, there was a sense in which any spotlight gave at least temporary nourishment to a choral director. The relationship between the case and his own energy was curious; he felt like a rubber toy that is alternately inflated and deflated according to the breathing habits of a whimsical child. Sam was used to performance and was never sorry to be appreciated. The support he was getting had an element of applause to it, but there was also the sideshow aspect he was the freak for whom everyone feels sympathy and— darkly, secretly—contempt.

The charges against him, the newspaper accounts, the prosecution's seeming vendetta were all mortifying, but even the squabbling between his own lawyers and Carl Morgenstern bothered Sam. If they scored points against each other as though they were in a game, then he was the ball. The school board wanted the teachers under control, the Ohio Education Association wanted a power base in Hamilton. Between these two positions—and their advocates—Sam was swatted, batted, stroked, smashed, caught. Hugh Holbrock had told Sam confidentially he thought Referee Zopff would rule for the board of education. The Shie team would then take the case into the court of common pleas (which was their right if they lost at the hearing level) where Holbrock was confident they would win. Sam had argued that Zopff could not possibly rule against him; the school board had failed to prove its case, and the defense had not even presented its side yet. But Holbrock had an antagonistic personal relationship with Zopff from a previous case, and he felt the referee would decide for the authoritarian establishment which was, as far as the defense was concerned, the board of education and its superintendent of schools.

Having dinner with friends was a relief, but it also reminded Sam of the pressure that stayed with him like a tumor. If he did not win, how long would they *be* his friends? Either he would become a social liability or he would literally be kicked out of school. That morning, before the hearings, knowing that sooner or later Phil would see a headline in the *Journal-News* or be told about the stories appearing almost daily describing his father's alleged toilet behavior, Sam and Mary had a talk with their son. They had sat him down after breakfast and tried to explain masturbation to the eight year old. He had seemed to understand some of what they said but had made no response. They couldn't tell if he knew more than he was showing or was just uninterested. He said he wanted to get to school early to finish a drawing he had started the day before. When Phil was gone, Mary had said, "He took it all right, didn't he?" Sam had shrugged.

By the time the waitress brought the green Jell-O covered with the stale whipped cream appliquéd from the aerosol can, the dinner had started to seem only a continuation of Sam's ordeal. Everyone, friends as well as enemies, was part of the barrage. "Look," he said, surprising himself as much as Mary and their dinner partners, "I'm a father too, just like the people on the school board. I have an eight-year-old boy, don't I? And I sure as hell don't want him to have a teacher who would make a pass at him. Not ever."

"We know that," Connie Beale said. "No one here doubts you or accuses you."

Sam, however, was not listening. "If we pick up and leave here, there will always be someone somewhere who knows about what happened back in Hamilton. Right? And no one will believe anything except that I was run out of here for a sex crime. I'll have to pick a spot to stand and fight, so it might as well be here. Where else?" Sam was almost finished before he began to sob.

The first defense witness was Connie Beale. In addition to recounting her meeting with Sam in Elder-Beerman's on the afternoon of his arrest, Ms. Beale, a pretty and vigorous young woman whose quick smile disguised the toughness she displayed in the witness chair, said she taught singing at Wilson Junior High. That meant she sent choral students on to Sam Shie at Taft; she said it was a great honor for any of her singers to be picked for the high school chorus. "I admire Sam Shie's teaching abilities very much. He makes superior music. I shall always try to be like him."

As a frequent visitor to the Shie home and a companion of the Shie family on weekend car trips, Connie Beale attested to the numerous times Sam needed to excuse himself or stop at gas stations for "my usual problem," as he had called it, to his everlasting regret, at the police station. Whether Sam Shie's friends were recollecting accurately or had decided, for his own protection, to convert his genital offense into an anal embarrassment—to reverse the maturation process and go backward from the adolescent to the infantile state where bowel control has not yet been achieved—they could not have asked for a more definitive spokesperson than Connie Beale. Without hesitation, she gave details on toilet habits as if they were simply, wonder of wonders, the most natural thing in the world.

On cross-examination, she withstood Morgenstern gamely. At first, the prosecutor was gentle, standing near Connie Beale while he established that she had no qualifications in administration, teacher evaluation, or supervision, that her only expertise was in music. "And in teaching itself," she said quietly. "That's right, Miss Beale," Morgenstern said, turning and walking away from her as if to conceal the fact that he was now, in effect, taking off his gloves. When he turned back to her, Morgenstern did not so much pose his question as throw it at her. "Now, Miss Beale," he said, completing his about-face as life imitated, if not art, at least the networks, "what would Sam Shie do if he walked into class and found a dirty word written on the blackboard?"

"I guess he'd do what the rest of us do. Erase it."

Morgenstern's voice went up a few decibels as he took his leave of network television. "Really, Miss Beale? Is that all? Wouldn't the word 'cocksucker' written on the blackboard affect Sam Shie's ability to perform his duties as a teacher?"

Daintily, Connie Beale looked down at her fingernails for a moment and then stared back at Morgenstern. "Not if mine hasn't been affected by 'motherfucker.'"

Not everyone in the hearing room cheered. There were also scattered cries of "such language!" and "shame!" Referee Zopff was quick with his gavel. Morgenstern asked again that the room be cleared so the hearings could continue in an atmosphere of impartiality instead of carnival. "I must admonish the audience once more," Zopff said. "Try not to respond vocally or I will have to clear the room. I want you to stay, this is your crisis as much as anyone's, but please—no reactions in here."

Morgenstern pressed on. "Now, you know, Miss Beale, what Sam Shie has been convicted of—a sex crime. So let me ask you this: *Would you put a pyromaniac back into a dynamite factory?*"

What a treacherous world Morgenstern evoked! In this analogy—this vision—masturbating is a sex offense so explosive in nature it could go off at any moment. High school students are mere sticks of TNT just waiting for their fuses to be lighted. Many parents in Hamilton no doubt were prey to visions like Morgenstern's, resigned to believing their own attempts to instill principles and self-control had failed, that the teachers at school were helpless or worse, and that their children awaited only time, place, and opportunity for spontaneous combustion to occur. The debts of repression in both generations paid off in the wages of sin. Morgenstern's metaphors were often colorful, but this one was forceful enough to evoke a gasp of recognition, even from an audience on Shie's side.

Connie Beale, however, held her ground. "No, Mr. Morgenstern, I would not put a pyromaniac into a dynamite factory, but this isn't that. I know Mr. Quisenberry had facts and information and advice. I simply disagree with the conclusions he came to."

"You have heard the principal of the high school, the assistant superintendent, and Superintendent Quisenberry all testify that the publicity *alone*—not what actually happened in that men's room but the publicity *alone*—would make it impossible for Sam Shie to continue to function normally in the classroom. Do you not know that, Miss Beale?"

"They are reasonable men whose reasoning has gone wrong. It happens."

"You have heard experts in education from Miami University say the man should not be allowed back in the classroom. They all say, the specialists *and* the administrators, he should not teach again. Are you aware of that, Miss Beale?"

"They're not teachers. I am. I teach the kids he teaches. I know how good he is—with his subject *and* the students."

Morgenstern decided to soften his approach. "Sam Shie is a friend of yours, isn't he, Connie?"

The use of her first name, which a lawyer would be considerably less likely to do with an adult male who was not a close acquaintance, did not exactly win over Connie Beale. "That's right, Mr. Morgenstern. He's a very good friend."

"You would do anything in the world to help him and Mary, wouldn't you?"

"Of course not," Connie Beale said.

Connie Beale won the skirmish, but the battle belonged to Carl Morgenstern and the board because of a circumstance in the case—a sort of bottom line—over which neither Connie Beale nor Sam Shie had any control. "If he goes back into the classroom and anything happens, if there's an incident with a student, or if a student just accuses Mr. Shie of making an approach to him, do you know who is responsible?" Morgenstern asked.

"It wouldn't happen. I know him. It never *has* happened."

"Ah, but if it did—just hypothetically, *if* it did, who is responsible?"

"He's responsible himself," Connie Beale said. "Mr. Shie is."

"No, he's not," Morgenstern said, "not ultimately. Where the buck stops is right over there—in Mr. Quisenberry's office, with the superintendent himself. That'll be all, Miss Beale."

Connie Beale had been pushed on cross-examination, but had yielded little if any ground. The staunchness of her support and her basic credibility would help Shie, even if Morgenstern's point about ultimate responsibility was valid. Outside the hearing room in the stair-top hallway, a revered Taft English teacher, Sheldon Levine, showed up with his father, a clothing salesman who had once painted steeples in Russia. ("It was the only job they'd give me, the *goyim* were afraid to climb that high.") Just like in school, teaching his beloved Whitman, Sheldon Levine was as alert as a man standing up in a canoe. His eyes flicked, rabbitlike, around the hallway and into the hearing room, but he only stood at the door and would not venture inside. "We don't really have time, my dad and I," he said. "We just dropped in to see how things were going. Sam understands I'm on his side. The real trouble is, all of us know that if they can do this now to Sam, they can do anything to anyone."

"That's right, you heard it like he told it," his father said, and the Levines, *pere et fils,* vanished back into the catalogue of Hamiltonia like paintings kept in the warehouse of a great museum until it is again time for them to be put on exhibit.

The defense called Dr. Roger Fisher, a Ph.D. in clinical psy-

chology and director of the Butler County Forensic Center, to
give his opinion on Sam Shie's emotional state. Obviously, Dr.
Fisher would not have been asked to testify had he found Shie
to be an unregenerate sex maniac or a raging schizophrenic, yet
his assessment, even the professional jargon, was believable beyond the bounds of what can usually be expected from expert
witnesses. Unlike most experts, including the ones called by the
prosecution, Dr. Fisher was not being paid. He also resisted
efforts by the defense to make Sam Shie sound like a psychological superman. He had examined Sam Shie in two lengthy sessions and had also administered a withering barrage of
psychological tests containing over five hundred questions. One
of his colleagues had interviewed Mary Shie, and afterward, in
a follow-up session, Dr. Fisher had talked to both Mary and
Sam.

"Mr. Shie's examination and the battery of tests he took show
him to be within normal limits," Dr. Fisher said. "He is suffering
from transient situational stress reaction. He is intermittently
depressed, morose, there is some crying. He is coping well
under pressure, and the stress seems limited to the temporary
circumstances he finds himself in."

"What is that stress the result of?" Randy Rogers asked for
the defense.

"A combination of community pressure, the financial difficulties of not working, and the uncertain future for his family and
himself."

"What is Mr. Shie's sexual pathology?" Rogers asked.

"I looked carefully for the presence of any sexual disorder or
condition that would cause him or others trouble. I discovered
no sexual pathology."

Dr. Fisher had attended several of the hearings and listened
to other witnesses, which was permitted in this process, but
would not normally be in a court trial. Rogers asked him if it
were possible to reconcile Officer Ferdelman's accusation with
Shie's own testimony that he had not been masturbating in the
men's room.

"The facts really are not all that different as presented by the two men," Dr. Fisher said. "The main difference is in interpretation. Motivation, needs, and personal stress all affect one's perception, as well as some notion of what it is one is supposed to be seeing."

"See what I told you?" a Garfield teacher whispered among the spectators. "Ferdelman was trigger-happy, just dying to bag a fag first day on the job."

"Isn't this a sad comment on humanity?" a little white-haired old lady, widow of an industrial patternmaker, whispered back. "I've got two daughters and four grandkids, all living in Hamilton, and every single one of us is appalled at what they're doing to this man, plus using those terrible dirty words to plant the power of suggestion thirty ways from Sunday."

"Now, Dr. Fisher," Rogers continued, "we're not conceding there was an erection; in fact, Mr. Shie denies it, but if there was one, if that is what Officer Ferdelman saw, what else besides masturbation could have caused it?"

"An inflamed prostate frequently gives rise, as it were, to an erection when sexual arousal is not present. Straining in the act of defecating can also cause an erection," Dr. Fisher said.

"Is there any place in the professional literature we can find this, to confirm your opinion, Dr. Fisher?"

"Certainly, it's all in Masters and Johnson." From the spectator rows came an amused stirring, but no eruption, and Dr. Fisher continued. "It's awfully hard to tell what was going on in there, especially when the officer who had been hired to find misconduct says he only saw masturbation out of the corner of his eye for a few seconds."

"But what if the incident they allege was true?" Rogers asked. "What if he *was* masturbating? What effect would it have on your opinion as to Mr. Shie's state of mind?"

"No effect," Dr. Fisher answered. "I've treated many people who have such problems and they continue their careers in very satisfactory ways."

Morgenstern, cross-examining Dr. Fisher, asked whether psychologists were not concerned in their work with role models. Dr. Fisher said they were. "Then how can you, as a clinical psychologist, recommend in all good conscience that a man arrested for masturbating in a public rest room be returned to a high school classroom?" Morgenstern asked in a rising voice. "What kind of role model does a sex offender make?"

"Mr. Shie has not run from his problems, but faced them right here in this room. If he is a role model at all, that model is one of courage in the way he has faced this crisis."

"Oh really? Then it's all right to masturbate in a public men's room, is that it?"

"It is preposterous to think that students would conclude that it's all right to do anything that would cause someone to go through what Mr. Shie has had to endure here."

Morgenstern now made two rare slips, the first Freudian and the second a sarcastic remark delivered impatiently. Whether or not these slips would affect the final outcome of the case, they revealed starkly the attitude of the prosecutor and, by extension, the board of education. "Well, then," Morgenstern said, "you think that it's perfectly okay to put Mr. Shie back in the rest room?"

The audience laughed, and a school board employee quickly whispered to Morgenstern that he had said "rest room" when he meant "classroom." "Oh, classroom, of course," Morgenstern corrected himself, but could not resist continuing into his second slip. "We'd *like* to put him back in the rest room!" The audience tittered at Morgenstern's joke. "Strike that, I withdraw that remark," Morgenstern said to the court stenographer.

But Robert Dunlevey was on his feet. "No, absolutely do *not* strike that. It shows exactly what the school board's thinking is here."

"Okay, don't strike it," Morgenstern said, sighing. "Can you answer the question, Dr. Fisher?"

"Yes sir," Dr. Fisher said, "I think it would be perfectly all right to put Mr. Shie back in the classroom. I would say that is just where he belongs."

Morgenstern was ready to pop the big question—the question that, as far as anyone in Hamilton knew, had nothing to do with Sam Shie himself but that underlay the hearings, the newspaper coverage, and the entire controversy. It wired Hamilton into a nationwide network of concern, and it interconnected, through the ancient medium of sexual anxiety, conservatives with those liberals who, like Carl Morgenstern himself, could often be counted on the civil libertarian side of many other issues. Extreme opposites were found with linked arms here. For this campaign, moral majoritarians could be discovered almost literally in the same bed as those on the far left who viewed sexual freedom as a late, wilting bloom of decadent bourgeois culture. But Carl Morgenstern was no one's zealot. The way he posed his question was not as a challenge to a hostile witness, but as a genuine, wondering, only residually skeptical inquiry into the nature of human development. He even removed the dark glasses that had hidden his eyes throughout the hearings. "Then is it your considered opinion, Dr. Fisher," Morgenstern asked, "that there is no harm to our children if we allow homosexuals or lesbians to teach in our public schools?"

Dr. Fisher had already done his considering, and he answered immediately. "Yes sir, that's right. I know many homosexuals who are already in the Hamilton schools, and they are good and responsible teachers. I don't think they should be deprived of their livelihood."

"All right," Morgenstern said, putting the dark glasses back on, "what if there is notoriety—should they still be allowed to teach?"

"The fact of notoriety would lessen any potential risk to students just because everyone would be on guard, so I'd say yes, in case of notoriety I still think they could teach effectively."

Morgenstern pointed out that notoriety brought other problems along with it into the classroom. He then embarked on a doomed though interesting course. He asked how Shie had scored on the psychological tests, and Dr. Fisher said he had scored well within the normal range. Morgenstern said he realized these were not tests on which a subject scores high or low but rather gives some indication as to his mental and emotional state. In view of that kind of evaluation, he asked if Dr. Fisher would reveal answers to individual questions. Dr. Fisher said he could not do that because it would violate doctor-patient confidentiality. "Then you will give us your opinion on Mr. Shie's psychological state," Morgenstern said, "but you won't show us how you arrived at that opinion, is that right?"

"To talk about individual answers by a patient would be a gross misuse and misapplication of the questionnaire," Dr. Fisher said. "These tests are designed to give overall indications of a subject's condition, not to be pulled apart, question by question, out of context. The individual answers mean little by themselves anyway."

"Is that so?" Morgenstern asked, about to show that he had done his homework quite well. "I happen to think it would be very interesting indeed to know Mr. Shie's answers to the questions about his sex life, attitude toward masturbation, toilet habits, his dreams, how he reacts to trouble, whether he always tells the truth, whether he is attracted mostly to members of his own or the opposite sex, and so forth. If I can't ask questions about how you arrived at your conclusions, then I cannot cross-examine you."

Although Dr. Fisher still insisted on the privacy of Shie's individual answers, Morgenstern's point was not lost. Dr. Fisher was an expert, and he had personally examined the defendant. But his conclusion was only an opinion and not an objective tabulation that the school board and the referee had to abide by religiously.

In rebuttal, Morgenstern called Fisher's old boss, Professor William Shipman of Miami University, also a clinical psychologist. Dr. Shipman reviewed in detail the circumstances surrounding Shie's arrest, saying they indicated "a homosexual sort of situation." He dismissed the strong support many Hamiltonians were giving Shie by saying that "there are sections of the community that are sympathetic to deviant behavior." When asked if homosexuals should be allowed to teach school, Dr. Shipman was unhesitating. "No," he said. "We certainly do not need enticement to homosexuality facilitated by schools. No question about it, I would not hire anyone to work with adolescents who had some question about sexual direction."

With histrionic aplomb, Hugh Holbrock casually baited a trap for Dr. Shipman on cross-examination. Amazingly, since Dr. Shipman was hardly an unsophisticated witness, he stepped right into Holbrock's trap, giving the audience one of its better laughs and cutting the legs right off his earlier testimony. "Now, Dr. Shipman," Holbrock began, "you've described for us a pattern of behavior—hanging around a known homosexual rest room, staying far too long in there, wearing bright red shorts, masturbating in full view of another man—you've described this hypothetical pattern as being consistent with homosexual behavior, have you not?"

"That is correct," Dr. Shipman said.

"Of course, you've never met the defendant, Sam Shie, have you?"

"That is also true, Mr. Holbrock, but it is not hard to spot a personality who conforms to the deviant behavior that has been earlier described here."

"Oh, I see," Holbrock said, sensing he was about to capitalize on an occupational hazard of Dr. Shipman's. "Well then, sir, it should be no great difficulty for you to point out Mr. Shie for us. Will you do so?"

"Objection," Morgenstern said, trying to protect the witness from smugness, the contagion that sometimes seems as indigenous to Dr. Shipman's line of work as black lung disease is to coal mining. "This is completely immaterial."

"I'm not so sure," Referee Zopff said. "Let's hear the answer if he has one."

Undaunted, the witness leaped blithely into Holbrock's snare. "That is the man there," the worldly Dr. Shipman said, pointing past the plump, usually jovial defendant to the tall and slender, caustic defense lawyer, Randy Rogers. No two men in the whole hearing room were more dissimilar.

"Well, isn't that remarkable?" Hugh Holbrock said, suddenly switching roles to become the host of a panel show and beaming at the hearing room spectators, who conspired to stay silent until he finished. "Thank you very much, sir. All right, will the *real* Sam Shie please stand up?" Just like on television, it was

Randy Rogers who shifted his long legs, but it was Sam Shie who rose to the ovation of what had become the studio audience.

"And so," Holbrock continued when Referee Zopff had at last and, it seemed, somewhat reluctantly achieved quiet in the hearing room, "this is what the citizens of Hamilton have paid you eighty dollars an hour for, Dr. Shipman. To read over the old hearing transcripts, apply your expertise to every phase of this case, spend nineteen hours in preparation and testimony, and here in this room now, for a total of one thousand five hundred and twenty dollars, fail even to identify the defendant you are helping to destroy, is that right?"

"My fee is quite appropriate for what I am going through here," the chastened psychologist said. "I have never been treated with such humiliation and insults."

Holbrock looked very pleased. "I hope you mean me."

"Yes, I do."

"Good. No further questions."

At last Syrilla Everson had her day—but it was more like a moment—in court. She had been pro-Shie from the beginning, but as the hearing continued, she worried more and more that there would be reprisals for her testimony on Shie's behalf. As a liberal in a conservative community, Mrs. Everson had often felt under siege. One of her friends had wondered, when the case began, whether the Shie adherents would disappear into the woodwork like termites or come out and be mowed down. Mrs. Everson herself was rather afraid of being mowed down, but she never even considered disappearing. For her testimony at the hearing she was a chic but careful sonata in green, from her jade earrings to her ultra-suede suit to her unaccustomed high heels. Mrs. Everson told a brief anecdote about Sam Shie's ability to bring a young girl out of her depression through music. "He is highly respected by everyone, and we need Mr. Shie at Taft," she concluded.

Not in disrespect, but in simple acknowledgment of their long, if suspended, friendship, Morgenstern called Mrs. Everson by her first name during cross-examination. He was also gentle, as if trying to effect a reconciliation rather than score points for the prosecution. "You're a very good English teacher, Syrilla," Morgenstern began.

Mrs. Everson barely trembled when she said, "Thank you."

Instead of asking for her credentials as he had for all the other witnesses, Morgenstern recited them himself. "You have a B.A. from Michigan, and then you have your Master's in English. I believe most of your courses were in journalism and English, is that correct?"

"That is correct," Mrs. Everson said.

"Well, did you ever take any courses, Syrilla, in evaluation or supervision?" Morgenstern was almost contrite about establishing, as he did with all the teachers, that they were qualified by training only in their own subjects and not in evaluating the performance of other teachers.

"No, I did not."

"All right. Well, you're a good friend of Sam Shie's, aren't you."

"No, I am not." Mrs. Everson would have stared more affectionately at Torquemada. "I thought I was a better friend of yours, Carl."

Morgenstern sighed. "No further questions."

Two Taft students were heard briefly. A boy said, affectingly, that Mr. Shie was an excellent teacher highly thought of by his students. A girl said simply, "We want our music teacher back. He's the best." When Morgenstern asked if there were any vulgar jokes around Taft about Shie, she answered, "Some—just by the boys."

During several days' recess before the final witnesses for the defense were heard, two things happened to place Hamilton's school system in a national context. First, Dr. Donald Helms, the assistant superintendent, resigned to become deputy superintendent of the East Baton Rouge Parish school district. The Louisiana job, with 70,000 students (to Hamilton's 13,000) represented a big promotion for the much-traveled Helms. The migration south was an opportunity for Helms, of course, not only to advance his career but to remove himself from the battle-scarred turf of Hamilton on which he had—considering the School Bond issue, the "back-to-basics" backlash, integration quarrels, and now the Sam Shie controversy—done extremely well to survive. Superintendent Quisenberry praised Helms, regretted his leaving, and said it was a great honor for one of the largest school districts in the South to raid his own school system since it reflected favorably on the accomplishments of the Hamilton administrators.

The second development was the NBC broadcast of the "Today" show segment that had been filmed in Hamilton. The advent of a TV crew in a town far from the two coastal film enclaves can confer respectability, even authority, on an otherwise questionable local practice. The subsequent actual broadcast not only confers, it practically canonizes. "Two years ago," the NBC correspondent began, "the schools in Hamilton, Ohio, were in an educational crisis." Superintendent Quisenberry was then presented, saying that there had been a "complete breakdown" in both disciplinary and academic standards before he took over. (In his Washington sanctuary, secure in the federal bureaucracy, his predecessor, Dr. Peter Relic, might have allowed himself a furtive wince.) Both verbal and physical assaults on teachers had become frequent, a condition Quisenberry, like many school officials, traced to the Vietnam War: "Opposition to the war by young people led to a lack of respect for all authority, including teachers."

The segment went on to show students and teachers in and out of class while the narration described the return to authoritarian structures in the school system. The report, documenting a national trend, did not include Quisenberry's local critics, nor did it mention Sam Shie, whose case was rending the community and whose fate was being argued only a few feet from the office in which Superintendent Quisenberry was filmed. It is easy enough to see irony in the juxtaposition of a television crew breezing through town to film an alleged triumph while next door an unseen drama partaking both of farce and tragedy is being played out. Such a juxtaposition is the irresistible kind that television itself specializes in. The "Today" show staff, however, was only responding to a national mood and looking for some way to visualize it.

The problem was not in their ignorance of Sam Shie, but in the assumption that the "back-to-basics" campaign amounted to much more than a pendulum effect and a rather sloganized one at that. Hamilton was presumably as good a community as any to dramatize the campaign—others have their own Sam Shie cases, their contending factions and gaping ironies—but the changes were neither as interesting nor as controlling as the continuities. The cycle of educational theory and practice had simply wheeled around once again to discipline. Continuity, the bane of daily journalism, simply has to be forgotten, pushed out of sight and mind, when headlines and montage are needed to provide the latest vision. A mirage, after all, is never just an idle image but a projection of what we hope or fear will be there when we get there. So the back-to-basics trend itself became significant if only as a dream that the hickory-stick past could be joined to a fundamentalist future.

"Are there some people," the NBC correspondent asked Quisenberry instead of finding them for himself, "who say that you are insensitive at best and at worst a fascist?" Quisenberry allowed he had heard some criticism of his methods, but "we just felt we had to restore our house." The NBC correspondent closed with the observation that "the changes, so far at least, get high marks."

As proof that "Today" was touching a national nerve, the school board and Quisenberry were embraced in phone calls from all over the country. North Carolina, Michigan, Kansas, San Diego, Seattle, New York. What administrator, teacher, or parent, in what county, precinct, suburb, or slum would *not* want to know the secret of getting children both to obey and learn? "It's a real tribute to our system to get this sort of publicity," Quisenberry said. "The fact that Hamilton is, in a manner, leading the way, is something we ought to be proud of." A new fairy tale, "The Pied Piper of Hamilton," was in the making.

Next door in the hearing room, the old fairy tale was still playing to a packed house. Teachers were proud Hamilton had

been chosen for "Today" but tended to smirk about the difference between appearance and reality. Math scores were up
slightly, they said, language skills were down, and "motherfucker" still led the hit parade in the hallways and cafeterias of
their schools. The defense now finished its case with a triple-
header of William Beckett, Taft basketball coach Marvin Mc-
Collum, and the defendant himself.

The retired president of the Beckett Paper Company was the
first to testify on the sixth day of the hearing. William Beckett
was foursquare behind Sam Shie, but that did not mean he was
not still William Beckett. He made it clear that although he
would honor the subpoena to appear as a witness on Shie's
behalf, he would be damned if he was going to sit around in the
hearing room all day until it pleased the defense to call him.
Accordingly, they called him first.

Beckett had sent a letter to all school board members, as well
as to the *Journal-News* (which refused to run it on the grounds
that they did not print circulated mail, an indignity that Beckett's father and grandfather would surely not have had to endure), in which he supported the teacher against his accusers.
The letter was entered into evidence at the hearings. "I am
troubled," he began, "by the matter of Samuel Shie." No one
had ever charged William Beckett with inattention to propriety,
and he was probably the first person since Shie had arrived in
Hamilton ten years earlier to refer to the teacher by his full
Christian name. "Even if some temporary aberration affected
Mr. Shie, and he performed an act considered reprehensible in
our society," Beckett urged the board to remember the "years
of inspiration and uplift to hundreds of young people who
learned under Mr. Shie to love and perform good music." Destroying Shie could only hurt Hamilton, Beckett said, and he
concluded his letter with a phrase that summed up precisely
what had been lacking throughout the proceedings. Beckett
pleaded that the board, in its disposition of the Shie case, dem-
onstrate a "fine moral understanding." In three words he clari-
fied what the hearings had taken six days and well over three
hundred thousand words to obscure.

In his spoken testimony, Beckett said he knew Shie from occasional church choirs and Christmas choral presentations and that his reputation was very good. He thought Shie could remain in Hamilton and teach effectively, regardless of the publicity accruing to the criminal charge, which still was "not substantiated." Completing his prepared support for Shie, Beckett sat grimly, waiting to be cross-examined.

The confrontation between William Beckett and Carl Morgenstern symbolized the division of Hamilton. The town's leading conservative pitted against one of its most outspoken liberals. The chairman of the board, an old-line, old-family Episcopalian, who had fought for decades to keep unions out of Hamilton, facing the Jewish lawyer, who had once almost succeeded in unionizing the police force itself. The two could be expected to take opposing sides on virtually any public issue—and many private ones as well—and here they were, predictably enough, on opposite sides. But who would have predicted that *these* would be the opposite sides they would choose? The encounter was brief but pointed. Morgenstern was less than reverential as he established that Beckett had never graduated from college but had left MIT after three years; so who was Beckett, went the implication, to judge the worth of a teacher?

When Morgenstern, who was not intimidated by Beckett's seniority and standing in the community, challenged the industrialist to say he would hire a homosexual in his paper mill, Beckett answered that he would, adding that homosexuals and lesbians could also be good teachers. "I regret the problems that arise from homosexuality," he said, "but though personally distasteful, homosexuals should not be discriminated against in hiring. I also believe a man can make a mistake, recognize it, and continue to be a productive member of the community." It was difficult for Morgenstern and Beckett to argue further because almost literally they did not speak the same language. Shortly, the antilibertarian liberal gave up, and the prohuman rights conservative primly left the stand, as well as, very quickly, the hearing room.

As not only a male teacher but the basketball coach, Marv

McCollum possessed exactly the masculine image the defense
was anxious to project. McCollum was the unusual combination
of soft-spoken and long-winded, the first earning the respect of
athletes who were used to coaches who yell, and the second
endearing him to students and friends even as they looked at
their watches and crept toward the door. He was solemn as he
said Sam Shie could come back to Taft and nothing terrible
would happen. McCollum began spiraling into a tale as he made
the point that he would teach gladly with Sam Shie if he returned, because he had had many colleagues in his nineteen
years at Taft—ever since the school started—and he could
never imagine refusing to teach with any of them.

When he was asked if Shie's condition, assuming there was
one, would influence young people or prevent students from
taking his courses, McCollum spoke slowly and quietly, almost
chewing each word to make it last longer. "I don't think what
Sam has been accused of would stop or delay anyone from
taking his course, or from getting the most out of it," McCollum
said. "Incidents of use and abuse of alcohol, which we have a
fair amount of, are far more likely to influence students nega-
tively than what Sam's accused of. Nothing Sam has done has
changed my attitude toward him, and frankly I think the sin-
gling out of the teaching profession in this case amounts to
character assassination by an administration and a community
that does not have the right to throw those stones. In the nineteenth and early twentieth centuries, teachers weren't allowed
to smoke, women couldn't teach if they were married, yet
human rights and equality demanded . . ." It was not mere rhetoric, and it was all true as far as Shie's supporters were concerned. But since the defense knew the school board was weary
and didn't want even the most well-meant lecture, they turned
the coach over to Morgenstern for cross-examination.

"What if a member of your basketball team were indecently
exposed?" Morgenstern asked. "You're known as a strict disciplinarian, so what would you do?"

"Well, can I tell you a little story about this?"

"God, please no," Morgenstern beseeched, "anything but one

of your stories!" For almost the only time during the hearings, the spectators laughed good-naturedly on behalf of both sides.

Referee Zopff ruled that McCollum could tell his story if he kept it brief, but that was like asking a miler to sprint. McCollum said each case in life was unique and should be handled individually, which he always tried to do with his players. "I remember the time twenty years ago," he said, "when the principal of the old Hamilton High had his house bombed, or gently grenaded, by some pranksters who were really good kids at heart, by the way, because one of them eventually became a Rhodes Scholar, which was why the principal called me in and asked what I thought we ought to do, which made me think of Voltaire."

"It's the reincarnation of Casey Stengel," Morgenstern said. "Okay, I surrender." But McCollum had stood up for his friend and, at whatever length, had made his point.

The final defense witness—at last, after pathos, anger, accusation, and hysteria—was Sam Shie. When Oscar Wilde rose in his own doomed cause to tell the court of "the love that dare not speak its name," he had at least half of London listening to him (while the other half were afraid he would speak their names), but the moral climate was one of contempt and revulsion. When Sam Shie took the stand, he had all Hamilton reading about him, the sympathy (judging from the mail printed by the Journal-News) of many, and the moral climate contained at least as much outrage at his tormentors as disgust at what he was alleged to have done. Wilde's testimony was a defiant affirmation of a way of life whose validity it would take the world several more generations to acknowledge. Shie's was merely an affirmation of his right to live and work in Hamilton. Yet both men were scourged by the authorities in their communities. Happily married and a devoted father (the nouns also applied to Wilde, but hardly the adjectives), Shie made no brief for homosexuality, which he insisted had no application to him. His testimony, under the circumstances, was directed not toward gaining sympathy—he had enough of that—but toward the creation of an atmosphere that would permit him and his family to continue living in Hamilton.

Preeminently, as he repeated the denials of the by now old charges, Shie appeared spotlessly normal. Since the hearing had no jury, the jury was the whole town. It was not Referee Zopff Shie had to convince, but the students of Hamilton that he could still teach them and the parents of Hamilton that he could be trusted with their children. What he needed was not eloquence, just the earnestness of a man out of work hoping to get back to a job he loved. In trying to discredit Officer Ferdelman, his original accuser, Shie was precise but casual. "First of all," he said, "I didn't masturbate in Elder-Beerman's rest room. Secondly, I wasn't wearing red gym shorts but only a pair of regular underpants my wife bought me."

"Where did she buy them?" Hugh Holbrock asked.

The spectators were starting to chuckle even before Shie spoke. "Elder-Beerman." Now the audience, the school board itself, and even the lawyers were all discharging weeks of tension in their small roar of delight. Referee Zopff gaveled for order and threatened to question Shie by himself if everyone wasn't quiet.

"I have caused no problems in Hamilton," Shie resumed. Midway, his voice threatened to spill out his feelings, but he quickly zipped it back into his throat. "I have given offense to no man, woman, or child. I have taught classes I treasured in a school I am proud of. People say I have made good music and done a good job with their children. I sit here accused of something I did not do, and if I leave Hamilton it will follow me everywhere, yet if I stay here I have some chance of living it down. Still, now, after all, I continue to want to raise my son here. Could someone please tell me why I can't go back to my students, my work, and my music?"

The cross-examination was subdued. Morgenstern asked if Shie felt there was a conspiracy against him by the witnesses and the school board.

"It's not a conspiracy. They're just wrong. Officer Ferdelman made a mistake. When a mistake is made, police officers have a tendency to stick together."

"That's for sure," Hugh Holbrock said.

"Have you had any difficulty with the *Journal-News* before?" Morgenstern asked. "Have they covered your concerts well? Be fair to them when you answer."

"I have never had any difficulty with the *Journal-News*. As for fairness, I think I'm a lot fairer to them than they are to me."

"Amen," Hugh Holbrock said. "Let's all pray."

"You said you wanted to protect your family from publicity. Then you insisted on a public hearing. Why?" Morgenstern was hammering at a familiar theme.

"I chose a public hearing to see why you people decided to terminate my contract after ten years of service. I wanted the people of Hamilton to hear the little facts in the case. A private hearing implies there's something to hide, which there isn't. I had already lost everything when you took my job away, so I figured this might as well be out in the open. If I was wrong about the no-contest plea, I'm sorry. I've paid for it. I only meant to prevent embarrassment to the school, my students, and my family. I'm a music teacher, not a lawyer."

After summations in which both sides saw the case in the simplest possible terms, the hearings were over. Morgenstern repeated his opening arguments that Shie had been caught by a policeman while masturbating, had been convicted in court, and should now be sent on his way out of the Hamilton school system. Holbrock and Dunlevey maintained that nothing had been proved, that the community needed Sam Shie, and that a great and loyal teacher was being persecuted.

The hearings ended, but the case remained a litmus test for the community. Whether or not Sam Shie had exposed himself in the Elder-Beerman men's room, the rest of Hamilton had surely done so in the months that followed. On the Sunday after his testimony, when Coach McCollum walked into his church, the president of the church council stood to greet him and, shaking McCollum's hand warmly, congratulated him for his courageous stand on behalf of Sam Shie. The next day at school McCollum was visited by the statistician who had voluntarily kept records for all major Taft teams since the school was founded in 1959. A respected citizen and zealous sports fan, the statistician told McCollum that because of his testimony for Sam Shie, he was not going to compile statistics for the Taft basketball team any more.

Ten days after the hearings ended, Referee Zopff completed his review and handed down his decision. Sam Shie, he said, was guilty both of masturbating in the men's room and of perjuring himself in sworn testimony about the incident. But he should not, Zopff concluded, lose his job. Instead, Shie should be reinstated immediately with full back pay for the term of his suspension. That was all Shie had ever asked for. Like many mediators, Zopff had given the language to one side and the victory to the other.

Both sides took heart. The school board said Zopff had agreed with them on the facts of the case, though they reserved the right to disagree with his conclusion. The Ohio Education Association and Sam Shie himself felt they had won the case since Zopff's recommendation was exactly what they had been working toward. At a public meeting two weeks later, the board of education voted to reject the referee's conclusion and proceed with their own plan to fire Shie. It was the first time in forty-one years that a local school board in Ohio had refused to comply with a referee's decision. The defense lawyers immediately appealed the case in the Butler County court of common pleas.

Sam Shie could not teach any more in Hamilton. He kept a few music students—three for voice and two for piano—and the teachers' association gave him some secretarial work to do. "The broad-minded people in Hamilton will soon forget this," Sam Shie said. "The narrow-minded will make my life miserable. We have to decide which there are more of. The funny thing is, I'd still like to go back and teach the chorus at Taft, but the board will never let me. One way or another they're going to win and they know it."

From various friends and anonymous donors, the Shies received over four thousand dollars. Sam could not find a steady job anywhere. "There's no place I haven't looked for work—

any work—between here, Cincinnati, Dayton, and Columbus," he said, seven months after the school board had fired him. "I'm next in line as service rep for the phone company, and I have an application in with the Baldwin piano people. I've registered with a music teacher placement service in Chicago, but nothing's come of that. I have my up days and down days now. One of my voice students is coming along beautifully with Menotti. Another is just a kid, but he does 'Battle Hymn of the Republic' real well."

What he called his worst down day came when the Butler County court of common pleas refused to implement Referee Zopff's decision that Shie be reinstated. The court ruled that the school board could do what it wished in the hiring and firing of teachers. The teachers' association announced an appeal immediately. The Shies made plans to leave town.

After being out of work for a year, Sam Shie was hired to teach music in a smaller school system on the other side of the state. He still hoped to win in the appellate court and at least get his back pay from Hamilton. Even after another year had passed, he would occasionally go back to Hamilton for weddings of his former students. "They'll ask me to be organist and play Bach, Brahms, or Purcell's 'Trumpet Voluntary' for them. I try not to think about the school board and all that vindictiveness. We were just a middle-class family trying to establish ourselves and maintain stability, we were never on some big career move to get ourselves way up in the world. Although the transition away from Hamilton, from the school I was so devoted to, has been difficult, it could have been worse. Mary is a pillar of love, and Phil is growing up strong and happy. We're only a little over an hour from Pittsburgh."

During the Civil War, widely perceived in Hamilton to be a war not only for preserving the Union but ending slavery, most of the town managed to support blacks' right to freedom while denying their right to equality. In 1862 the school board considered the following proposal: "Resolved, that it is the opinion of the members of the board of education that the children of

Lionel Epps (Creole) are not entitled under the laws of the state of Ohio to admission into the schools of this city, set apart for white scholars." The resolution did not pass until a heated debate had taken place. In the coming century, differentness was never easy for official Hamilton to confront, whether it came in the form of race, social innovation, or presumed sexual preference.

When the shaft of differentness loomed over the town, the first instinct was to expunge it, as with the soldier who was hanged in the 1790s for leaving Fort Hamilton to see his girlfriend. If differentness could be proven to be good for business, it could be embraced, as with the invasion of the Fisher Body Company, which brought grief to the minority of industrialists but higher wages and more merchandising to everyone else.

Each change, even when accepted, rang a kind of bell in Hamilton, harking to a custom or moment in the town's past, appearing finally as a form of permanence, of continuity, a historical resonance rather than a phenomenon without precedent. When the community split its high schools in two during the 1950s, one on either side of the Miami River, it was returning to the *status quo* of the 1850s and earlier. When the corporate mergers of the 1960s and 1970s deprived the town of home-grown businesses, the complaints echoed those of the nineteenth century, the citizens blaming their troubles on Eastern bankers and Washington politicians. Outsiders, in fact, were always responsible for the troubles of Hamilton. As in other communities, real problems were caused by outsiders, those alien influences who disrupt what would have been local harmony. Since everything bad originated elsewhere, it had to be a wonder this country was not perfect.

Sam Shie was an insider when he brought Hamilton beauty, and he was honored. When he became an embarrassment, he was shucked as an outsider. The familiar extremes of the town had been visited upon Sam Shie the way they were upon everyone who was different or presumed to be. These were Hamilton's gifts to Sam Shie: affection, rejection. His friends made him a martyr; it was an honor he could do without. As the town had loved him, it had thrown him off. Throwing him off, the school board took stock of itself once more.

When the 1970s gave way to the 1980s, the board did what it had done in the 1860s; it decided there should be only one high school in Hamilton. Unlike the 1860s, the consolidated school accepted both blacks and whites. But one teacher said the result was merely "citywide turmoil because the poorer kids who can help on teams get sheltered in easy classes while the rest of the blacks and the Appalachian whites get lost in the chain of failure." The cure of one disease appeared as the incubation of another. Problems brought by the differentness in race and background were still to be solved. The divisions Mayor Witt had perceived remained unhealed. Sam Shie's appeals languished in the courts. "But even if I win I've lost," he said from his home across the state. "I can never go back there. I'm just thankful life does go on outside Hamilton, Ohio."

Life went on inside the town as well. The restoration of a single high school meant Taft and Garfield could no longer play each other. With intracity competition ended, the new rival became Middletown, slightly smaller, equally avid, fifteen miles northeast of Hamilton. As always, Hamilton remained united against outsiders, divided against itself.

AUTHOR'S NOTE

In certain instances, in order to protect individuals' privacy, names have been changed. All the events, however, did take place.

For their cooperation, their candor, for the privilege of observing their lives and permission to do so, I am lastingly grateful to the people of Hamilton.

ABOUT THE AUTHOR

Peter Davis graduated from Harvard University. He was an Emmy and Peabody Award-winning writer/producer for CBS News. He won an Academy Award for his film *Hearts and Minds*. He lives in New York City with his wife, Karen Zehring, and their four children.